**VOLUME 26   NUMBER 3   2020**

# Time Out of Joint:
# The Queer and the Customary in Africa

Edited by Kirk Fiereck, Neville Hoad,
and Danai S. Mupotsa

# A QUEERING-TO-COME

**Kirk Fiereck, Neville Hoad, and Danai S. Mupotsa**

Next I had to learn how to control my ancestors. If you can't control your ancestors, they can destroy your body. In the beginning, before I understood how to work with my ancestors, I used to roar like a lion when [the spirit of Nkabinde—an ancestral spirit—was] moving up my spine and gripping the back of my neck. . . . So I had to struggle with the spirit of Nkunzi and learn to keep him under control and this went on for nearly two months of [izisangoma] the training and I am still learning.
—Nkunzi Zandile Nkabinde, *Black Bull, Ancestors and Me: My Life as a Lesbian Sangoma*

My lover's nipples meet me affectionately,
a wound my body had not known it missed.
I am caged with her. And I am with him.
The three of us rolling under covers
on a three-quarter mid-morning bed.
We laugh. Tickle. Hands stroking.
Feeling out where we bleed into each other.
She does not know he is here.
He touches her.
She does not know that we are three.
Or four. Or five.
That we bleed into many, sometimes
—Vangile Gantsho, *red cotton*

I return to the experience of the quotidian, to how I would like to experience the quotidian. A quotidian that is the possibility of gathering into a livable, pleasurable social. We gather to practice freedom as we work across difference.
—Keguro Macharia, "Pleasure (in 5 Movements)"

*GLQ* 26:3
DOI 10.1215/10642684-8311743
© 2020 by Duke University Press

This special issue has a performative relation to the concerns it hopes to bring to the fore: the problems of finding a usable past for both the lived experience and the study of African sexual subjects, and how queer theory elaborated from Africa can inform queer theory's Euro-American silent ethnocentrisms (see Camminga 2017; Matebeni 2014; Matebeni and Msibi 2015; Mupotsa 2015; Musangi 2018; Nyanzi 2013; and Osinubi 2016). Our three opening epigraphs—from a memoir, a poem, and something that approaches a manifesto, respectively—suggest some of the lineaments of the queer customary: its temporal complexity containing ancestral time, the present, and invitations to futurity. Both caged and free, experientially singular but "bleeding into many," the queer customary not only invokes the historical determinants of what Keguro Macharia (2017) above terms the *quotidian* as it lodges in the body, but also suggests an undoing of those determinants in freedom as a practice. The epigraph from Nkunzi Zandile Nkabinde's memoir animates a cosmology beyond the imaginaries of secularism and invites a consideration of sexual and gendered self-fashioning that draws on indigenous religious practices and experiences that defy the conservatism often attributed to matters deemed "traditional." In turn, Vangile Gantsho's poem holds a similar proliferation of hauntings in something more like the apparently synchronic time of the erotic encounter refusing the hetero/homo binary and its attendant bourgeois couple form, or at least suggesting that such forms are riven with contradictions. Finally, the Macharia quotation from "Pleasure (in 5 Movements)" sutures those two experiences of the everyday into a more social desire for freedom "across difference."

We hope that these three epigraphs together capture what we are calling the *African queer customary*. That said, it is possible that we might come to find that the queer customary is out of joint with itself, and that the more political work of the quotidian, the customary, must remain deferred or aspirational. As Sokari Ekine (2013: 78) notes, "Two distinct yet interlinked narratives dominate discussions of queer sexualities: one claims that queer sexualities are 'unAfrican' and the other treats Africa as a site of obsessive homophobia." We hope to deploy an idea of the customary and its more complex, improvisatory notion of time to do something else—to see how African sexual subjects might make and remake themselves under conditions not of their making, holding onto African singularities but hopefully also opening up into elsewhere.

John Comaroff and Simon Roberts (1981: 78) defined the customary as "the undifferentiated repertoire of the normative." Mahmood Mamdani ([1996] 2018: 25) argued for "customary law" as "the theory of decentralized despotism."

This issue hopes to work the former definition against the latter, disarticulating the customary from its colonial and, in many instances, postcolonial codification/ossification into customary law. We define the *queer customary* as those practices and desires and their representations that reference (while inhabiting and inflecting) the heteronormativity of customary categories. Simultaneously, the *queer customary* refers to queer studies' secret normativities—even in their ostensible antinormative guise—thus transgressing the expected boundaries and forms of the field. Queering the customary specifically entails the unsettling of expected roles, subjectivities, and forms of personhood that are normatively proscribed by customary practices—within queer studies as well as other local communities—and discourses that are simultaneously enabled by those very same practices and discourses.

This special issue addresses key topics at the intersection of queer studies and ideas and practices of "the customary," more specifically, with a geographic focus on the continent of Africa. As such, we hope to further some of the ideas raised in Ashley Currier and Thérèse Migraine-George's (2016) essay on the intersection of African and queer studies in the recent *Area Impossible* issue of *GLQ* (Arondeker and Patel 2016). Such ideas include how queer studies/theory is strengthened through understanding queerness from/within Africa. What presumptions within Euro-American queer studies/theory scholarship contribute to Afro-pessimist and/or Afro-optimist scholarship and viewpoints? What of an Afro-pragmatist perspective, and how might Afro-queer scholarship chart such an ostensibly impossible path? How might the customary be a space for political pragmatism? Or perhaps the queer customary might be an idealist pragmatism oriented toward ideals-to-come like queer democracy, or freedom—ideals to strive for, but that nonetheless must forever be beyond our reach lest they repeat the failures of the European Enlightenment from which they also derive. Our hunch is that an understanding of gender and sexuality as at least partially customary forms and processes can illuminate the normativity debates in Euro-American queer theory in novel ways, as well as challenge the legal liberalism that has increasingly come to stand in for much of queer politics today.

Obviously the queer customary is not only African. As same-sex-desiring and gender-variant subjects in much of the North Atlantic world and beyond are unevenly and contestably becoming subjects of legal liberalism through state recognition and international human rights law, the queer customary remains and shifts in those spaces, too: the tea dance, the turkey baster, the pride march, the rise of "throuples" in queer communities that inhabit while transgressively inflecting coupledom, dating apps, and on and on, are all potential sites of and for what could be called the *queer customary.* Macharia (2017) plays with the queer customary as pleasure:

> Ordinary. Banal. Quotidian.
>
> Ordinary:
> adjective
> 1. of no special quality or interest; commonplace; unexceptional:
> 2. plain or undistinguished:
> 3. somewhat inferior or below average; mediocre.
> 4. customary; usual; normal:
>
> Banal:
> adjective
> 1. devoid of freshness or originality; hackneyed; trite:
>
> Quotidian:
> adjective
> 1. daily:
> 2. usual or customary; everyday:
> 3. ordinary; commonplace:

By invoking the customary, we distinguish this category from the hegemonic realm of customary law, which has sometimes been particularly oppressive with regard to nonconforming genders and sexualities. The customary exists "beneath and beyond" as well as "before and belatedly" to overlapping regimes of customary, constitutional, and international law (Hoad 2016: 10). Customary practices and discourses are not just those authorized by customary norms, although they many times reference them, inflecting them toward unexpected ends that are not overdetermined by customary authority, and sometimes working the different sites and levels of customary authority against each other. For example, Stella Nyanzi and Margaret Emodu-Walakira (2009) explore how Baganda women take the customary practice of widow marriage (for instance, when a woman's deceased spouse's brother marries her) as a highly ambivalent issue—as both a kind of "evil" and "solution" with regard to women's adjustments to widowhood in relation to issues of property and inheritance (also see Okech 2019). Nyanzi (2013: 953) later asks, "What is this 'traditional family'?," noting the variety of nuclear and extended family models, all of which trouble heteropatriarchal national fantasies and are often the fantasy-object from which homophobic law and policies emerge (also see Macharia 2013 and Tamale 2009). This beneath and above is again echoed in Neo Musangi's (2018) recent article on how women in their family married women.

When South African Olympic athletes Caster Semenya and Violet Rase-boya married in January 2017, they had a "customary" wedding with the acceptance and participation of family members, which included *lobola* (bride-price) exchange and Caster's family welcoming Violet as their *makoti* (newlywed bride). As Michael W. Yarbrough's (2018) work shows, in South Africa the transactions between civil and customary law in the making of ideals of same-sex marriage reshape forms of personhood, intimacy, and relation. This is what Xavier Livermon (2015) refers to as "useable traditions. Likewise, Malawians Tiwonge Chimbalanga Kachepa and Steven Monjeza were engaged in a "customary" ceremony in 2009. The practices surrounding the event expressed overt community buy-in or self-determination of the customary (White 2015). This included the local pastor serving as an *ankoswe* (traditional marriage counselor) and the admission of Tiwonge into the church congregation as a woman (Biruk 2014), woman here referring to a sexuated position as "bride" (see Muptosa 2015; Musangi 2018; Mupotsa in this issue) that is not biologically determined or contained within a "dual sex-gender system" (see Oyĕwùmí 1997). Such practices were and are oblique to hegemonic customary authority and community norms that may have assigned Tiwonge a male gender before successfully performing the markers and gaining general recognition of her womanhood as a bride by church congregation members. In this way Tiwonge and those in her community collectively both disarticulated customary practice from customary authority and inflected community normativities, themselves never singular or monolitic in their constant (re)interpretation.

Other examples of the queer customary can be found in the shifting roles of authority embodied in the practices and politics of traditional healers in South Africa (Nkabinde 2008). Additionally in South Africa, Xhosa-speaking black gay men from lower-class, middle-class, and poor families in townships have been choosing to undertake *ulwaluko* (male initiation and circumcision rituals). Those undergoing customary rites of passage are engaged in processes that generate a range of contested, ordinary, and plural forms of sex, gender, sexuality, performance, experience, relation, persons, and intimacy (see Qambela Forthcoming). These plural forms were undeniably entwined with these customs. What is "queer" emerges within the vernacular of these rituals and traditions (Qambela 2019). It also refers to ways of using and inhabiting space (Ombagi 2019). While these subjects are regularly marginalized during these processes because of their sexuality, their desires to undergo these customs were not determined solely by the hegemonic notions of masculinity that such customs are intended to enforce. Rather, these young men trouble the heteronormativity of manhood by reengaging the semiotic processes of these customary practices and discourses (Fiereck 2018).

We have assembled a multidisciplinary representation of scholars from literary studies, anthropology, and sociology, with a focus on contributions from scholars based in African institutions. A special issue on the topics of African queerness and the customary is timely. The African Studies Association recently formed a Queer African Studies Association. *Research in African Literatures* just published their first queer issue (Hoad and Osinubi 2016). The Center for Constitutional Rights saw its case against Scott Lively for his role in the drafting of the Ugandan "Kill the Gays" bill finally dismissed in 2017 on jurisdictional grounds, but more such cases are on the horizon as Uganda reconsiders the bill at the moment of writing. Given these developments, it will be increasingly necessary for all gender and sexuality scholars who focus on queerness to understand where specific idioms and forms of cultural particularity—such as the antinormativity debates, customary forms, traditionalisms, and tribalisms—overlap and, most critically, where precisely they diverge. Here one must extend the Foucauldian insight that any sexuality is a classed sexuality to the other powerful forms of group belonging (see Nyanzi 2013).

This special issue presents a series of theoretically informed articles that are situated within existing scholarship on queerness in a range of African contexts, without taking the designation African for granted, and explore the "non-normative" (Matebeni and Msibi 2015), or secret normativities of particular strands of Euro-American queer theory that are customarily antinormative. Such "secret normativities" exist in the uncritical adoption of performativity theory that ignores the normative structure of the performative. As Jacques Derrida (1995) reminds us, such a structure requires an exhaustive normative context for a successful performative to instantiate that which it names, even an antinormative one (Morris 2007). For example, in Euro-American queer studies, there is an unmarked (secret) normative assemblage of personhood (which includes norms of body, psyche, self, subject, individual, and public and personal personae) that structures both normative and antinormative performativities (El-Tayeb 2011).

The suppressed presence of the customary disarticulates existing African and queer studies as a focus on the customary renegotiates the constitutive "outside" of both queer liberalisms and African ethnonationalisms. As same-sex-desiring and gender-nonconforming African subjects use indigenous and queer studies' customs in their self-fashioning, they contest the secret normativities and ethnocentrisms of Euro-American queer studies scholarship, or even undo some of the heteropatriarchal norms of African ethnonationalisms. Those ethnonationalisms, similar to customary law, are/were partly produced by colonial and postcolonial encounters and enterprises. Simultaneously, that coinhabiting of queer and customary practice positions such subjects as not entirely assimilable to codes of legal liberalism, the right to culture or self-determination notwithstanding. The recursive, quotidian temporality of the customary resists both the teleological temporality of LGBTQIA+ citizenship and the anchoring eternities that tradition, invented or otherwise, brought into being. This recursive quotidian space of the customary lives beyond and beneath the spaces of governmentality: to bring the customary formally into the law renders it no longer customary. The customary is not civil society either, yet civil society actors can inflect and transgress those norms in registers we would label as the queer customary. We inevitably risk the romance of the incommensurate, but also realize that despite the commensurabilities that the operations of law and capital make inevitable, particularly when they act in concert with one another, that there is nonetheless space for dissonance—in a word: noise.

The essays in this special issue address inter alia how customary queer cultural production might serve as a basis from which to critique late capitalist forms of value production (material, ethical, and semiotic) and exchange. The queer customary is nothing if not an urgent engaging of the conditions of the reproduction of everyday life right now. On this contorted and moving time/space of the queer customary, we are bound to a series of enabling and constraining inheritances. We inherit the always already multiplicity of this issue's objects of focus. We inherit "the customary," as we do "the queer," in their multiple temporal and spatial disjointedness. We struggle with the ongoing legacies of colonialism, settler colonialism, and racial capitalism that weaponize nature and ourselves against one another, alongside more recent violent histories sewn long ago of both industrial and financial capital—of identities and datafied selves; of commodified bodies and derivativized, specular persons. All of these histories and their deployments are ones that preclude any simple or unified notion of the queer or the customary.

In this special issue, Macharia's article stretches across temporalities in a Kenya partly routed through the black diaspora to think the inheritance of intimate disorganization and its potentialities through disjointedness, but also urges us to forget or abandon the study of a racist and colonial archive of sexuality and, *pace* Ann Stoler (1995) and Joseph Massad (2007), perhaps even sexuality itself, especially in the form of the homo/hetero binary, which can rightly be seen as an ongoing imperial project, which replicates its injuries in every invocation of its histories, no matter how critical.

What can/must be abandoned in ways that are not just the production of alibi? Is it possible to forget entirely or ignore the colonial archive of sexuality? Or will those abandonments necessarily return as hauntings (Matebeni 2014)? We would like to abandon the fantasy of representativity—both geographic and temporal as well as semiotic. What of the unrepresentable, the atemporal, the unconscious of the antagonisms of everyday life for everyone, everywhere? Most queer African studies, with a few important exceptions like the work of Wendy Belcher (2016) on Ethiopia, are twentieth-century focused, though an idea of the customary with its lost origins and persistent reworking of past practices messes with any easy historical periodizing.

Spatially, as one website would have it, "Africa is [not] a country."[1] There are 57 countries on the continent, and close to 2,000 languages are spoken, with over 250 in Nigeria alone. What appears in this special issue on the queer customary is not even a scratching of the surface. If we think of "Africa" in the *longue durée* of the colonial encounter, two strands of historiographic thinking can be isolated: first, "Africa" was always and already queer, in the sense that African sex and gender norms and practices did not look like those of the emergent white, middle-class nuclear family (itself more of an ideological phantasm in the West than a lived reality for most people), and these differences in sex and gender norms may have been constitutive of racial and "civilizational" difference rather than merely evidence of it. This imputation of African queerness underwrote in frequently dystopian ways the ideological claim/justification of colonialism as an ostensible "civilizing mission." It is not churlish to point out that humanitarian and human rights initiatives find a precursor in this earlier instance of well-intentioned Westerners telling African people what they should and should not do with their bodies. Relatedly, the South African historian Jeff Guy (1997) explains the emergence of customary law in what becomes the South African province of KwaZulu-Natal as "an accommodation of patriarchs." However, T. J. Tallie's (2019) recent book, by highlighting the agency of Zulu women in resisting the attempt to eradicate ilolobolo (bridewealth), certainly complicates Guy's assertion. How such accommodations prefigure something like a global family values coalition that underlies the drafting of recent legislation in Nigeria and Uganda is a question worth posing. Alongside that fantasy stood what Marc Epprecht (2008) has established as the cognate but contradictory fantasy of "heterosexual Africa." The field of queer African studies has inevitably inherited some epistemic habits from the endurance of a heteropatriarchal nationalism (Ekine 2013). Sharon Holland (2012: 56) has demonstrated "how the transatlantic slave trade altered the very shape of sexuality in the Americas for everyone." How the African diaspora influences, reframes, and transforms an object of conjuring like the African queer customary marks the site of another begged question.

Queer theory and to lesser but still significant extent queer studies has been mostly a knowledge project of the North Atlantic world of the last thirty years or so. That fact is an inheritance that is difficult to shake, though Macharia (this volume) urges us to try, without collapsing into a nativism that disavows its colonial history in ways that are more repetition than rupture. We hope that these essays can work an idea of the customary with its sense of adaptiveness to inherited normativities, but working multiple levels of authority within the customary to make these normativities anew can be an intellectual resource in, for the want of a better shorthand, "white" and "Western" queer theoretical thinking on its self-professed central intellectual problem—the normative—hetero and homo. Recent years have seen the inauguration of a project under the banner of "theory from the South," though obviously there has always been theoretical thinking from what is now designated the global South (Comaroff and Comaroff 2011). So in addition to making "South" contributions to queer theory of and from the North, we hope to advance that project of theory of, from, and for the South queerly, using the African queer customary as a kind of lever. What does it mean that queer studies' inheritance of custom can be understood to be the antinormative stance with regard to the antinormativity debates? This issue asks readers to attempt new ways to think of and with these inheritances and how they continue to haunt us in ways that we cannot yet fully grasp. We hope the queer customary can also become a way to engage various articulations of queer and diaspora (Allen 2012; Tinsley 2008; El-Tayeb 2011). Some of these approaches can also mean a refusal, or a walking away, as Grace Musila (2019) tells us.

What we hope the queer customary would enable is neither a simple antinomy between normativities and their antis, nor an oversimplification by parsimonious readings of the work that "cultural particularity" and notions of "the local" have traditionally done in scholarship defined by David Graeber (2014) as "vulgar Foucauldianism." In the place of these approaches, the authors we have collected here rework such antinomies and frugality. They do so by inhabiting and inflecting an African as well as a Black Atlantic history of diagnosing and rehabilitating pathological norms to attempt to turn the machineries of chattel slavery as well as industrial, postwar political regimes of nationalism and financial capitalisms' focus on race-as-property as well as circulation as an exclusive space of capital accumulation against themselves.

We begin the special issue with Danai Mupotsa's "Conjugality," the essay that most thoroughly lays out the time/space of the customary in analytic and meditative terms by asking what forms of knowledge inhere in the hybrid form of an African "bachelorette party," allowing the impossibility of the translation of cultural idiom to become visible. Macharia's "belated : interruption" follows and outlines the stakes of what it might mean to both finally and only start to think African queerness in a venue such as this one.

Next, Ruth Ramsden-Karelse's "Moving and Moved: Reading Kewpie's District Six" gives readers a sense of when national and civic appropriations of queerness as forms of self-fashioning that were aspirational, customary, unevenly tolerated—both partially normative and defiantly transgressive—are archived and redeployed in a landscape of shifting interests from giving a new national constitution a historical life to processes of gentrification. The case study is South African, but liberal constitutionalism, national appropriations of queerness, and processes of gentrification have much wider geographies. For example, these readings of the queer customary are similar to the granting of legal personhood to environmental entities like rivers and mountains in New Zealand and India (Fiereck 2017), which references indigenous norms of personhood but inflects them in new ways. The emergence of environmental personhood in liberal constitutionalisms globally mirrors the processes Partha Chatterjee (2004) identified in his division of post-colonial sociality into political society and civil society. In his examples, humans in political society address conditions of injustice produced by civil society. In this way, the environmental customary as well as the queer customary reference aspects of sociopolitical processes that the constitution of civil society produced as suppressed presences throughout the colonial and postcolonial periods and aim to rework them toward unpredictable, decolonizing ends.

Edgar Fred Nabutanyi's "(Un)Complicating Mwanga's Sexuality in Naki-sanze Segawa's *The Triangle*" takes a recent novelistic retelling of the story of Mwanga, the last kabaka (king) to rule Buganda—and the story of the most explicit instance of African queerness being used to justify colonial rule in the history of the British Empire—to suggest that the alterity of the past can neither be used to find an authentic African precolonial queerness nor to assert that such a thing could never be. Phoebe Kisubi Mbasalaki's "Through the Lens of Modernity: Reflections on the (Colonial) Cultural Archive of Sexuality and Gender in South Africa," an essay in productive tension with Macharia's, searches for traces of African customary queerness in a colonial archive that wishes to eradicate precisely such practices, desires, and forms of knowledge.

Cal (Crystal) Biruk's "'Fake Gays' in Queer Africa: NGOs, Metrics, and Modes of Theory" reads the NGO world as a site of the customary where the figure of the "fake gay" emerges in "ritualized practices associated with neoliberalism (monitoring and evaluation, paperwork, counting) [that] operate as queer sites of multiplying possibilities and emergences." In "After Performativity, beyond Custom: The Queerness of Biofinancial Personhood, Citational Sexualities, and Derivative Subjectivity in South Africa," Kirk Fiereck tracks multiple scales of determinism and freedom in positing citational sexualities and derivative subjectivity as terms that reveal "how black LGBTQ-identified and other gender non-conforming South Africans juxtapose the queer with the customary as well as the financial as they constitute forms of queer biofinancial personhood that are paradigmatic of financialized capitalisms globally."

The special issue concludes with Laura Edmondson's "The Fabulous Pan-Africanism of Binyavanga Wainaina," an essay that analyzes Wainaina's only play, *Shine Your Eye*, to rethink questions of theatricality, visibility, and queer agency in the context of Wainaina's commitment to a queer pan-Africanism. Wainaina was Kenyan, but his pan-Africanism moves beyond the confines of national space. Binyavanga Wainaina died much too young on May 21, 2019: a complicated figure of African queer celebrity, whose exceptionality usefully contrasts with our focus on the quotidian.

We see these essays as both invitations and caveats: carefully delineated points of possible entry into the growing experiential and epistemological archive of African queer self-fashioning as it deploys the customary with all its ambivalences in the context of dystopian and enabling global forces.

## Notes

1.   See *Africa Is a Country*, africasacountry.com (accessed January 21, 2020).

## References

Allen, Jafari S. 2012. "Black/Queer/Diaspora at the Current Conjuncture." *GLQ* 18, no. 2: 211–48.

Arondeker, Anjali, and Geeta Patel. 2016. "Area Impossible: Notes toward an Introduction." *GLQ* 22, no. 2: 151–71.

Belcher, Wendy L. 2016. "Same Sex Intimacies in the Early African Text *Gädlä Wälättä Peṭros* (1672): Queer Reading an Ethiopian Woman Saint." *Research in African Literatures* 47, no. 2: 20–45.

Biruk, C. 2014. "Aid for Gays: The Moral and the Material in 'African Homophobia' on Post-2009 Malawi." *Journal of Modern African Studies* 52, no. 3: 447–73.

Camminga, B. 2017. "Categories and Queues: The Structural Realities of Gender and the South African Asylum System." *Transgender Studies Quarterly* 4, no. 1: 61–72.

Chatterjee, Partha. 2004. *The Politics of the Governed: Reflections on Popular Politics in Most of the World*. New York: Columbia University Press.

Comaroff, Jean, and John L. Comaroff. 2011. *Theory from the South: Or, How Euro-America Is Evolving toward Africa*. Boulder, CO: Paradigm.

Comaroff, John L., and Simon Roberts. 1981. *Rules and Processes: The Cultural Logic of Dispute in an African Context*. Chicago: University of Chicago Press.

Currier, Ashley, and Thérèse Migraine-George. 2016. "Queer Studies/African Studies: "An (Im/)possible Transaction?" *GLQ* 22, no. 2: 281–305.

Derrida, Jacques. 1995. *Specters of Marx: The State of Debt, the Work of Mourning, and the New International*. Translated by Peggy Kamuf. New York: Routledge.

Ekine, Sokari. 2013. "Contesting Narratives of Queer Africa." In *Queer African Reader*, edited by Sokari Ekine and Hakima Abbas, 78–91. Dakar: Pambazuka Press.

El-Tayeb, Fatima. 2011. *European Others: Queering Ethnicity in Postnational Europe*. Minneapolis: University of Minnesota Press.

Epprecht, Marc. 2008. *Heterosexual Africa? The History of an Idea from the Age of Exploration to the Age of AIDS*. Durban: KwaZulu-Natal Press.

Fiereck, Kirk. 2017. "The Queer Custom of Non-Human Personhood." *Queer-Feminist Science and Technology Studies Forum* 2, no. 1: 39–43. http://queersts.com/forum -queer-sts/.

Fiereck, Kirk. 2018. "Queer Customs, Customarily Queer." *Medicine Anthropology Theory* 5, no. 1. www.medanthrotheory.org/read/10018/queer-customs-customarily -queer.

Graeber, David. 2014. "Anthropology and the Rise of the Professional-Managerial Class." *Journal of Ethnographic Theory* 3: 73–88.

Gantsho, Vangile. 2018. *red cotton*. Tshwane, South Africa: Impepho Press.

Guy, Jeff. 1997. *An Accommodation of Patriarchs: Theophilus Shepstone and the Foundations of the System of Native Administration in Kwa-Zulu Natal*. London: Institute of Commonwealth Studies.

Hoad, Neville. 2016. "Queer Customs against the Law." *Research in African Literatures* 47, no. 2: 1–19.

Hoad, Neville, and Taiwo Osinubi, eds. 2016. "Queer Valences in African Literatures and Film." Special issue, *Research in African Literatures* 47, no. 2.

Holland, Sharon P. 2012. *The Erotic Life of Racism*. Durham, NC: Duke University Press, 2012.

Livermon, Xavier. 2015. "Usable Traditions: Creating Sexual Autonomy in Postapartheid South Africa." *Feminist Studies* 41, no. 1: 14–41.

Macharia, Keguro. 2013. "Queer Kenya in Law and Policy." In *Queer Africa Reader*, edited by Sokari Ekine and Hakima Abbas, 273–89. Dakar: Pambazuka Press.

Macharia, Keguro. 2017. "African Pleasure (in 5 Movements)." *Gukiwa*, November 7. gukira.wordpress.com/2017/11/07/african-pleasure-in-5-movements/.

Mamdani, Mahmood. (1996) 2018. *Citizen and Subject: Contemporary Africa, Decentralized Despotism, and the Legacy of Late Colonialism*. Princeton, NJ: Princeton University Press.

Massad, Joseph A. 2007. *Desiring Arabs*. Chicago: University of Chicago Press, 2007.

Matebeni, Zethu. 2014. *Reclaiming Afrikan: Queer Perspectives on Sexual and Gender Identities*. Johannesburg: Modjaji Press.

Matebeni, Zethu, and Thabo Msibi. 2015. "Vocabularies of the Non-normative." *Agenda* 29, no. 1: 3–9.

Morris, Rosalind. 2007. "Legacies of Derrida: Anthropology." *Annual Review of Anthropology* 36: 355–89.

Mupotsa, Danai S. 2015. "Becoming Girl-Woman-Bride." *Girlhood Studies* 8, no. 3: 73–87.

Musangi, Neo S. 2018. "Homing with My Mother/How Women in My Family Married Women." *Meridians* 17, no. 2: 401–14.

Musila, Grace A. 2019. "Against Collaboration: Or the Native Who Wanders Off." *Journal of African Cultural Studies* 31, no. 3: 286–93.

Nkabinde, Nkunzi Zandile. 2008. *Black Bull, Ancestors and Me: My Life as a Lesbian Sangoma*. Johannesburg: Jacana.

Nyanzi, Stella. 2013. "Dismantling Reified African Culture through Localized Homosexuality in Uganda." *Culture, Health, and Society* 15, no. 8: 952–67.

Nyanzi, Stella, and Margaret Emodu-Walakira. 2009. "The Widow, Will, and Widow-Inheritance in Kampala: Revisiting Victimisation Arguments." *Canadian Journal of African Studies/La Revue Canadienne des Études Africaines* 43, no. 1: 12–33.

Okech, Awino. 2019. *Widow Inheritance and Contested Citizenship in Kenya*. London: Routledge.

Ombagi, Eddie. 2019. "Nairobi is a Shot of Whiskey: Queer (Ob)Scenes in the City." *Journal of African Cultural Studies* 31, no. 1: 106–19.

Osinubi, Taiwo. 2016. "Queer Prolepsis and the Sexual Commons: An Introduction." Special issue, *Research in African Literatures* 47, no. 2: vii–xxiii.

Oyěwùmí, Oyèrónkẹ́. 1997. *The Invention of Women: Making an African Sense of Western Gender Discourses*. Minneapolis: University of Minnesota Press.

Qambela, Gcobani. 2019. "'Mna Ndiyayazi Uba Ndizotshata Intombazana', 'I for One Know That I Will Marry a Woman': (Re) Creating 'Family' and Reflections on Rural Lesbian Women's Experiences of Child Rearing and Kinship." In *Queer Kinship: South African Perspectives on the Sexual Politics of Family-Making and Belonging*, edited by Tracy Morison, Ingrid Lynch, and Vasu Reddy, 106–18. Pretoria: UNISA Press.

Qambela, Gcobani. Forthcoming. "'There Is Only One Place for Me. It Is Here, Entabeni':

_Inxeba_ (2017), _Kalushi_ (2016), and the Difficulties of "The Urban" for the New South African Man." _Social Dynamics_.

Stoler, Ann Laura. 1995. _Race and the Education of Desire: Foucault's_ History of Sexuality _and the Colonial Order of Things_. Durham, NC: Duke University Press.

Tallie, T. J. 2019. _Queering Colonial Natal: Indigeneity and the Violence of Belonging in Southern Africa_. Minneapolis: University of Minnesota Press.

Tamale, Sylvia. 2009. "A Human Rights Impact Assessment of the Ugandan Anti-Homosexuality Bill 2009." _Equal Rights Review_ 4: 47–57.

Tinsley, Omise'eke N. 2008. "Black Atlantic, Queer Atlantic: Queer Imagining of the Middle Passage." _GLQ_ 14, no. 2–3: 191–215.

White, Hylton. 2015. "Custom, Normativity and Authority in South Africa." _Journal of Southern African Studies_ 41, no. 5: 1005–17.

Yarbrough, Michael W. 2018. "Something Old, Something New: Historicizing Same-Sex Marriage Within Ongoing Struggles in South Africa." _Sexualities_ 21, no. 7: 1092–1108.

# CONJUGALITY

Danai S. Mupotsa

## "Proper" Sex

*W*hen my cousin got married, she asked me to arrange a separate bachelorette party for her cousins and friends while my mother and aunts arranged a kitchen tea party. I walked off the plane from Johannesburg and drove straight to my aunt's townhouse in the city center of Harare to a family barbeque of at least three generations of women, on my mother's side. On arrival, I was struck by a sensorial nostalgia. It was like the parties I grew up attending where the children played on their own, generally unaware of the other activities at hand. As I grew older, I was invited to look and, eventually, participate. Friends and cousins all under the age of thirty-five were called upstairs to a bedroom, where we would receive life lessons. On this occasion, these lessons were opened with a prayer. The first half of the speech was about the good management of the body. Our instructor, Auntie Eve, told us that, while she hoped we knew by this time to wear things like deodorant and to shave our armpits and pubic areas, it is always good to revisit and perfect our practices. Auntie Eve showed us the tools for body management. As you enter marriage, these teenage lessons were even more important. No husband wants to touch you anywhere, no less down there, if you are smelly. Cleanliness is next to godliness, after all, for sex talk, here, is repetition of lessons on the proper constitution and regulation of a sexuated body. By *sexuated* I refer to the sense of being sexually located, as described by Bibi Bakare-Yusuf (2003), who calls for a phenomenological account of African women's experiences that is attentive to how sexed and gendered positions are produced in located relations.

On the following night, I arranged for us to spend an evening partying in the VIP section of a popular night club. In a private room we could have a drink and a laugh while playing some generic bachelorette party games. Typical games involve testing the bride on their knowledge of their groom and testing the various

*GLQ* 26:3

DOI 10.1215/10642684-8311758

© 2020 by Duke University Press

friends and family on their knowledge of the bride—sort of a competitive sport in intimate knowledges. Two games I chose proved controversial. Never Have I Ever is a rather common drinking game and party classic that involves taking turns stating something that one has never done, and then all those who have done it drink and perhaps share the tale. We followed this game with another that involved preset questions to which each guest wrote down an answer and placed it in a hat. Once collected, the group would decide who wrote which answers. Our group was soon established as marked with two distinctions, the "virgins" and the "whores," as through various linguistic codes such as jokes, sarcasm, and repetition it was clear that we all understood that "proper" women (see Hungwe 2006) were either virgins or at least held the decorum to act as such—an unspoken and shared knowledge that virginity was this sort of private fiction.

The bachelorette party shares structural and affective parallels with other customary rituals that Black women pass through in a cumulative process of getting married in South and Southern Africa. These weddings and the attached rituals are often read as different, and the dualism of modern/traditional is often and easily applied or implied when people observe and describe them, despite the actual ways that the categories are incoherent and unstable. Kopano Ratele (2007) reminds us that cultures are contested networks of encodings and objects that people inhabit, yet it is precisely a set of claims about this culture that reinforces the social forces that make heterosexual sex (even here, in its form as inference through the performative act of talk) "proper." I view these rituals as a continuum or as a process of becoming that is not simply an entry but a continuous process of symbolic, material, psychohistorical and temporal entry to the proper but never quite/never right. The play of silence and speech, or the play across the dichotomy of the customary and the otherwise, relates to what Elizabeth A. Povinelli (2006: 4) refers to as autological and genealogical imaginations: the *autological subject* refers to "discourses, practices, and fantasies about self-making, self-sovereignty, and the value of individual freedom associated with the Enlightenment project of contractual constitutional democracy and capitalism," while *genealogical society* refers to "discourses, practices, and fantasies about social constraints placed on the autological subject by various kinds of inheritance." Povinelli offers a third concept, the *intimate event*, which, "as opposed to *intimacy*, is simply the way in which the event of normative love is formed at the intersection—and crisis—of [the autological and genealogical] discourses" (4). The bride occupies the positions of both the autological and the genealogical, while the wedding presents us with the intimate event.

In her influential essay "Thinking Sex," Gayle Rubin (1984) asks us to think about sex historically by drawing together Marxist and psychoanalytic readings about how sex and gender come to be reproduced in a hierarchical dual sex-gender system. The argument Rubin presents as to how immorality organizes a sex/gender system is useful in considering the ways women articulate their relation to being proper in the rituals I analyze here. The proper sticks to certain forms of social organization, such as marriage, that get fixed as the ideal: monogamous, heterosexual, able-bodied, and reproductive. The fixing of women's sexual desire within the narratives of romance and heteronormative marriage maintains a persistence in South Africa for some scholars because of a dominance of "westocentric meanings of sex and sexuality" (Steyn and van Zyl 2009: 5). Following the passing of the Civil Union Act of 2006 that makes provision for same-sex marriage (Judge, Manion, and De Waal 2008), this "proper" also elaborates itself as or, rather, extends its surface as elaborating, perhaps, a form of citizenship in South Africa (also see Scott and Theron 2017). And yet, most people's lives are not arranged within the proper enactment of such a social arrangement (see, e.g., James 2017; Macharia 2013; Nyanzi 2013).

In many accounts of the practice of *lobola* and its persistence,[1] there is something always implied as a crisis in relation to how we understand the liberal subject (e.g., Gqola 2017: 116–17). In such accounts, lobola potentially threatens access to equal rights for women (Ansell 2001) or produces contradictory meanings in the present, for instance, where men are able to appropriate the intentions of the process (Shope 2006). For others, the effects of a rising consumer culture shape all wedding rituals, including the ways people practice lobola, so the opportunity for a couple to share the costs of the process here works as a further expression of their romantic love, and in sharing these responsibilities the couple here performs an extension of their equal rights (van Dijk 2017). Read in this way, customary practices alongside civil marriage are both in and out of contradiction with what Pumla Dineo Gqola (2016) has named the New South African Woman and Gcobani Qambela (forthcoming) has named as the New South African Man.

Michael Yarbrough (2018) not only historizes same-sex marriage alongside contestations in the history of customary law in South Africa but also notes that, for many Black lesbian and gay-identified South Africans, struggles about kinship and marriage and the political claims for same-sex marriage draw on ideals of romantic love that are not in contradiction with claims for recognition of marriage through customary law. Xavier Livermon (2015: 17) echoes Yarbrough in suggesting that "for black queers one important site for making claims to sexual autonomy rests in accessing forms of African tradition and redefining what constitutes African culture." This view of custom extends a definition of African culture as "traditional authority" (see Comaroff and Comaroff 2018) "to produce the customary as the site of circumscribed community self-construction through the possibility of the appeal to multiple authorities beneath and above the rule of Law" (White 2015: 1010).

Opening a volume on sexualities in Africa, Signe Arnfred (2004) suggests that we make attempts to understand sexuality/ies in Africa by taking an epistemological orientation to the category Africa as one produced through moral codes that place it and Africans as repetitively becoming, continuously subjects of history as other in relation to the invention of a European subject (Lewis 2011). This signification is retained in the consolidation of area studies and queer studies (see Currier and Migraine-George 2016) and in orientations to queer Africa (see Ekine 2013). The epistemological orientation Arnfred (2004: 15) reads foundational authors of disciplinary knowledge forms in the human, social, and biological sciences as responsible for articulating what they observed of kinship and sexuality in Africa with a number of problematic assumptions that are interpolated into the present:

1. The assumption of heterosexuality, taking for granted the impossibility of same-sex relations because "no penis, no sex"
2. The assumption that stable sex and gender differences exist, in a hierarchy where men are superior and where sex happens between men and women in something that we now call compulsory heterosexuality
3. The assumption that immorality is defined by the purpose of sex: good sex is that which is procreative, while bad sex is that which is for pleasure

To this list I would add the process of becoming, or entering the social and historical for the bride (regardless of their sex or gender), who is the primary subject of my analysis, through the reading of rites of passage or rituals, like marriage somehow matches up to psychoanalytical development maps. The cartography of these maps relies on the ritual producing a coherent subject as bride, adult, or even sexually mature, and these maps are also decidedly linear. Initiation is readily seen as a rite of maturation for brides, who pass through a process that enables them to birth legitimately, thereby legitimizing female sexuality and reproduction (Becker 2004: 40). The child, as a sign of a future, marks the legitimacy of this cartography (Edelman 2004). I am interested in the ways that sexuality is therefore assumed to be accumulated through rehearsals of initiation, education, social-ization, and practicing and how the legitimacy of proper sex in turn offers a new status, as bride or wife.

While customary rituals offer the possibility of passing through sex, gen-der, and sexuality as communally related processes, on the other hand, rituals such as bachelorette parties are often read as individualistic, if not individualizing practices. The bachelorette in becoming-bride is a visual centerpiece who through love, romance, and consumption gets to demonstrate transformation into the status of bride in an uninhibited and hypersexual manner. On the subject, Beth Monte-murro (2003) makes the argument that the bachelorette party is a departure from its precedent, the bridal shower (like the kitchen tea party), principally because of the ways the bride is able to publicly express relation to sexuality and pleasure.

In this article, I read several scenes where I observed parties and pro-cesses of becoming-bride (see Mupotsa 2015) with the intention of thinking both about the figure of the bride and about the (sexual) relations made through the term *conjugality*. I have attended several bridal showers, all involving cisgender women receiving lessons on what it means to become bride. In my initial reflec-tions on these scenes, I noticed how, in these homosocial spaces and during these advice ceremonies, through various kinds of communication very normative ide-als about proper sex were exchanged, yet various other things were happening and being communicated. The phallus imagined or otherwise seemed to remain at the center of what was understood as a proper sexual relation, yet I was witness to groups of women practicing sex or doing what I later discuss as dry humping, in continuity and excess of this normative frame. Because these rituals, or inti-mate events (Povinelli 2006), rest so densely within the crises of autological and genealogical discourses, I could only come to think about dry humping as a dense knot of sociality, or conjugality, that is both within and in excess of the grammar of proper sex.

Yarbrough (2018: 1094) notes that current struggles for the recognition of relationships for Black lesbians and gay-identified South Africans share "much in common with contemporaneous struggles of their heterosexual counterparts, and these commonalities reflect ongoing tensions between more extended-family and more dyadic understandings of African marriage." The tensions Yarbrough notes fall in line with the tensions, or play, as I have put it, around autological and genealogical discourses. Thinking in parallel with Yarbrough's consideration of same-sex marriage in South Africa, I aim to elaborate this position through the discussion of conjugality I offer here. The complex dynamics are produced at the contestation of the ideas of two persons in love, against an understanding of marriage as dyadic and involving the family that are sutured to the sexual relation made through the figure of the bride, regardless of gender. Scholars who observe the historical changes in customary practices such as lobola note the ways shifting labor relations imposed by racial capital produce and enforce divisions of labor, sex, and power or, in transforming masculinities, reshape the meaning of marriage. While only men can initiate marriage (see Hunter 2010; Mwanmanda 2016; Yarbrough 2018: 1093–94) in many common understandings of the practice, my argument here begins with the premise that the bride *is* the marriage across these social relations—the bride, regardless of gendered identity, is the conjugal relation. The implications here are that there is something about sex (proper and otherwise), as it is articulated, as a relation, or sexuated position, around which other relations are forged, that exceeds the notions of sex as property of person within these intimate events.

## "Making Tea"

Wedding rituals, through the scandalous use of language and bodies (see Felman [1980] 2002), enact the process or at least the desire for a project of territorialization. "Making tea" is one such process. Many parties that I grew up attending with my mother were called "kitchen tea parties." These parties were hosted usually by an older and/or married aunt for a soon to be or recently married woman. These parties shared many characteristics with the parties we attended during and after lobola negotiations, as well as what I understood, at least from visual and media culture, as the bachelorette party. Women would make delicious food, such as samosas and sausage rolls, and a lot of wine, beer, and cider would be going around. There would be music and dancing and some degree of debauchery after and occasionally during the formal exchanges. Women would bring such gifts as crockery and tableware and offer unsolicited advice about how to manage the new home. Many years later I adopted the style of the kitchen tea, sans gifts, and sat with a group of women, some of whom were in the state/stage of becoming-bride. We discussed the process of getting married. The memories we shared about being at these parties as children were animated and exciting; they elicited the intensity of an "almost-secret" pleasure.

My research began with an awkward autoethnographic commitment, one that shares kinship to "writ[ing] in transit, shuttling between times and places," and as a "missive from the Black queer space that *demands to be thought, but refuses to be known*" (Shange 2019: 41). Writing this article has taken time, demanded forms of speech and language that bundle different audiences and grant those audiences different rites of access to forms of knowing, what Keguro Macharia (2016: 188) offers as "the sly native, the trickster native, the desiring native, the sage native, the agential native, the undeveloped native, the homosexual native, the queer native, the deracinated native . . . the native who wanders off." In the time of the research and the time of writing this article are temporal lines where I have occupied various nonnormative vocabularies (Matebeni and Msibi 2015) and positions of queer woman entering heterosexual marriage, divorced queer woman, and lesbian woman. The entanglements of my positions (my life, lived experience), as a practice of fugitive autoethnography, move across this account.

It was not actually until one afternoon, during the focus group discussion I mention earlier, that I recognized the force of this orientation in approaching personal, intimate, yet public performances of sex, such as the wedding ritual itself. The group of women was composed of friends, some more familiar than others. I opened our discussion by asking if the group understood the process of lobola, and the conversation was soon animated with experiences of being both in and out of the status of bride at various social occasions. Because I began the work with a sense that I did not actually know what happened during lobola negotiations, it came like a smack to the face when the memories recounted felt so very familiar. While there was something specific about being in the location of the bride and feeling like this was actually about you, it was a full range of accounts, memories, and scenes that this and other rituals accumulated as shared and rather impersonal narratives about being a girl or woman that we had experienced socializing with our friends and families.

Molemo had been living with her partner for years and was finding the process of getting married as unfamiliar as I initially had. For instance, their families had several meetings to negotiate the lobola—this in itself was not unusual. As lobola was negotiated, the families also negotiated the white wedding with regard to such aspects as who would pay for it and what it would involve. Again, this was frustrating but not necessarily unusual. What she found really interesting was that in each meeting she was asked to relate a version of herself as bride that "played virgin," so she would in principle "move in" with her partner once they were actually married. Moving in would be a gesture performed at each of these family meetings through sound bites of advice about married life. On the last of these meetings the sound bite arrived as a strong suggestion when Molemo's mother-in-law talked to her about making tea. The mother-in-law never once made direct reference to sex or sex acts but instead talked to Molemo about how important it was to make tea for your husband, because this was the way to sustain a happy marriage. She also explained that making tea was a way of making marriage legitimate, because if they were to make tea with regularity it would be no time at all before they would have children to give proper form to the union. As Molemo shared the encounter, we smiled, laughed awkwardly, and turned to each other in shared recognition, because even if we were not actually there, we knew the story well.

"Making tea" is the most creative expression of the kinds of advice that one receives on these occasions. Described to and directed at me quite often, to *make tea* is an expression to the bride of the task of keeping your future husband sexually satisfied. Making tea goes further because it works on the presumption that, despite "known" conditions, you have fulfilled the performance of bearing a solid prior innocence of sex and, further, that you recognize that sex is part of other socially reproducing tasks like cooking. Making tea is about pleasure, because no husband is satisfied with a sexually passive wife. Yet to be sexually active is more specific: do not be too assertive, for if you are to make tea, you perform your sexual desire by being seductive, perhaps use props like lingerie and perfume. "On Fridays, why don't you leave work early and send the kids to a friend or relative," when making tea, making love, alludes to making babies. Other advice: "Prepare husband's favorite meal, and set aside his favorite whiskey." "Meet husband at the door, partially dressed." Yes, making tea is romantic love. "Be sure to call husband *baby, darling, sweetie, sugar, daddy*," yes.

Making tea is not simply a direction, a process of being hailed, as Ratele (2007) suggests. I regard it as a process of territorialization, one that rhetorically acts out the desire to produce "bride" through the performance of sexuated and ethnolinguistic boundaries. One becomes, or in becoming-bride is offered potential to become, a historical subject. Making tea enables a subject to develop and fail to pass through an ideal image. While Black womxn are invited to represent "culture," we make tea to also inherit one, as "women have no tribe" (Vail 1989: 15). We can take the change in dress at traditional wedding ceremonies as an example. Following successful negotiations, the couple is invited to change from one set of traditional attire to another when the bride is received by her new family. The bride is literally "changed" by her new in-laws, a visualized transformation from tribelessness to the fashionable, modern belonging to a tribe. What constitutes "traditional" dress is a negotiation of imagination, aspiration, fashion, and taste (see Motsemme 2003) and a demand to cohere a sense of the self that belongs to a recognized ethnolinguistic category of difference (Bell 1998: 465). The wedding ritual places (Black) women as a kind of "presence/absence" (Spillers 1984), as the ritual is framed around the movement of women from one territorial claim to another. Making tea as ritual places women at the center of a scene that forms a structure of kinship through language and the law in a project to project the aspiration of difference. The songs sung and spoken on these occasions articulate the anxiety of these messy becomings. The tensions are eased at the height of the ritual as the bride is invited to join the clan of their husband, learn the language, and prepare for a life of social reproduction animated by advice ceremonies and exchange of gifts.

Sibonile Edith Ellece (2011) looks at making tea through the ritual advice ceremonies of *go laya* in Botswana. Ellece makes a correlation between the relative unsafety of women in marriage and the advice women are given in these ceremonies. This argument centers on the concept of the "marital fool," where "'foolishness' represent[s] traditional feminine values of subservience, long-suffering, tolerance and passiveness" (44). Nonhlanhla Dlamini (2009) looks at songs, *umstimba* in Swazi/SiSwati, that serve a congruent set of purposes of advising women entering marriage. The songs are individual and communal, so that the work of articulating an individual experience of marriage is interrupted, sometimes literally by the voice of another, to constitute the performance of these songs, and the advice given through this mode of performance comes to bear the weight of thick contestation rather than offering a simple instruction in passivity. Dlamini (2009: 139) give several examples of this, for instance, in the bodily movements of women, pointing to the breast, which enacts a "corruption" of what she views as male-authored texts. Through the song, la Dlamini (aunty or mother Dlamini), who is being observed by Dlamini (2009), attends to how her body has been constituted in history and discourse as immoral, and proceeds to express her mistreatment in marriage through the demand for her body to experience pleasure. Dlamini (2009) examines language and the body in renditions of performances that, while reconstituting sexual difference and an attendant hierarchy of sex-gender and compulsory heterosexuality, relate girl-woman-bride as a sexuated subjectivity, holding an awareness of being in, around, outside of place.

Social historians have referred to advice ceremonies like this in such terms as *initiation rites* and *sexual socialization*, to measure and describe transformations of societies in the region (see Delius and Glaser 2002; Erlank 2004). In these accounts, sexuality as a field relates to young people who through these rites or processes of sexualization are able to variously enter adulthood. In Natasha Erlank's (2004: 77–78) account, initiation rites come into crisis with the introduction of Christianity for African people, as it both opened and closed spaces to engage with sex, for instance, with regards to sexual pleasure. While there were spaces to publicly foreground the ideal of sexual pleasure for Black people prior to the colonial encounter, missionary Christianity brought perspective on sexual difference, domesticity, and femininity that emphasized abstinence and chastity. The church took a position toward initiation schools, which would otherwise have educated girls about sex, and because of this position the church became increasingly concerned with the form of instruction they took. Sexuality as a subject about youth also meant the introduction of sex education, narratively presented as "science" in schools to sexually differentiated groups.

Erlank's analysis relies on a spatial demarcation between the countryside and the city, which in her and many other analyses would experience different paces of change in the nineteenth and twentieth century. In part, this assumption relies on the presumption that in the countryside forms of relation and family structure could retain prior and continuous coherences. The other part is demonstrated in the account by Peter Delius and Clive Glaser (2002: 27) of the processes of sexual socialization "that existed in African societies in South Africa in the past [and] the way these were transformed under the impact of Christianity, conquest, migrant labor and urbanization." Delius and Glaser addressed an audience of social historians and Africanists to account for a flimsy dearth of work in the field of sexuality and noted that attempts to do this kind of work often reference or borrow the methods of anthropologists whose work more often described the sexual lives of the societies that they studied. One of the key inheritances of this mode of reference is that, as anthropologists describe sexuality in reference to closed social systems, empirically and methodologically, social historians inherit the presumption that sexuality is learned in relation to becoming, or entering a social system of belonging. That is, sexuality is accumulated and is also a point of entry into kinship.

*Initiation* and *education* are terms that Delius and Glaser (2002) used to understand socialization. We are to understand that children learn about sex and in turn develop a sexuality. Children as such do not have a sexuality but enter the social by seeing and practicing sex, coming into knowledge about it and, through rites, become legitimate or mature sexual subjects in adulthood. We are given the example of "mummy/daddy" games that children would play in precolonial contexts as one form of practice (Delius and Glaser 2002: 32). This form of play is variously described in relation to closed social groups, so we inherit the assumption that it is specific to the coherent ethnolinguistic group it was related to describe and is presumably not a generalizable aspect of childhood across temporal and spatial boundaries. We also learn that the play itself is not real sex, just mere rehearsal.

## The "Real Housewife"

When Nomathemba got married, I was set the task of finding a "Zambian," a collo-quial term for a woman—who in this case was actually a Zambian national—who would run a two-hour class on proper sex in marriage. As friends, we awk-wardly gathered and proceedings followed. The Zambian arrived quite early and demanded that the still sober crowd gather in a circle as she placed Nomathemba at the center and proceeded to demonstrate a technique that she called the "lazy man." She understood sex as an act we were obliged to do with our husbands, and male pleasure in sex was not just expected but natural. For women, pleasure should be achieved as well, but it is necessary that we be coy about this pleasure. Your husband should not be expected to give you pleasure—to be a husband is to be a "lazy man."

The lazy man is what is perhaps more commonly referred to as the "cow-girl" (front and reverse) where the (future) wife in this case straddles the (future) husband, and they are able to participate with at least the nonexpectation of much movement on the husband's part. As you are responsible for moving, you are in a privileged position to make sure that your special spots are stimulated, and you can rather furtively guarantee that you have an orgasm. So, we took turns learning how to straddle the teacher-as-metaphorical lazy man on the ground and, through subtle movements in the hips and upper body, not only leading our man to climax but with subtlety and demureness also managing to achieve completion ourselves. This is the "lazy man."

The lazy man "sticks" (Ahmed 2004) as a narrative script that forms or structures emotions. By this, I refer to the narrative that structures desire and articulates the process by which we are pulled or orientated toward another. There is perhaps nothing all that desirable about a lazy man, and yet it forms a strong part of the encounters that we have with what it means to have our desires recip-rocated in the form of love, "the normative version of which is the two-as-one inti-macy of the couple form" (Berlant 2012: 7). In the Zambian's account, sex is so saturated with the phallus that no activity is required from the person symbolically possessing that particular pound of flesh. Only one kind of genital organ "counts," so as it stands, "'real sex' is nearly always associated with the penis" (Ratele 2011: 399). If you recall my charge that sexuality has been read as a linear cartography, on this line in the phallic phase, adult sexuality comes to be organized around a male-female difference where men possess a phallus and women are castrated, since their genitals are never to be found. By implication, the language we have to understand sexual subjectivities can only articulate female desire, and the sexual relation through the logic of this One (Gallop 1988: 125–26), the "One" referring to the status of the phallus as the single signifier of sexual difference.

Unable to locate a Zambian for a bridal shower for Ntombifuthi, another friend, I went to the internet and sought the services of Joy, a consultant for Pure Romance, an in-home direct sales company that sells "intimacy aids" and/as "empowerment" to women.[2] Joy was rather lovely, and I have since had the pleasure of sitting with her to discuss how she came to this work. She told me her sister had a bridal shower, and a Pure Romance consultant presented her wares to them. She was amazed, and was most attracted to what she was saying because the consultant was teaching her and other women things that others do not teach them, "educating women about things that your mother won't tell you, or your grandmother."[3] Joy, like the unnamed Zambian, was a Black woman in her mid-forties who had worked as a consultant with this company for just under a year at that time. She believed in the "three Es" that they sell to women: entertain, educate, and empower, for what they teach is pleasure for women, nothing to make them "dirty" or "promiscuous." For both Joy and the Zambian, sex and its pleasures are for marriage.

Black women's power is articulated in the language of gender equality as the form of agency that breathes the democratic present to life by placing love as duty and obligation to family, culture, and nation (Clark 2006). Gqola (2007: 117) refers to this articulation of power as guided by a "cult of femininity" that affirms what we "share" but forms a conservative and nontransformative public discourse that we receive as "women's empowerment." The contradiction for Gqola is that women are placed in public as highly empowered but remain contained by limiting notions of femininity in the private sphere.

Joy worked for a major publishing house and sold Pure Romance on the weekend and during her free time. There are differences in scale between what Joy and Aunty Eve or the Zambian did, because Joy worked for a multinational corporation, but there are also many similarities. The aunties, many of whom are not blood or even closely kin relation, have generally always been a friend or friends specifically hired to attend a party and teach sexual knowledge. Many of the aunties I met at these parties growing up, I understood then as I do now, were gender-nonconforming or trans women. They were aunties, like "Auntie Tiwo," as she was referred to during her hearings (Biruk 2014: 458).[4] Their sexual knowledge, gathered in the term *Auntie*, is something that is part of the "production of Black queer common sense across gender and generation [that carry] fleshy dimensions" described by Savannah Shange (2019: 41). This is a commonsense knowledge, asserted in Zethu Matebeni and Thabo Msibi's (2015) claims of "vocabularies of the non-normative" and Stella Nyanzi's (2013) claims of the multiple routes or forms of assertion same-sex–loving individuals claim in various African countries. While these aunts (when I grew up) did not sell actual toys, creams, or clothes to enhance sex acts, their time and expertise were compensated in cash. (And in many recent experiences, these aunts now also trade in sex toys.) It is also the case at these parties that the range of objects gifted share qualities with those of Pure Romance. That is, the pot sets and crockery gifted to the becoming-bride are directly sold to the gifter by a woman present, who like Joy works part time for a direct sales company. These parties are generally a time when women present their entrepreneurial savvy as part-time dressmakers or importers of specialist goods from China or Dubai. The attachment to an object like Tupperware, for instance, is tied to the very ritual in practice and the affective dimensions that it presents to the audience (see Vally 2014). The heady mix of knowledge, power, and morality proposed by Joy not only speaks to how women are trained to sell these products but also broadens a longer relation between notions of empowerment in Black women's intimate public spheres.

Pure Romance sells the "three Bs": beauty, bedroom, and body. Super Stretch Lips and the Real Housewife are silicone vaginas, and they are a really big sell. Women buy them as gifts for their partners. Joy did not know if these men used them. When we met, Joy had recently purchased one herself, for her husband for Valentine's Day:

> He shouldn't know about it. He should think that I am just busy. I will tie him up and blindfold him. Super Stretch Lips—I think that is an excellent idea. For those days when you just don't feel like it. And you can just sit on him as if you are busy with him. Either giving him a blow job or sitting on him as if you are having sex. I think it will work. The Housewife works the same way.

I was surprised by the number of silicone vaginas sold on the evening of my friend's party. I was alarmed because they were sold on the promise that one could substitute their own mouth, anus, or vagina for the silicon one in the case of "really not wanting to," rather than as a gift substitute for anyone, really, despite their genital/sexual configuration or practice, to invariably use with or instead of their own body parts. The silicone vaginas were sold as appendage/replacement in a re/performance of the lazy man. After my side-eye judgment, I have been thinking of Joy's account of the usefulness of Super Stretch Lips and the Real Housewife in the terms of a "prosthetic embodiment" (Berlant 2008: 151), which expands or stretches the frame of "women's empowerment."

The Real Housewife extends further the meanings I outline above, more specifically in reference to Black women's relation to the good or "proper" line. Shireen Ally's (2013) reading of commodity culture and colonialism emphasizes the iconographic assemblage of maid-madam and machine to argue that domesticity is produced and articulated in multiple valences and relations to labor. Domesticity as a discourse that frames femininity, proper sex, the organization of space, and the constitution of sexuated persons informs the ways that freedom to consume and have proper sex are the same. Domesticity is a discourse that literally and figuratively enables white women to historically be properly feminine but for Black women remains more significantly shaped by labor as "hired hand" in domestic labor in the South and Southern African experience. The word play we can do with the "real" housewife is plenty when we read the location of being-housewife as being/becoming produced by hired hands as prosthesis: "If, in the post-imperial centers, the servant would be figured as antithetical to modern white suburban domesticity, in the colonies, the black servant would become iconic of the same. Servants and detergents would thus together share a specific, what I will argue may be called a prosthetic, relation to the 'housewife'" (Ally 2013: 329).

## Dry Humping

This article's aim is to present conjugality as an assemblage that gathers or drags "proper sex," "making tea," and "the real housewife" as continuous figurations of "the bride." Along with thinking about the epistemological frames by which we come to know the African bride as a particular kind of figure, marked by the signifier *African*, it is also my aim to foreground the ways or forms of knowing the world possessed, enacted, intuited, or performed by those of us who have been variously located in proximity with that category. In this sense, two epistemological lines run across this article simultaneous, along which conjugality as a continuous intimate event enables or orients our view to autological and genealogical forms of subjection. The subject of this conjugal relation appears under conditions where the liberal individual subject is simultaneous with the emergence of ethnolinguistic difference as "culture," which emerges coconstitutively with sexual difference, or "gender" within a male/female distinction. It is in this sense that I read the co-occurrence of customary law/same-sex marriage and the extension of the consumer wedding to Black people as constituent to the rights of proper citizenship, with the coincidence of the persistence of the law of society or of the father, where marriage and the rites/rights to it remain a site of struggle.

In her discussion with Katherine McKittrick, Sylvia Wynter revisits her formulations of Man1, Man2, and Man3. This genealogical project offers us tools to consider the forms of knowledge that are made in the conversations I offer as examples, along with the assumptions about the person, science, knowledge, sex, and sexuality that are articulated in scholarship that has examined "sex education" for Black women. Wynter locates various epistemological ruptures: the secularization of humanism, the Copernican leap, Darwinism, Frantz Fanon's sociogeny, and the 1960s, marked by the ruptures of postcolonialism and poststructuralism. Wynter noted that "the figure of the human is tied to epistemological histories that presently value a *genre* of the human that reifies Western bourgeoisie tenets; the human is therefore wrought with physiological and narrative matters" (Wynter and McKittrick 2015: 9).

The emergence of *homo humanitas* and *homo politicus*, which are then followed in the context of liberal monohumanism with *homo economicus*, is often assumed to follow an abandoning of *homo religious*, but Wynter notes a continuity rather that a total severing. In this way we might think about the heady mix of religion, capitalism, and science in the advice and lessons I have discussed here, in the signifier *Africa*, and in the ways that custom is a remainder that "escapes" but also enables the emergence of the secular liberal monohumanism retained in these analyses of sex education—the signifier *Africa* is one that then comes to still contain animism, understood here as a belief that not just humans but material objects and other species possess a consciousness. Africans' appropriation of science, modernity, or even Christianity, when articulated within the dichotomy of modernity/tradition, rearticulates the charge that the remainder of animism distances Africans from secular liberal monohumanism. It is in these terms that I read the assemblage of conjugality as "dragging" these two temporal lines.

Harry Garuba (2003: 263–64) notes the ways that social scientists who study "the state, culture, and society in postindependence Africa have observed various aspects of [a] cultural practice of assimilating the diverse instruments and dimensions of European modernity, such as its science and technology as well as the . . . state and its political machinery, into the matrix of traditional ritual and culture . . . [a] practice [that] has broadly been referred to as the 're-traditionalization of Africa'." Garuba observes two concurrent and related premises to this re-traditionalization; "the first involves the assimilation of modern forms into traditional practices by a 'traditional' elite; and the second refers to . . . the recuperation of traditional forms and practices . . . and their incorporation into the forms of Western modernity" (265).

In Mark Hunter's (2010) evaluation of transformations of masculinity in South Africa, for example, it is the imposition of traditional authorities through the machineries of taxation, which enable colonial authorities to force those who through waged labor become "men." The crises "between men" that follow happen with regard to the practice of lobola, because previous forms of status and hierarchy are interrupted by the imposition of a cash economy. Young, working men now in a position where they can rely on an income no longer rely on the support of fathers and uncles, and here a new subject of masculinity is produced. Oyèrónké Oyěwùmí's (2004: 4) case against the use of gender as a concept is made through a critique of the nuclear family, describing it as a specifically European form and as the gendered family par excellence: "Thus, while daughters self-identify, as female, with their mothers and sisters, sons identify with their fathers and brothers. . . . The spatial configuration of the nuclear family household as an isolated space is critical to understanding feminist conceptual categories." Oyěwùmí's analysis refutes biological essentialisms, revealing that anatomy is not necessarily destiny, as there are various kinds of statuses or positions that are available in the family, when the family is not necessarily understood to be nuclear. That is, there may be statuses in the family that are not necessarily based on a male/female distinction, and a patriarchal status might be placed on someone we would identify as "woman."

This case against "woman" is echoed in Nkiru U. Nzegwu's (2006) analysis of the concepts of "family." Nzegwu opens her book with the view that, within the linear temporality of African nation states, the family becomes the site of contesting tradition (also see Macharia 2013), and here the positions "daughter" and "wife" come to be legally subordinated statuses because of the universal adoption of the nuclear family as the epistemological site from which culture as difference and as categories of gender emerge. Nzegwu (2006) is cautious not to assume that this means there are no hierarchies, echoing Bakare-Yusuf (2004), but it seems important to me to sustain this critique of woman as a category. I earlier mention Rubin (1984), who establishes an important vocabulary about how certain forms of sexual relation become proper and others are relegated as otherwise. Rubin's analysis also sets the scene for us to understand how this proper relation is made, through the incest taboo, whereby that proper relation necessarily relies on the transaction of women between men.

Ifi Amadiume (2005: 84) challenges the universality of this transaction as an origin story for patriarchy, principally querying the linear progression from "barbarism to savagery in primitive sexual promiscuity, to matrilineal descent to matriarchy and mother-right, and finally, to masculine imperialism in patriarchy; monogamy and the nuclear family" relied on by most scholars of kinship. Amadiume, whose aim is to first discount a prevailing view that patriarchy and matriarchy are total social systems, further argues that "the matricentric unit is an autonomous production unit; *it is also an ideological unit*" (88, emphasis mine). This means that we have a co-occurrence of the subject through the tripartite "mummy, daddy, me," and another through other concepts of the family that are closer to "mother, daughter, son." This is an important remainder, one that I believe remains alongside that of animism.

What is codified to customary law, and articulated within the frame of secular monohumanism, is that, along with losing sight of these forms of subjection as related to what it means to be a person, much less how many families are socially organized as not nuclear, we also often miss the remainders of an animist orientation to the world. Garuba (2003: 266) wrote that he has "chosen to describe the practice of *continually re-enchanting the world* as a manifestation of the animist unconscious," developing animist materialism and animist unconsciousness as a magical worldview. This remainder I believe is contained in what Audre Lorde (1984) has described as "the erotic" and M. Jacqui Alexander (2005) as "the Sacred."

Kaja Silverman (1984) reads feminist psychoanalytic attempts to place in structure and language a vocabulary for women's pleasure. In these accounts, it is *jouissance*, a pleasure that exceeds the law because it is illegible in the language of the phallus. As women, we escape the repression of the phallic phase because our genitals are apparently so difficult to find. As it is, men as the phallus are wholly consumed by the symbolic order and an identification with the law, while as women we potentially disidentify with the phallus as it eternally fails to represent us (Berlant 2012: 57). The *jouissance* that we can experience outside of the law is made possible during the performance of proper sex because what we do learn in becoming-bride is the work of femininity as masquerade. Masquerade is the proper sex that we perform due to our understanding of what it means to be intelligibly feminine in the symbolic order, yet as we mask our own experiences of pleasure, say, as is the case in the lazy man, we are able to reveal the extent to which we recognize that our absorption into that logic is at best superficial.

Nzegwu (2011) is interested in African eroticism as something that exceeds the hegemony of Western influence and logic, retaining an animism like Garuba (2003) describes. The Zambian and Auntie Eve are specialists in teaching from such a perspective, in the sense that they emphasize that the lessons they offer in spaces intimately zoned for womxn only are formed of generations of oral tradition that has at its central goal the expectation that sexual pleasure for men and women is a social good. Nzegwu (2011) does not intend a pure bifurcation of "African" and other sexualities and their logics but is attentive to the ontological possibilities of a narrative structure about sexuality that privileges the minor literatures that spread during these rituals and exceed certain forms of analysis and explanation. Nzegwu notes that these ontologies have two principles that emphasize fertility and pleasure (259). Much like feminist readings of psychoanalysis, the grammatical structure prioritizes fertility as proper sex for women, and yet again Nzegwu observes forms of language hidden in these major grammars that place stronger emphasis on female pleasure outside of the fulfillment of a procreative wish.

At a kitchen tea party for an older cousin when I was fourteen years old, I was again called into the room where an auntie pointed to me among the others and asked me what I knew about sex. I stood still and listened as she told me that I would need to learn her lessons if I was ever going to keep a man. She asked if I thought I was pretty, repeatedly, and then chastised me for my vanity before I could answer. The auntie then explained that I had better listen to her because it did not really matter how pretty I was, if I did not listen then even "Shatricia" could steal my man. *Shatricia* is a name made up of the Shona verb *kushata*, which means "to be ugly," and the proper name *Tricia*. Combined, the fictional figure of the ugly but sexually knowledgeable Shatricia was set as a motivation for me to acquire sexual knowledge. This auntie then had us on our backs and our knees in a range of poses we were meant to hold and practice for the future. At the end of the event, as our mothers looked on, partly drunk and deep in laughter, the auntie then asked my mother if she could return later in the week to show me how to pull myself. *Pulling* refers to the practice of stretching the inner labia. Accounts of the practice and techniques vary in relating its main purpose. When offered the chance to learn, I was curious; it was an opportunity to talk about sex and discover my own body, albeit with a somewhat callous and intrusive auntie figure, so I eagerly albeit anxiously said yes. Mathabo Khau (2009), in conversations with girls in Lesotho, concluded that they found their experience of pulling conformist, as proper girlhood was constructed in relation to proper sex. Guillermo Martínez Pérez, Brigitte Bagnol, and Concepción Tomás Aznar (2014) instead look to labia pulling as ritual that presents opportunities for a different relation to sexuality for women, principally because of the homoerotic and autoerotic techniques of the practice.

For Nzegwu (2011) and Sylvia Tamale (2005) practices like those that Auntie Eve and the Zambian teach, such as labia stretching, make us more aware of the vagina. In these practices we are introduced to self-stimulation, and the labia are explicitly made into sex toys. Extending this view, Nzegwu offers a reading of rituals that perform and practice the "devouring vagina," a positive re/forming of the "lazy man" which emphasizes the vagina as "'mature and experienced,' 'taunting' (referring to dexterous pelvic movements during intercourse), 'assertive,' 'firm,' 'tight,' 'moist,' 'warm,' 'rhythmic,' 'textured' and pulsating'" (2011: 265). The knowledge of the body that Auntie Eve and the Zambian confer has the intention of demystifying the body and sex yet retains the rhetorical form of science fiction that Donna Haraway (1989) argues frames our relation to the body. For Haraway, bodies are material-semiotic and generative, and their boundaries are made only in social interaction. To "know" the body is a process of putting in language a certain subjectivity. For women, the process of subjection is the process of entering the symbolic in language, which has been demonstrated to lead to a subordination of women's desire, the "body is charted, zoned and made to bear meaning" (Silverman 1984: 325).

Dry humping is a literal reference to the techniques we rehearsed with the Zambian. As I described earlier, we sat on the floor and straddled each other to learn the technique of the "lazy man." The process as practice, or rehearsal for the real thing, enabled these moments of stimulating ourselves and each other. The permission to dry hump, rehearsing autoerotic and homoerotic pleasures, comes from the extent to which the central meaning of the ritual is articulated determinedly around proper sex. In another example, once Joy left Ntombifuthi's party, the drinking kicked into gear. The group of increasingly incoherent women passed their advice to her in turns. As her cousin reminded her not to be the one who gives her husband blow jobs (that dirty work is for the side women), at that precise moment two women present turned to each other and leaned in for a kiss. While not open for the whole group to observe, three of the remaining seven women sat outside with me on the veranda and recounted their fantasies of kissing other women and then begged me to kiss them "to practice."

What does it mean "to practice"? At the time of the incident, I called a lesbian friend because I was upset at being at the center of particular forms of objectification for a group of women who are otherwise to continue heterosexual lives—the incident bore the feeling of a wrong articulated by Awino Okech (2013) in her reflections on the ways friendship permits forms of heterosexism to permeate in African feminist activism and solidarities. And yet, it seems too easy to consider the forms of sociality that occurred as simply a part of the rite of passage toward the goal of proper sex. It has apparently been quite difficult to find African lesbians (see Currier and Migraine-George 2017), and Taiwo Adetunji Osinubi (2018) thinks about recent, more assertive representations of African lesbians as claiming forms of political authority. A small amount of work on same-sex–loving women and the word *lesbian* as an identitarian claim exists (see, e.g., Matebeni 2008, 2011; Gunkel

2010; Imma 2017), and there is also work that attests to how African women loving women can be legible in forms outside of sexuality as property of the person,
what Heather Love (2009) describes as a frame and as a loss prior to the modern
individual subject (see, e.g., Morgan and Wieringa 2005). I think thinking so long
and hard about conjugality, with these scenes, is my attempt to gather all of this.

Neville Hoad (2016: 2) wrote that, while *customary law* refer to customs
codified within the law, there is "an archive of the customary [that] may provide
intellectual and affective resources to reimagine African sexual sovereignty." I
noted earlier that, while the taken-for-granted position is that women cannot initiate marriage, there is a history of woman-to-woman marriage in many African
contexts. Notably, in the declaration of the banning of woman-to-woman marriage
in 1974, Nigeria made use of the colonial repugnancy clause (Oomen 2000). Hoad
(2016: 8) notes that, for scholars like Amadiume (1987), these marriages are not
to be considered as sexual arrangements, echoed by Ashley Currier and Thérèse
Migraine-George (2017: 139), who note Amadiume's (1987) caution against Lorde's
(1984: 50) reference to these marriages as part of a trans-historical, intergenera-
tional history of Black women's erotic lives and attachments. In their account of
these marriages, Wairimu Ngaruiya Njambi and William E. O'Brien (2005) refute
the argument that these social arrangements of the household were purely agential
arrangements for women, for example, to ensure the rights to children or a means
to ensure inheritance. They also problematize the term *female-husband* and make
the main argument that these marriages *do* involve affective bonds. Despite these
observations, Njambi and O'Brien (2005) are still cautious in thinking of these
arrangements as interrupting heterosexuality as the proper form for sexuality, or
in considering these arrangements as forms of sexual relation where, even while
people are structurally (in the familial relation) in forms where heterosex happens,
other forms of sex may be transacted. This way of thinking about other kinds of
familial form and relation and sexual relations differs, for example, from the ways
Gloria Wekker (2006) examines how sexual relations and familial arrangements
can be arranged outside the frames of the proper that I have here described.

Also thinking about Gikuyu woman-to-woman marriages, Neo Sinoxolo
Musangi (2018: 403) approaches the question of these arrangements with the leading question, *How are you called?*:

> I privilege the *how*—rather than the *what*, or perhaps even the *why*—of
> my family life through a generation of women beginning with my grand-
> mothers, by way of my mother. I use the question "Witawa ata?" or "How
> are you called?" as an entry for an inquiry into the thing now known as

woman-to-woman marriage, its logic of care, and how this relationship could potentially enable us to rethink community formation and kinship ties.

"How are you called?" might gather the frames of conjugality I am trying to drag across this article. Natasha Thandiwe Vally (2015) offers a short reading of group theory as "form as confusion." I reference this to refer to the ways that dry humping confirms the narrative closure of proper sex in becoming-bride but also presents other confusing stimulations. In group theory, you identify organizing principles that you use to order the $x$ in mathematical equations. These principles would be the patterns we come to recognize that help us solve the equation or understand the mathematical question, patterns that we come to recognize and form meaning from. Vally (2015: 67–68) presents the four rules a mathematical sentence needs to obey to be a group—closure, associativity, identity, and inverses—to emphasize the ways that forms rely on axiomatic assumptions about the thingness/thinghood of their content. Making tea demonstrates the four rules as a form and, in turn, reveals pleasure as the reiteration of that form that "captures a way of being a something unbound to an identity that circulates" (Berlant 2011: 13). Dry humping is similar form because of the way it rehearses and returns us to the scene of making tea and its attachments. Yet, I conclude with the gentle suggestion that dry humping reiterates the scenes of pleasure that confuse the very language that attempts to confine identity, sexuality, or even desire. I worry about presenting a vocabulary for dry humping that claims certain meaning to it, as a *what*, but instead suggest that, if we pull apart the axiomatic assumption that sexual development is necessarily attached to coherent group identity, or kin, the figure becoming-bride in making tea productively confuses some of the ways we read sexuality.

## Notes

Some of the names of interviewees in this article are pseudonyms.

1.  *Lobola* refers to the process of negotiations undertaken between the families of the bride and groom. The negotiations, if successful, lead to a contract (either verbal or written, and at times both) about the form of gifts that will be passed from the family of the groom to the family of the bride to make the marriage legitimate. The emphasis on the term *negotiation* is intended perhaps to signal that the relationship formed in the conversation is ongoing, so in many instances the full amount is never paid directly or immediately, as these conversations continue in the life of a marriage,

presumably seen at this stage as one formed between families rather than between individuals. These negotiations also support patrilineage, so in fact it can be argued that what is negotiated is the reproductive labor of the wife and the guarantee that the children born in the union are legitimate.

2. See www.pureromance.co.za/about-us/our-history/ (accessed February 12, 2012).

3. Interview with "Joy," February 10, 2015, Rosebank, Johannesburg.

4. Steven Monjeza and Tiwonge Chimbalanga Kachepa, aka "Auntie Tiwo," were charged for their alleged same-sex marriage in Malawi in 2009–10. During the hearings, Tiwonge was described by many witnesses as a "proper woman," which meant commonsense understanding of Tiwonge's gender; this made her and Steven's relationship legible outside of its recognition as a homosexual one.

## References

Ahmed, Sara. 2004. *The Cultural Politics of Emotion.* London: Routledge.

Alexander, M. Jacqui. 2005. *Pedagogies of Crossing: Meditations on Feminism, Sexual Politics, Memory, and the Sacred.* Durham, NC: Duke University Press.

Ally, Shireen. 2013. "'Ooh, Eh Eh . . . Just One Small Cap Is Enough!' Servants, Detergents, and Their Prosthetic Significance." *African Studies* 72, no. 3: 321–52.

Amadiume, Ifi. 1987. *Male Daughters, Female Husbands: Gender and Sex in an African Society.* London: Zed Books.

Amadiume, Ifi. 2005. "Theorizing Matriarchy in Africa: Kinship Ideologies and Systems in Africa and Europe." In *African Gender Studies: A Reader,* edited by Oyèrónké Oyěwùmí, 83–98. New York: Palgrave.

Ansell, Nicola. 2001. "'Because It's Our Culture!' (Re)Negotiating the Meaning of Lobola in Southern African Secondary Schools." *Journal of Southern African Studies* 21, no. 4: 697–716.

Arnfred, Signe. 2004. "Re-thinking Sexualities in Africa: Introduction." In *Re-thinking Sexualities in Africa,* edited by Signe Arnfred, 7–29. Uppsala: Nordic Africa Institute.

Bakare-Yusuf, Bibi. 2003. "Determinism: The Phenomenology of African Female Existence." *Feminist Africa* 2: 8–24.

Bakare-Yusuf, Bibi. 2004. "'Yorubas Don't Do Gender': A Critical Review of Oyèrónké Oyěwùmí's *The Invention of Women: Making African Sense of Western Gender Discourses.*" In *African Gender Scholarship: Concepts, Methodologies, Paradigms,* edited by Signe Arnfred, 61–81. Dakar: Codesria.

Becker, Heike. 2004. "Efundula: Women's Initiation, Gender, and Sexual Identities in Colonial and Post-colonial Northern Namibia." In *Re-thinking Sexualities in Africa,* edited by Signe Arnfred, 35–57. Uppsala: Nordic Africa Institute.

Bell, Vikki. 1998. "Taking Her Hand: Becoming, Time, and the Cultural Politics of the White Wedding." *Cultural Values* 2, no. 4: 463–84.

Berlant, Lauren. 2008. *The Female Complaint: The Unfinished Business of Sentimentality in American Culture*. Durham, NC: Duke University Press.

Berlant, Lauren. 2011. *Cruel Optimism*. Durham, NC: Duke University Press.

Berlant, Lauren. 2012. *Desire/Love*. New York: Punctum Books.

Biruk, Crystal. 2014. "Aid for Gays: The Moral and the Material in 'African Homophobia' in Post-2009 Malawi." *Journal of Modern African Studies* 52, no. 3: 447–73.

Clark, Jude. 2006. "Looking Back and Moving Forward: Gender, Culture and Constructions of Transition in South Africa." *Agenda* 20, no. 68: 8–17.

Comaroff, John L., and Jean Comaroff, eds. 2018. *The Politics of Custom: Chieftainship, Capital, and the State in Contemporary Africa*. Johannesburg: Wits University Press.

Currier, Ashley, and Thérèse Migraine-George. 2016. "Queer Studies/African Studies: An (Im)Possible Transaction?" *GLQ: A Journal of Lesbian and Gay Studies* 22, no. 2: 281–305.

Currier, Ashley, and Thérèse Migraine-George. 2017. "'Lesbian'/Female Same-Sex Sexualities in Africa." *Journal of Lesbian Studies* 21, no. 2: 133–50.

Delius, Peter, and Clive Glaser. 2002. "Sexual Socialisation in South Africa: A Historical Perspective." *African Studies* 61, no. 1: 27–54.

Dlamini, Nonhlanhla. 2009. "Gendered Power Relations, Sexuality, and Subversion in Swazi Women's Folk Songs Performed during Traditional Marriage Rites and Social Gatherings." *Muziki* 6, no. 2: 133–44.

Edelman, Lee. 2004. *No Future: Queer Theory and the Death Drive*. Durham, NC: Duke University Press.

Ekine, Sokari. 2013. "Contesting Narratives of Queer Africa." In *Queer African Reader*, edited by Sokari Ekine and Hakima Abbas, 78–91. Dakar: Pambazuka.

Ellece, Sibonile Edith. 2011. "'Be a Fool like Me': Gender Construction in the Marriage Advice Ceremony in Botswana—A Critical Discourse Analysis." *Agenda* 25, no. 1: 43–52.

Erlank, Natasha. 2004. "'Plain Clean Facts' and Initiation Schools: Christianity, Africans, and 'Sex Education' in South Africa, c. 1919–1940." *Agenda* 18, no. 62: 76–83.

Felman, Shoshanna. (1980) 2002. *The Scandal of the Speaking Body*. Palo Alto, CA: Stanford University Press.

Gallop, Jane. 1988. *Thinking through the Body*. New York: Columbia University Press.

Garuba, Harry. 2003. "Explorations in Animist Materialisms: Notes in Reading/Writing African Literature, Culture, and Society." *Public Culture* 15, no. 2: 261–81.

Gqola, Pumla Dineo. 2007. "How the 'Cult of Femininity' and Violent Masculinities Support Endemic Gender Based Violence in Contemporary South Africa." *African Identities* 5, no. 1: 111–24.

Gqola, Pumla Dineo. 2016. "A Peculiar Place for a Feminist? The New South African Woman (NSAW), *True Love Magazine*, and Lebo(gang) Mashile." *Safundi* 17, no. 2: 119–36.

Gqola, Pumla Dineo. 2017. *Reflecting Rogue: Inside the Mind of a Feminist*. Johannesburg: Jacana.

Gunkel, Henriette. 2010. *The Cultural Politics of Female Sexuality in South Africa*. London: Routledge.

Haraway, Donna. 1989. "The Biopolitics of Postmodern Bodies: Determinations of Self in Immune System Discourse." *differences* 1, no. 1: 3–43.

Hoad, Neville. 2016. "Queer Customs against the Law." *Research in African Literatures* 47, no. 2: 1–19.

Hungwe, Chipo. 2006. "Putting Them in Their Place: 'Respectable' and 'Unrespectable' Women in Zimbabwean Gender Struggles." *Feminist Africa* 6: 33–47.

Hunter, Mark. 2010. *Love in the Time of AIDS: Inequality, Gender, and Rights in South Africa*. Bloomington: Indiana University Press.

Imma, Z'etoile. 2017. "(Re)Visualizing Black Lesbian Lives, (Trans) Masculinities, and Township Space in the Documentary Work of Zanele Muholi." *Journal of Lesbian Studies* 21, no. 2: 214–41.

James, Deborah. 2017. "Not Marrying in South Africa: Consumption, Aspiration, and the New Middle Class." *Anthropology South Africa* 40, no. 1: 1–14.

Judge, Melanie, Anthony Manion, and Shaun de Waal, eds. 2008. *To Have and to Hold: The Making of Same-Sex Marriage in South Africa*. Johannesburg: Fanele.

Khau, Mathabo. 2009. "Exploring Sexual Customs: Girls and the Politics of Elongating the Inner Labia." *Agenda* 23, no. 79: 30–37.

Lewis, Desiree. 2011. "Representing African Sexualities." In *African Sexualities: A Reader*, edited by Sylvia Tamale, 199–216. Cape Town: Pambazuka Press.

Livermon, Xavier. 2015. "Usable Traditions: Creating Sexual Autonomy in Post-apartheid South Africa." *Feminist Studies* 41, no. 1: 14–41.

Lorde, Audre. 1984. *Sister Outsider: Essays and Speeches*. Trumansburg: Crossing Press.

Love, Heather. 2009. *Feeling Backwards: Loss and the Politics of Queer History*. Cambridge, MA: Harvard University Press.

Macharia, Keguro. 2013. "Queer Kenya in Law and Policy." In *Queer African Reader*, edited by Sokari Ekine and Hakima Abbas, 273–89. Dakar: Pambazuka Press.

Macharia, Keguro. 2016. "On Being Area-Studied: A Litany of Complaint." *GLQ* 22, no. 2: 183–89.

Matebeni, Zethu. 2008. "Vela Bambhentsele: Intimacies and Complexities in Researching Black Lesbian Groups in Johannesburg." *Feminist Africa* 11: 89–96.

Matebeni, Zethu. 2011. "Exploring Black Lesbian Identities in Johannesburg." PhD diss., University of the Witwatersrand.

Matebeni, Zethu, and Thabo Msibi. 2015. "Vocabularies of the Non-normative." *Agenda* 29, no. 1: 3–9.

Montemurro, Beth. 2003. "Sex Symbols: The Bachelorette Party as a Window to Change in Women's Sexual Expression." *Sexuality and Culture* 7, no. 1: 3–29.

Morgan, Ruth, and Saskia Wieringa, eds. 2005. *Tommy Boys, Lesbian Men, and Ancestral Wives: Female Same-Sex Practices in Africa*. Johannesburg: Jacana.

Motsemme, Nthabiseng. 2003. "Distinguishing Beauty, Creating Distinctions: The Politics and Poetics of Dress among Young Black Women." *Agenda* 57: 12–19.

Mupotsa, Danai. 2015. "Becoming Girl-Woman-Bride." *Girlhood Studies* 8, no. 3: 73–87.

Musangi, Neo Sinoxolo. 2018. "Homing with My Mother / How Women in My Family Married Women." *Meridians: Feminism, Race, Transnationalism* 17, no. 2: 401–14.

Mwanmanda, Sharon. 2016. "Representing Lobola: Exploring Discourses of Contemporary Intersections of Masculinity for Zimbabwean Men in Cape Town: Lobola, Religion, and Normativity." MA thesis, University of Cape Town.

Njambi, Wairimu Ngaruiya, and William E. O'Brien. 2005. "Revisiting 'Woman-to-Woman Marriage': Notes on Gikuyu Women." In *African Gender Studies: A Reader*, edited by Oyèrónké Oyěwùmí, 145–65. New York: Palgrave.

Nyanzi, Stella. 2013. "Dismantling Reified African Culture through Localised Homosexualities in Uganda." *Culture, Health, and Sexuality* 15, no. 8: 952–67.

Nzegwu, Nkiru U. 2006. *Family Matters: Feminist Concepts in African Philosophy of Culture*. Albany: State University of New York Press.

Nzegwu, Nkiru. 2011. "Osunality' (or African Eroticism)." In *African Sexualities: A Reader*, edited by Sylvia Tamale, 251–70. Cape Town: Pambazuka Press.

Okech, Awino. 2013. "In Sisterhood and Solidarity: Queer African Feminist Spaces." In *Queer African Reader*, edited by Sokari Ekine and Hakima Abbas, 9–31. Dakar: Pambazuka.

Oomen, Barbara. 2000. "Traditional Woman-to-Woman Marriages, and the Recognition of Customary Marriages Act." *Journal of Contemporary Roman-Dutch Law* 63, no. 2: 274–82.

Osinubi, Taiwo Adetunji. 2018. "The Promise of Lesbians in African Literary History." *College Literature* 45, no. 4: 673–84.

Oyěwùmí, Oyèrónké. 2004. "Conceptualising Gender: Eurocentric Foundations of Feminist Concepts and the Challenge of African Epistemologies." In *African Gender Scholarship: Concepts, Methodologies, Paradigms*, edited by Signe Arnfred, 1–8. Dakar: Codesria.

Pérez, Guillermo Martínez, Brigitte Bagnol, and Concepción Tomás Aznar. 2014. "Autoerotism, Homoerotism, and Foreplay in African Women Who Practice Labia Minora Elongation: A Review." *International Journal of Sexual Health* 26, no. 4: 314–28.

Povinelli, Elizabeth A. 2006. *The Empire of Love: Toward a Theory of Intimacy, Genealogy, and Carnality*. Durham, NC: Duke University Press.

Qambela, Gcobani. Forthcoming. "'Born in Alice. Raised in Port Elizabeth. Exiled in

Johannesburg': *Inxeba, Kalushi*, and the Difficulties of the African 'Urban' for the New South African Man." *Social Dynamics*.

Ratele, Kopano. 2007. "Native Chief and White Headman: A Critical African Gender Analysis of Culture." *Agenda* 21, no. 72: 65–76.

Ratele, Kopano. 2011. "Male Sexualities and Masculinities." In *African Sexualities: A Reader*, edited by Sylvia Tamale, 399–419. Cape Town: Pambazuka Press.

Rubin, Gayle. 1984. "Thinking Sex: Notes for a Radical Theory of the Politics of Sexuality." In *Pleasure and Danger: Exploring Female Sexuality*, edited by Carole S. Vance, 267–319. Boston: Routledge and Kegan Paul.

Scott, Jessica, and Liesel Theron. 2017. "The Promise of Heteronormativity: Marriage as a Strategy for Respectability in South Africa." *Sexualities* 22, no. 3: 436–51.

Shange, Savannah. 2019. "Play Aunties and Dyke Bitches: Gender, Generation, and the Ethics of Black Queer Kinship." *Black Scholar* 49, no. 1: 40–54.

Shope, Janet H. 2006. "Lobola Is Here to Stay: Rural Black Women and the Contradictory Meanings of Lobola in Post-apartheid South Africa." *Agenda* 20, no. 68: 64–72.

Silverman, Kaja. 1984. "Histoire d'O: The Construction of a Female Subject." In *Pleasure and Danger: Exploring Female Sexuality*, edited by Carole S. Vance, 320–49. Boston: Routledge and Kegan Paul.

Spillers, Hortense J. 1984. "Interstices: A Small Drama of Words." In *Pleasure and Danger: Exploring Female Sexuality*, edited by Carole S. Vance, 73–100. Boston: Routledge and Kegan Paul.

Steyn, Melissa, and Mikki van Zyl. 2009. "The Prize and the Price." In *The Prize and the Price: Shaping Sexualities in South Africa*, edited by Melissa Steyn and Mikki van Zyl, 1–17. Pretoria: HSRC Press.

Tamale, Sylvia. 2005. "Eroticism, Sensuality, and 'Women's Secrets' among the Baganda: A Critical Analysis." *Feminist Africa* 5: 9–36.

Vail, Leroy. 1989. "Introduction: Ethnicity in Southern African History." In *The Invention of Tribalism in Southern Africa*, edited by Leroy Vail, 1–18. London: James Currey.

Vally, Natasha Thandiwe. 2014. "Spending Time." Paper presented at the WISH Seminar Series, Wits Institute for Social and Economics Researcher, University of the Witwatersrand, October 13.

Vally, Natasha Thandiwe. 2015. "Grouping Theories: A Response to the Johannesburg Workshop in Theory and Criticism (JWTC) Panel on 'Confusion as a Form.'" *Social Dynamics* 41, no. 1: 66–68.

van Dijk, Rijk. 2017. "The Tent versus Lobola: Marriage, Monetary Intimacies, and the New Face of Responsibility in Botswana." *Anthropology South Africa* 40, no. 1: 29–41.

Wekker, Gloria. 2006. *The Politics of Passion: Sexual Culture in the Afro-Surinamese Diaspora*. New York: Columbia University Press.

White, Hylton. 2015. "Custom, Normativity, and Authority in South Africa." *Journal of Southern African Studies* 41, no. 5: 1005–17.

Wynter, Sylvia, and Katherine McKittrick. 2015. "Unparalleled Catastrophe for Our Species? Or to Give Humanness a Different Future: Conversations." In *Sylvia Wynter: On Being Human as Praxis*, edited by Katherine McKittrick. Durham, NC: Duke University Press.

Yarbrough, Michael. 2018. "Something Old, Something New: Historicizing Same-Sex Marriage within Ongoing Struggles over African Marriage in South Africa." *Sexualities* 21, no. 7: 1092–1108.

# MOVING AND MOVED

## Reading Kewpie's District Six

**Ruth Ramsden-Karelse**

*I*n 1998, the recently established Gay and Lesbian Archives of South Africa
(GALA) acquired approximately 600 photographs from Kewpie, born in 1941 in
District Six, Cape Town.[1] The Kewpie Photographic Collection, as it is now known,
includes sixteen photographs taken on a single sunny afternoon and dated 1973,
which like many in the collection feature Kewpie and a few of her friends from a
larger group, whose lead I follow in referring to them using female pronouns and as
sisters or the girls of District Six. Assigned to the male sex at birth, the girls presented and expressed themselves according to conventions of femininity, to vary-
ing extents and in different combinations. Many of them worked as hairdressers,
performed onstage, intermittently lived with each other, spent weekends together
camping and playing sports, and organized and attended fancy-dress club nights
and exclusive parties called "drags."

In these sixteen photographs, in crocheted tops, brightly colored flares,
sheer maxi dresses, and beehives, Kewpie and her sisters smile and laugh on various streets in and just beyond the district. They stand with hands on hips and arms
around each other, lie down on the road and across boots of cars, lean against palm
trees and buses, and perch on railings and bicycles. Occasionally they are watched
from the corner of the frame, and then, as the afternoon turns into evening, they
pose with arms around a few passers-by. Considering these images, in which they
alternatingly appear and sometimes cast vaguely recognizable shadows, we might
imagine the girls passing a camera among themselves and taking turns to call out
affirmations or instructions as they capture one another on film.

The reverse of each photograph in this series bears a description, handwritten by Kewpie. In most of these she notes the date they were taken, or perhaps
printed or captioned, and describes herself and her sisters in spaces beyond the
location they depict—a location she thereby rewrites with possibilities she imag-

*GLQ* 26:3
DOI 10.1215/10642684-8311772
© 2020 by Duke University Press

Figure 1. "Kewpie on the Parade." AM2886/130.10. GALA Queer Archives
and Kewpie Collection.

ines actualized in the spaces beyond it. Leaning against a palm tree, Kewpie is
"modelling Dior Gown Paris 73" (fig. 1), while a couple of the girls posing with
a bus on the Cape Town Parade are "on tour to Germany 24.3.73" (fig. 2). At the
Cape Town Station, Kewpie and her sister are "in their new Movie, Girls will be
Boys Boys will be Girls 73" (fig. 3). Balancing on a bicycle and drinking from
champagne coupes as the sun sets and children stare from the sidelines, Kewpie
and another sister are competitors in "the S.A. Mixed Games" and "the first multiracial SA games, Pretoria 1973" (figs. 4 and 5).[2] These final two descriptions of a
bright postapartheid future make explicit the element of futurity in Kewpie's other
descriptions of herself and her sisters as fashion models and film stars, as well as
the implied critique of her present that is marked by its distance from the spaces
in which she imagines these glamorous possibilities actualized.

Forty-five years after these sixteen photographs are dated, images of Kewpie began to reappear in the area of Cape Town they partly depict—a place that
many continue to call District Six. During the week leading up to September 24,
2018, Jarrett Erasmus of the Burning Museum Arts Collective decorated buildings

Figure 2. "Julie Andrews and Patti on the Parade." AM2886/130.13. GALA
Queer Archives and Kewpie Collection.

in which Kewpie was born, lived, or performed onstage with large-scale wheat-
paste portraits (for more information, see Tan 2018). Each new public artwork
marked a pause along the 2018 route of the Heritage Day March organized annu-
ally by the District Six Museum, where the first public exhibition of one hundred
images from the Kewpie Photographic Collection had opened four days earlier. An
article published on the GALA website summarized the spirit in which this march
was dedicated to Kewpie and themed "Reclaiming with Pride," suggesting that "in
a sense" it facilitated the "return" of Kewpie's "legacy to her home" (Tan 2018).
*Home* here is District Six, the place where Kewpie was born and lived and where
many of her photographs were taken, including the series of sixteen mentioned
above. It is also, as this series demonstrates, a place from which she imagined
herself elsewhere.

The District Six Museum exhibition gave rise to increased digital acces-
sibility of the collection. Whereas previously only a handful of photographs were
available via its website, GALA provided fifty-four to the Digital Transgender
Archive and shared others from a dedicated Instagram account in the months
leading up to the exhibition,[3] which was featured, during its run, in articles pub-

Figure 3. "Kewpie and Julie Andrews on the Parade in Cape Town." AM2886/130.3. GALA Queer Archives and Kewpie Collection.

lished online by sixteen local and national media outlets, and one international. The renewed vigor with which Kewpie's archive was made increasingly public followed a nearly twenty-year hiatus after its acquisition, facilitated by Jack Lewis, producer and director of *A Normal Daughter: The Life and Times of Kewpie of District Six*, an independent documentary film released noncommercially in 2000. Kewpie's photographs were catalogued with information she gave in 1999, in response to Lewis's questions about locations and people shown (these descriptions are included in captions for each photograph printed here). In addition to the Kewpie Photographic Collection, GALA holds footage shot for *A Normal Daughter* and over six hours of audio recordings of Lewis interviewing Kewpie in 1996 and Mark Gevisser interviewing Kewpie in 1998.[4] These efforts to conserve Kewpie's archive for posterity might be understood in terms of the spirit in which GALA was founded in 1997, "to address the erasure and omission of LGBTIQ stories from public institutions such as official archives in (South) Africa" (GALA, n.d.). In the project of writing a history of gender and sexual diversities in support of an

Figure 4. "Kewpie on a bicycle in Combrinck Street." AM2886/130.9. GALA Queer Archives and Kewpie Collection.

Figure 5. "Patti in Invery Place." AM2886/130.4. GALA Queer Archives and Kewpie Collection.

inclusive future for a new South Africa, District Six has had particular resonance given it has, since its destruction by the nationalist government over a period of approximately sixteen years, beginning in 1966, come to function as a symbol of lost diversity, integration, and urban cultural production. Although current scholarship on District Six and on gender and sexuality in South Africa varies greatly, there has been a tendency to describe the district, in keeping with this symbolism, as home to a way of life or culture, variously described as "gay" or "queer," generally accepted if not celebrated by its wider community (see, e.g., Gevisser [1994] 2012: 27; Leap 2002: 224–25; Visser 2003: 127; Tucker 2009: 77–78; Munro 2012: 114; Pacey 2014: 114).

The Kewpie Photographic Collection has become somewhat embedded in this, referenced as a rich archive of documentary evidence. Although some studies have reproduced individual photographs and short excerpts from the audio recordings featuring Kewpie, critical engagement has been minimal, and in their entirety, these materials complicate the ways they have been circulated. Across the audio recordings, Kewpie gives a contradictory account of her life in District Six. On one hand, there is a sense of possibility, freedom, and community that has been lost along with the district. On the other hand, there is a sense of confinement, a sense that she was, before its destruction, yearning but unable to leave the district and that she and her sisters lived precariously within it. This ambivalence is evident in the sixteen photographs discussed above, in which Kewpie poses confidently with her sisters, looking fabulous on public streets in and near to the district and yet, in handwritten captions, imagines they are elsewhere: Paris, New York, Germany. References to the collection as documentary evidence fail to account for the ways Kewpie uses photography to rewrite District Six—in this series of photographs, for example, with the possibility of being adored as fashion models, film stars, and athletes.

After its four-month Cape Town run was extended to six, the exhibition *Kewpie: Daughter of District Six*, curated by Tina Smith and Jenny Marsden, opened in Johannesburg in May 2019 (curated by Tina Smith, Jenny Marsden, and Karin Tan). At a series of related events, organizers from GALA and the District Six Museum expressed their openness to other readings of the Kewpie Photographic Collection, commenting that the exhibition offered just one possible narrative. It also constitutes only one public-facing component of a range of related memory work led by both organizations, from which more nuanced and complicated narratives continue to emerge. In Johannesburg, the exhibition was adapted to incorporate some of these, notably through the inclusion of video footage of events and workshops that took place during the Cape Town run. District Six Museum curator Tina Smith (pers. comm., May 23, 2019) commented that she sees the exhibition as "an entry point, a moment of introduction."

In that spirit, this article proposes an alternative reading of the Kewpie Photographic Collection, one that centers the strategy of rewriting District Six evident in the series of sixteen photographs discussed above. Privileging their creative rather than documentary functions, I propose that Kewpie uses both photography and oral testimony to make and remake the world around her. While I recognize the political merit of remembering District Six as particularly hospitable to gender and sexual diversities, I move away from doing so. Instead, I remain attentive to the differing and at times contradictory ways Kewpie presents herself, her sisters, and District Six more broadly in order to consider how she reconfigures her world as part of what I understand to be a larger collaborative project. I therefore limit my focus to photographs featuring the girls of District Six, even though they make up only a portion of those named in Kewpie's descriptions of the photographs, and to the interviews with Kewpie from which short excerpts have been reproduced in scholarship.

It is worth noting that, although Kewpie has been identified as a gay man, a cross-dresser, and a *moffie* (e.g., in Tucker 2009; Chetty [1994] 2012; Reid 2013), there is no record that she identified as such. She insisted, in fact, that "people can't say I'm a man, they can't say I'm a woman,"[5] and in her usage, *gay* is never attached to *man* or *men*. We might understand *gay*, somewhat inexactly, as referencing the specific imbrication of having been assigned to the male sex at birth and expressing femininity in a way that is at least in part understood as making visible a sexual orientation toward men whose gender expression aligns with conventions of masculinity. Thus Kewpie and her sisters, including those who had what she calls the "sex change," are gay; the men with whom they typically had sexual relationships are not. *Drag*, for Kewpie—never *cross-dressing*—describes gays sartorially expressing a particularly glamorous mode of femininity, as when she declares that the girls "didn't just dress up: they used to *drag*" (Lewis 2000). And while the relatively recent reappropriation of *moffie* might be broadly understood as a political statement engaging with an ironic, camp tradition containing elements of self-mockery, its use as a derogatory marker for (individuals read as) men considered lacking in characteristics associated with manliness is evident in Kewpie's various recollections of being targeted—or not—with the term as an insult.[6]

Remaining attentive to the terms Kewpie uses to describe herself and her sisters, I refuse the aforementioned terms with which she has been described. I want to suggest that the terms used by Kewpie indicate complex modes of identification and expression that exceed and undermine the coherency of the terms used by others, and that might hold as yet unexplored possibilities for making livable lives that exceed the logics of hegemonic discourses on gender and sexuality. Furthermore, by dwelling with contradictions in Kewpie's photographs and oral testimony, I aim to refuse the certainty with which they have both been fixed in critical discourse in a fairly narrow position—ironically, as evidence of District Six's "openness"—and to offer instead an alternative public circulation, a new theoretical space in which Kewpie's legacy might move around.

I take up this idea of "moving around" from the account Kewpie gives of how she came to live her "gay life" as one of the girls of District Six. It begins with a search for spaces in which she could move more freely: "Wherever I could move around."[7] Using this as a point of departure, I consider two different senses of movement in the collection and propose that Kewpie uses both to create spaces in which she can access forms of freedom. The first concerns ways of moving beyond District Six in the realm of imagination, through performances of an elsewhere that are imbricated in what I call the District Six Star System. The second concerns finding ways of physically inhabiting space through corporeal movement in her locale.

Contestations over freedom and movement have been constitutive elements of the popular history of this locale. The inner-city area named the Sixth District of Cape Town in 1867 had become increasingly densely populated since emancipation thirty-four years prior, when, it is often noted, many invested their compensation in local residential property to embark on a new career of profiting, as "slum landlords," from those who had been counted among their former human property (e.g., O'Connell 2015). District Six is typically remembered as home to a "mixed" community of descendants of enslaved people, immigrants, artisans, laborers, and merchants that benefited from close proximity to the city and the port.[8] Following the 1901 forced removal of residents legally considered "African,"[9] most of those remaining—including Kewpie and her sisters—were classified by the term in the Population Registration Act of 1950 with both a liminal and residual function: "Coloured."

Kewpie was still living in the district in 1966 when it was declared "Whites Only" under the Group Areas Act. Most photographs in the collection were taken over the following period of about sixteen years, during which approximately sixty thousand residents were forcibly removed as the area was almost completely bulldozed and renamed Zonnebloem (Dutch for "sunflower"). While it is unclear exactly when Kewpie moved or was removed,[10] it is clear that by the early 1980s she lived about ten kilometers away, in a room adjoining the hairdressing salon where she worked in Kensington. A family friend had opened this salon with Kewpie as manager at some point in the 1960s, the decade in which the nationalist government succeeded in establishing its location as a "model Coloured township," having forcibly removed from the area then known as Kensington and Windermere the largest concentration of Cape Town residents classified "African," including some of those forced out of inner-city areas such as District Six at the turn of the century.[11]

Through its heavy investment in the regulation of movement across space and its intermediary placement of those formerly classified "Coloured," apartheid legislation structured both Kewpie's forced movement from District Six and the constrained freedom she had to move to Kensington, which was contingent on the forced movement of others. In the Kewpie Photographic Collection and audio

recordings in which she is featured, there is a sense of limited conditions of possibility. But there is also a sense that she reworked limited existing freedoms to
create conditions of greater—although still limited—possibility. She accessed
restricted spaces, for example, by performing affluent glamour beyond the enclosed
space of the cinema in which it was available to her, taking up and transforming
the iconography of stardom to construct a kind of celebrity using every mode of
photography she could access.[12]

Kewpie's accounts of these strategies of reworking limited existing freedoms is rooted in a sense of lost possibility, articulated in descriptions of an opportunity she received and was denied as a fourteen-year-old dancer taking extracur-
ricular lessons at the University of Cape Town Ballet School. The place she was
invited to travel for further study—"overseas"—functions as the imagined elsewhere promising glamour and adoration, with which she rewrites District Six in the
series of sixteen photographs discussed above. In audio recordings in which she is
featured and in *A Normal Daughter* (Lewis 2000), Kewpie repeatedly emphasizes
that, had she been able to accept the invitation, she "would have been a retired
dancer today." She "regretted" this "all [her] life long," and although she would
have "love[d] to" go overseas, she never again had the opportunity.[13] Instead, she
remained in District Six and found ways to inhabit it that felt less restrictive.

Kewpie explains that her father prevented her from accepting the invitation "because of [her] being gay," thereby "rejecting [her] gay life as well."[14] She
"wanted [dance] to lead her somewhere," but after her "father's rejection" she
"couldn't go on with it."[15] So she decided to "bang back into [her] gay life" (Lewis
2000), searching for spaces in which she could move more freely, corporeally if not
overseas: "Wherever I could move around."[16] She started sneaking out from her
family home "to go dancing at night"—"the rhumba, the salsa, the cha cha . . . and
most of all the jazz"[17]—at clubs and parties where she would "meet up with different gays" (Lewis 2000). She explains that dancing was a case of survival—"it
was in my veins, in my body, in my life. I just couldn't live without it then"—
and that she used it as a strategy to cultivate a kind of celebrity within the space
she remained.[18]

Because Kewpie was "always entertaining" people by "danc[ing] around"
and singing and dancing in variety shows, cabarets, and Moffie Konserts, from
the age of "fifteen or sixteen," she "became known as Kewpie, Kewpie, all around
District Six."[19] In *A Normal Daughter* (Lewis 2000), she remembers the first Kon-
sert she saw: "It was fantastic to see what *moffies* could do onstage. They were
artists. They were beautiful. They were attractive. And they could perform." Her
description of onstage performance as "fantastic" suggests its power, however

ephemeral, to reify the imagined or unthinkable—in this instance, the ordinarily abject *moffies* describes "artists" who are "beautiful" and "attractive" precisely because "they could perform." Similarly, it is because of Kewpie's "fantastic" performances that people "came to love" her.[20] In *A Normal Daughter*, she recalls her first time onstage: "I had applause, standing applause, standing ovation" (Lewis 2000)—she performed, she explains elsewhere, "for the ovations."[21]

Performers in Moffie Konserts were billed as the names they adopted after stars, usually those audiovisually imported to the district by its seven cinemas, known as bioscopes, which from the 1940s mostly screened Hollywood films. Kewpie recalls that Hedy Lamarr, Yvonne De Carlo, Betty Grable, and Betty Hutton were the "main queens" of the older generation, and her photographs depict Kim Novak, Caroll Baker, Patti LaBelle, Sandra Dee, Joanne Woodward, Jean Shrimpton, Hayley Mills, Connie Francis, Shirley Bassey, Piper Laurie, Greta Garbo, Stephanie Powers, Sue Thompson, Diana Ross, Leslie Caron, Julie Andrews, Olivia de Havilland, Dolores Gray, Kay Kendall, Brigitte Bardot, Mitzi Gaynor, and—rather excitingly—Miriam Makeba.[22] Kewpie, sometimes Kewpie Doll, was so nicknamed as a child after the popular cherubic characters initially conceived of in 1909 and produced as dolls from 1912.[23] She is referred to as such by every interviewee in *A Normal Daughter* (Lewis 2000). When she started performing at events and in competitions, she adopted the stage name Doris Day after her "favorite star of that years,"[24] and later, presumably because the name Doris Day was already in use, she changed her billing to Capucine.

Through this performance of an imagined global, which we might think of as the District Six Star System, the girls redefined their own value. An interviewee in *A Normal Daughter* (Lewis 2000) explains that the Konserts showed "'n moffie se waarde: hy is werd ook om 'n film ster te wees" (a moffie's worth: he is worthy of being a film star). There is a sense, however, that this redefinition functioned precariously in spaces beyond the stage. Some of the girls achieved a sort of celebrity, appearing regularly in the daily *Golden City Post* newspaper and monthly *Drum* magazine between the early 1950s and the late 1970s, in interviews, sensationalist exposés of "moffie drags," reports of court cases and other scandalous goings-on, and articles detailing onstage competitions sponsored and reported as "moffie elections" by the *Post*—always with accompanying photographs.[25] Although these popular locally based sister publications circulated throughout sub-Saharan Africa, the coverage did not cultivate the sort of celebrity that might open up opportunities for the girls themselves to physically travel. Dhianaraj Chetty ([1994] 2012: 121) describes reporters' presumably unwitting juxtaposition of descriptions of "moffies" leading "lonely and bitter" lives, finding "solace" only "at the bottom of a bottle," with photographs in which they look fabulous: "At once demure, flirtatious, coquettish and playful." In tones oscillating between fascination and disgust, articles describe the girls in terms that are more sensationalist and pathologizing than celebratory.[26]

Kewpie edited this unsatisfactory coverage, archiving three glamorous press photographs of herself but none of the articles in which she is featured. And—in response to the failings of popular press, we might imagine—as a self-declared "bioscope fanatic," she took up the promise of Hollywood to construct her own celebrity.[27] As well as screening films, the District Six bioscopes were popular venues for live musical performance and cabaret and so, in a literal sense, facilitated Kewpie's celebrity. In her oral testimony, therefore, they often function as sites at which she and stardom coalesce: in her 1998 recollection, the Star Bioscope is both the stage for her own "fantastic" performance for which she received "applause, standing applause, standing ovation" and where she saw her "best movie ever up till today," *A Star Is Born* (1954).[28] It is, to be more specific, the promise of this film in particular that Kewpie takes up as she uses oral testimony and photography to play with its depiction of stars as simultaneously constructed and authentic, in remarkable ways.[29]

In one such instance, while being interviewed in 1996, Kewpie authenticates her celebrity as Capucine. She had adopted the stage name "as [she] saw her pictures," she tells Lewis. "I said, 'ooh, wow, look at Capo'—I used to call her Capo." Capucine later traveled to South Africa, Kewpie recalls, and they met backstage after her show at the Luxurama Bioscope in Wynberg:

> Walking into her, uh . . . walking into the what-you-call-it room. And she's sitting in the mirror. And us coming in, we walked up to the mirror, up to her, and she turned around and saw me. Well, then I was much more younger. I looked *exactly* like Capucine, and Capucine looked exactly like me. Without the . . . she's got the superfluous hair. And she was a sex change. She was from Paris, from France [. . .] She was a singer, entertainer— like a cabaret star. And she was astonished, she was stunned when she saw me in the mirror. She turned around and she spoke to me, and she took my hand and she grappled me. She couldn't believe, she said to me I was her double. Well, I was much more younger then. And after she left she got married to this millionaire . . . went back to Paris.[30]

In the only recorded discussion of her chosen stage name, Kewpie narrates the fantasy of substitution through which Capucine (from District Six) becomes Capucine ("from Paris, from France"). As part of the District Six Star System, the name might read as a reference to French fashion model and film star of *The Pink Panther* (1963) and *What's New Pussycat?* (1965) fame, whom we might presume Kewpie is reconfiguring as "a sex change" by participating in a tradition that privileges gossip as epistemology. But this Capucine, whose fame facilitates a kind of mobility that is (relatedly) physical (performing to the international audience) and symbolic (marrying the "millionaire") is, Kewpie tells us, a "cabaret star."

In her 1982 coauthored autobiography, April Ashley briefly mentions a "Capucine (not the film star but one of us)" whose "keeper was a very famous millionaire" (Fallowell and Ashley 1982: 67–68)—*us* referring to performers at Parisian club Le Carrousel, many of whom adopted the names of women film stars and toured internationally. The quarterly magazine *Female Mimics* (1965: 27) introduced the same Capucine—featured in thirteen photographic portraits alongside a description of the "change" that has made her "complete" ("after long painful months . . . *legally a woman!*")—as "the toast and talk of many continents" (for more information, see Zagria 2016). It seems likely that this is the Capucine whose name Kewpie took "from her pictures, before she arrived," and that these pictures were promoting her upcoming performance. Capucine the cabaret star takes up, transforms, and transports the iconography of the film star. Then Kewpie sees herself in the cabaret star's "pictures," and perhaps in her performance on the stage of a bioscope where Kewpie herself may have performed and where the film star may have appeared on screen, and in Capucine herself when she meets her in "the what-you-call-it room," that liminal space of transformation. Here—in place of the metaphorical mirror of the bioscope screen in which Kewpie would see herself reflected, in and as the film star—there is an actual mirror that the cabaret star is "sitting in." Its capacity as a mirror enables the transference, while the relay of taking up and transforming the iconography of the film star/cabaret star is accentuated by the sonic component of the relay of "Capo"/Kewpie. Kewpie's awe and astonishment, and her affection (for "Capo"), are reflected back to her in Capucine, who takes Kewpie's hand and tells her she is "her double."

Discussing the "mirror scene" as "a convention of transsexual autobiography," Jay Prosser (1998: 100) writes: "At an angle to Lacan's mirror phase, the look in the mirror enables in the transsexual only disidentification, not a jubilant integration of body but an anguishing shattering of the felt already formed imaginary body." Conversely, what is enabled by Kewpie's "look in the mirror" at Capucine, as "imaginary body," is more like a "jubilant integration" than an "anguishing shattering." Kewpie's "disidentification" is more akin to the process theorized by José Esteban Muñoz (1999) than to the one described here by Prosser. As what

Muñoz calls the disidentifying subject, Kewpie reworks, to quite literally read herself into, Capucine. As Kewpie the "bioscope fanatic" might metaphorically get lost in a film, Kewpie the star gets lost in Capucine; and Capucine gets lost in Kewpie, so that Kewpie is the purer, more authentic version of Capucine than Capucine herself—who has "the superfluous hair"—and so that it is also symbolically Kewpie who leaves, marries "this millionaire," and travels "back to Paris."

In the project of constructing an authentic version of her own celebrity, of which we might consider her recollection of meeting Capucine to be one aspect, Kewpie also uses photography. She archives, along with images in which she performs onstage and in which she describes herself and her sisters as "modelling," starring in films, and "on tour," two particularly interesting photographs of herself taken by Movie Snaps. This company of street photographers, who worked opposite the Cape Town General Post Office from the late 1930s to the early 1980s, would draw a chalk line on the pavement, and anyone who walked across it would have a photograph taken and would be given a ticket with a number on it, with which to return a few days later to purchase the portrait, printed by the photographers and stamped on the reverse with the same number. Kewpie recalls that "the majority of the Movie Snaps photographers knew the gays as well, you know, going shopping and walking around in town," and the collection includes at least eleven Movie Snaps images.[31] These typically depict the girls and other friends pausing and smiling at the camera, sometimes slightly bashful but more often delighted at being photographed (see fig. 6). Kewpie, on the other hand, seems to engage with the photographers more deliberately. In one particularly striking example, a young Kewpie wearing a velvet jacket over a buttoned-up polo shirt, her bleached hair held back by a fur hat, turns toward the photographer as she passes, head slightly tilted back, lips parted, staring straight into the camera (fig. 7). The effect is devastatingly glamorous.

This same sense of deliberateness is evident, I want to suggest, in the two Movie Snaps photographs of Kewpie briefly mentioned above (figs. 8 and 9). These are remarkably similar, although one is in black and white and the other in faint color. In both, Kewpie wears pumps, a buttoned-up shirt, and a stovepipe pantsuit with its low-collared jacket fastened. In both, she appears to be unaware that her photograph is being taken. Straight-faced and staring ahead, she continues walking, with her right foot forward and a large handbag clutched in her left hand. We might even say she appears to be unwilling, given she sports a different pair of oversized, dark sunglasses in each image. Kewpie's own desire to be photographed and to own the photograph—as she crosses the chalk-drawn line and returns a few days later to make her purchase—is transferred to the photographer, who is

Figure 6. "Patti and Olivia in Darling Street (Movie Snaps)."
AM2886/27. GALA Queer Archives and Kewpie Collection.

visually absent but whose framing gaze is made desirous of her image. She utilizes an existing and popular practice of street photography to perform a sort of celebrity-paparazzi encounter in which the celebrity, whose image is desired by others, is not paying to have her photograph taken. The celebrity knows her image is desired; it is so desired that she asserts some control with, for example, the sunglasses. With slight variations on a signature look—including the same style of pantsuit she "loved" and described as her "real fashion" and her always-bleached perfect beehive, the hairstyle for which notes to the *Kewpie* exhibition declare she was famous as a hairdresser—Kewpie performs authenticity as an aspect of the construction of her celebrity.[32] And she repeats this performance, at least twice.

The celebrity that Kewpie constructs here is bound up with her roles as onstage performer and hairdresser. Many of the girls of District Six worked as hairdressers—Kewpie was trained with Piper Laurie and later apprenticed Patti

Figure 7. "This was June in winter time in the city. Taken by one of the Movie Snaps." AM2886/10. GALA Queer Archives and Kewpie Collection.

LaBelle and Mitzi Gaynor—and an interviewee in *A Normal Daughter* (Lewis 2000) declares that "'n hairdresser sonder 'n moffie issie 'n hairdresser nie" (A hairdresser without a moffie isn't a hairdresser).[33] The exhibition *Kewpie: Daughter of District Six* included a re-created section of Salon Kewpie, replete with dark green chairs, elaborately styled wigs, and orange walls adorned with images of Hollywood stars. One of the salon walls featured Piper Laurie's description of her customers: "They will think of the movie and say, 'oh I want a Butterfield 8 style,' you know, something like that. Or they'll come and say, 'oh I want a Cleopatra hair style.' Then you automatically know what they were talking about." Her words suggest that the hairdresser has a kind of capital that allows them to "automatically" understand the reference of the customer, while the salon promises the customer

Figure 8. "This is a very good friend of mine, Cliffidia Tabaccan, in town. Could be Darling Street." AM2886/6. GALA Queer Archives and Kewpie Collection.

Figure 9. "I was on my way to work in the morning at Salon Kewpie in Kensington." AM2886/11. GALA Queer Archives and Kewpie Collection.

access, via the hairdresser, to the glamour of the aspirational star imagery with which it is decorated and that establishes possibility within the space. In her recollection, Kewpie opened the first hairdressing salon in Windermere and brought with her the necessary associated glamour: "I introduced Windermere to dancing. I woke them up."[34]

Former District Six Museum director Valmont Layne and trustee Ciraj Rassool (2001: 153) contend that what they describe as the "gay culture expressed" in hairdressing salons was only "more" accepted on the condition that "it was contained in that space or performed on stage." Studies that offer the girls' roles in circumscribed spaces (hairdressing salon and stage) as evidence that they were integrated into the wider community typically describe District Six in terms of freedom, hospitality, and openness. These descriptions often reference Mark Gevisser's ([1994] 2012: 28) suggestion that "gay life" may have been able to "flourish" in the district because the "hybridity" of a "society like that of the coloureds" prevented the establishment of any single prohibitive doctrine.[35] Gevisser's understanding of "coloured communities" as inherently open—"by nature fluid, hybrid and permeable"—relies on a conception of a condition we might call "colouredness" as "mixed-race" and therefore a kind of deviance that necessarily allows for other forms of deviance (Gevisser and Cameron [1994] 2012: 7). His comments reinscribe the categorical sexualization of "colouredness." The "interracial" sex between "a European male" and "a native female" banned by the Immorality Act of 1927 continues to haunt discussions of the category first legally defined— in terms of a lack—one year later. A popular joke goes, "God made the black man . . . the Indian, the Chinese and the Jew—but Jan van Riebeeck, he made the Coloured Man" (Adhikari 2006: 147).[36] And this sentiment continues to be circulated in scholarship, cloaked in the language of academia: "On a purely etymological level," one study explains, "coloureds are the product of inter-racial sex" (Tucker 2009: 71).

As an aspect of these conceptual associations through which the relationship between "colouredness" and other perceived forms of sexual deviance is naturalized, District Six has been established as the birthplace of what Gevisser ([1994] 2012: 28) calls "gay life" in "Western Cape coloured communities" (see, e.g., Isaacs and McKendrick 1992: 93; Rabie and Lesch 2009: 725; Tucker 2009: 68). Its depiction as such is related to its construction both as a symbol of lost diversity and as a surrogate ethnic homeland, which has been widely discussed elsewhere.[37] The implication is that the district provided fertile ground for Kewpie and her sisters—as indicated by the titles of both *A Normal Daughter: The Life and Times of Kewpie of District Six* (Lewis 2000) and the 2018 exhibition *Kew-*

*pie: Daughter of District Six.* This suggestion seems to be at odds, however, with the extreme scarcity of publicly available instances of self-representation by the girls of District Six. The Kewpie Photographic Collection and interviews featuring Kewpie are perhaps unique in this respect.[38] Where studies provide references to archival evidence of a "gay" or "queer" culture in District Six, therefore, these lead to materials featuring Kewpie more often than not.[39]

Engagement with these materials, however, has been selective. Although excerpts of interviews with Kewpie have been reproduced as evidence of general acceptance if not celebration, across the entirety of the recordings a more complex and contradictory account emerges. Kewpie does at times state that "gays" were "accepted" by their families and the wider community, and that people were "never rude" or "hostile" to her—but she also recalls being "pressurized" as a child and suggests that "any parent would be like" her father toward "their gay." She describes parents who, upon finding out their child was a "moffie," would "bushwhack them, hit them," or "bang bang bang the child every time, until they can't do it any longer." She states that no one used the term *moffie* derogatorily, in District Six: "There was no such unscrupulous names such around." Yet she also remembers that "here and there you would find the unscrupulous ones calling out 'hey moffie' and so on and so on," and that "the cultured coloured people" who were "afraid to use Afrikaans words" would instead call out, "There goes a queer."[40]

Kewpie describes being safe in District Six: people would never "push" her "around," or "discard" or "abuse" her, she says, "by uttering rude things towards" her. And yet she also recalls "discovering," as she grew up there, "how people can push you around"—and this included being physically attacked by men. She describes the "straight guys" or men "who used to go with gays" as generally married to cis women, extremely covert about their extramarital desires and "afraid to be seen with the gays." At best, Kewpie's account suggests, acceptance was granted proportionally to the coherency with which the girls performed femininity. She often follows statements such as "we were accepted" with the qualification "not as gays," says she was safe in public only because passers-by "thought [she] was female," and recounts that everyone who "met up with" Mitzi for the first time "accepted" her specifically because "they would never believe that she was gay . . . she was normal, like any woman."[41]

Evidently, the girls were also targeted with abuse, and in audio recordings from 1998,[42] Kewpie describes how she "pacified" other "gays" on the receiving end, "like babies in [her] arms . . . trying to make them feel that they're wanted. Not just pushed about and pushed around but they are wanted." In audio recordings from 1996,[43] at times Kewpie mentions violence in passing, as though it were an unremarkable fact of life for the girls of District Six; she mentions that Mitzi Gaynor had "that warmth and that love for each and every one, and even for who-ever used to bungle her around or wanted to smash her up or whatever" and that Doris Day "was always kidnapped around." She recalls having to move away from Rutger Street because a man "interfered" with Shirley Bassey, who was living with her at the time, and remarks that this man must have "taken advantage" of Bassey because "she was a gay." Explaining that "some of these gays were headstrong too, not wanting to go with these guys, so they were kidnapped," Kewpie initially says, "it wasn't that harsh." "But," she adds after a pause, "it was almost like being killed around, too." There is a disturbing implication, at times, that any acceptance granted in proportion to the coherency of their expression of femininity made the girls vulnerable to certain kinds of violence—domestic violence, sexual coercion— that were unremarkable because of the ubiquitous nature of gender-based vio-lence, because they were understood as ways in which "guys" might assert their authority over "headstrong" women.

Clearly, Kewpie describes the district in contradictory ways in these inter-views. She discusses danger and discrimination, but there are also moments in which she speaks in absolute terms about being safe, and adored, and free. Xavier Livermon (2012: 299–300) has made the case for a contextually specific under-standing of freedom referring to the ability of "black queers" to construct what Judith Butler has called livable lives, by bringing "dissident sexualities and gender nonconformity into the public arena." Particularly in light of Livermon's emphasis on the necessity of an understanding that this "cultural labor of visibility"—which is ultimately about recognition—"will not result in the curtailment of or loss of life," it is evident that Kewpie does not so much describe historic freedoms in Dis-trict Six as create spaces of freedom within it. We might think of her recollection of the district, in these interviews in which she expresses a desire to "lift [her] life up . . . and take the best part of it,"[44] in terms of what Eric Worby and Shireen Ally (2013: 467) describe as the dual senses of *recollect* in a "post-apartheid" archival project: "'recalling' the past (through the work of memory)" and "'re-collecting' the past (through the work of archiving)."

At times, Kewpie discusses the strategy she employs to "re-collect" the past as she recalls it. She explains that she has "overlooked" negative aspects of her life, elaborating, "I don't call that to my memory." She advises that "if people reject you, just throw them a blind eye," and describes responding in this way to her father "rejecting [her] gay life": "I just threw a blind eye his way . . . I just gave him the wink of an eye." If anyone "should have" discriminated against her, she says, she "would never catch the eye to them," so as not to "keep it in [her] mind and [her] brains."[45] She recounts experiences of violence and discrimination in District Six much more often in these audio recordings, in which she often sounds tired and speaks slowly, taking long pauses and giving her narrative more time to unfurl, than she does in video recordings in which she is featured. Given her recollection of the district is noticeably more positive in the latter, the visual terms in which she describes her curatorial strategy seem to allude to the camera's function as a technology of self-curation.

The camera, of course, is the technology Kewpie uses to create her archive of photographs, in which she creates spaces in which she can access forms of freedom. In the photographs previously discussed, for example, her performances of an imagined elsewhere allow her to move beyond her locale in the realm of imagination. Kewpie also uses this technology to perform a more corporeal kind of freedom, archiving many photographs in which the girls appear to physically navigate and interact with their surroundings with a confident and easy playfulness. In a series of four, she and Sandra Dee lie draped over the tall branches of a huge piece of driftwood on the beach at Strandfontein, mimicking the gesture of the washed-up tree's limbs with their own,[46] before standing, triumphant, on the uppermost branch (figs. 10a–c).[47] Other photographs in the series suggest they are on one of the camping trips Kewpie describes "all the gays" going on as "a gang, almost every end of the month, every holiday, every weekend, from Saturday night until Monday morning, come back to work Tuesdays." She says it "was fun, it was lovely, it was beautiful" because away from District Six there were "no harassings, no fighting, no aggressiveness, no one abusing nobody, and it was just beautiful." She remembers being able to move freely "on the beach, dancing on the beach, dancing in the water, dancing in the sand," adding, again, "and it was beautiful, it was lovely."[48]

In many photographs taken in the district, the girls convey this kind of corporeal—often gravity-resisting—movement in static images, finding ways to move around and be free within a space that doesn't allow them full freedom: the still, enclosed space of a photograph and, I'm suggesting, District Six. Considering Kewpie's search for spaces in which she could "move around," we might read photographs in which the girls perform a kind of freedom within certain confines or parameters as one such space. In two, taken on separate occasions, Kewpie swings around lamp posts (figs. 11 and 12).[49] Utilizing the quotidian to locate herself in a filmic tradition that offers the possibility of, if not escape, escapism in film-length installments, she appears to be relishing a momentary defiance of gravity to literally be free of her burdens and claim a spotlight—specifically, the

Figures 10a–c. "Kewpie with Sandra Dee
at Strandfontein." AM2886/98.2-4. GALA
Queer Archives and Kewpie Collection.

one overhead—as her own. In another photograph, Olivia climbs the tall Nelson
Street sign (fig. 13).[50] She clings on at the top, one hand resting on the metal rect-
angle, the other preventing her floppy sun hat from blowing away in "the south eas-
ter" (wind) that famously blew through the district. Her left leg is wrapped around
the sign for stability, the other contorted so that she appears effortlessly perched,
cross-legged, as she laughs.

  The labor of creating these images—both imaginative and incredibly physically demanding—is erased in the photographic object itself. To be successful,
the performance must look effortless: it is "fantastic," in the sense suggested by
Kewpie's recollection discussed above. In one particularly striking example, from
the series of sixteen discussed earlier, Kewpie appears to be jumping through a
tire in midair (fig. 14).[51] She playfully repurposes the tire, a once-crucial component of vehicular movement rendered useless, to perform movement through (rather

Figure 11. "Kewpie in Sir Lowry Road."
AM2886/129.8. GALA Queer Archives and
Kewpie Collection.

Figure 12. "Sir Lowry Road: Kewpie."
AM2886/131.4. GALA Queer Archives and
Kewpie Collection.

Figure 13. "Olivia." AM2886/131.7. GALA Queer Archives and Kewpie
Collection.

Figure 14. "Kewpie at Cape Town Station. Picture taken by Vicky."
AM2886/130.2. GALA Queer Archives and Kewpie Collection.

than with) it. She utilizes photography as a medium of "fantastic" performance: her otherwise impossible jump through the tire is made possible by the stillness of the image, in which it cannot end or fail. Both Kewpie and the tire are aloft, resisting gravity; the image conveys a sense of freedom as something felt in discrete moments, suspended in time by the photograph.

The medium of these photographs is crucial to the sense of corporeal freedom they depict. I suggest that it is also crucial to the ways the collection as a whole has been understood to depict historical freedom. A number of photographs show groups of the girls wearing bright colors and feather boas, for example, or oversized sunglasses and theatrical hats, standing or lying back on streets and pavements, often with arms or a leg outstretched (see figs. 15 and 16). Some include adults and children we might assume are neighbors or passers-by, thereby indicating the girls' visibility to the wider public. However, the photographs cannot evidence an understanding that this visibility "would not result in the curtailment or loss of life" (Livermon 2012: 300). To put it differently, it seems unlikely

Figure 15. "Olivia, Kewpie, Patti (all at back, left to right), Sue Thompson, Brigitte, Gaya, Mitzi (all in front, left to right) in Sir Lowry Road." AM2886/129.10. GALA Queer Archives and Kewpie Collection.

Figure 16. "Kewpie and Gaya (standing) in Sir Lowry Road." AM2886/131.1. GALA Queer Archives and Kewpie Collection.

Kewpie would archive photographs showing "curtailment or loss of life." In the audio recordings discussed above, on the other hand, she does in fact state that the girls were targeted with physical violence—in 1996, she even mentions that one of the girls was murdered—and she implies that the girls were targeted specifically because of their gender expression.[52] Reading the photographs as evidence of historical freedom, therefore, relies on an assumption that the girls would not be seen looking so fabulous in public if it was not accepted by the wider community. I understand the logic of this assumption to be false on two counts. First, it fails to recognize that, for people forced to the margins, fabulousness can be a survival strategy, as opposed to a luxury.[53] Second, it fails to recognize that people forced to the margins do not do things only because they are given permission.

This is the logic through which the collection has been presented, in its two most comprehensive public circulations thus far, as evidence of historical freedom. Casting Kewpie in the role of "daughter" in their productions of District Six, both *A Normal Daughter* (Lewis 2000) and the 2018 exhibition *Kewpie: Daughter of District Six* present the Kewpie Photographic Collection as a "family album," assigning to it the task Pierre Bourdieu (1990: 29) names as the latter's primary function: to affirm "continuity" and "integration." A flyer publicizing the "new queer film from South Africa" *A Normal Daughter* proposes that Kewpie's "lovingly preserved collection of snapshots" show that "gay life in District Six was open and out—an accepted part of this racially and religiously diverse community."[54] Notes to the 2018 *Kewpie* exhibition propose that "the photographs show" that "District Six was a place where same-sex relationships and gender nonconformity were largely accepted, and people could express themselves openly."[55]

In both instances, the photographs are read in terms of their documentary as opposed to creative function. Thus, notes to the *Kewpie* exhibition conclude that the "street-scene photographs" mentioned above "demonstrate the extent of integration of queer people into the broader District Six community."[56] But they neglect to ask why, if members of the wider public in Kewpie's photographs evidence integration, the girls are absent in photographs of the wider public in District Six. If what Crain Soudien (2001: 104) describes as "cross-dressing" was, as he claims (as current scholarship often does), a "noted feature of the social landscape," it is one that has been almost completely erased from the latter's photographic representation. The girls do not appear in the work of any of the photographers who sought to document the district at any point in its history, including, with some urgency, its final years, or in the family photographs that have lined the walls of the District Six Museum since its earliest days.[57] Alluding to the use of documentary photography of the district as a means of constructing a narrative, Soudien and Lalou Meltzer (2001: 72) suggest that we might gain a sense of its partiality by "looking for who is not represented in the representations of streets."

The girls are among those not represented in documentary photography of District Six, so they are not visible or integrated into the wider community in the narrative it constructs. In the Kewpie Photographic Collection, on the other hand, they are, and this version of the district, obviously, has greater appeal for many of those who have read it as documentary evidence. Implicit in presentations of a community in which Kewpie and her sisters were not just accepted but celebrated are certain imagined futures. Notes to the 2018 *Kewpie* exhibition, for example, propose that the photographs "challenge the popular notion that homosexuality is un-African."[58] But a reading of the collection as documentary evidence cannot fully accommodate Kewpie's use of photography as a creative strategy, in the ways I have outlined in this article. And claims that the culture it depicts was enabled, freed, or even produced by the district limits the extent to which the agency of its producers can be recognized.

At times, the audio recordings in which Kewpie is featured reveal tensions between the different ways she and her interviewers engage with her photographs, as she frustrates their attempts to comprehensively document by locating subjects in time and space. She typically formulates her responses to questions about when things happened, or how long for, inexactly, as in "eight or ten or twelve years,"[59]

Figures 17a and 17b. "Kayna (Mrs. Salie) in her garage." AM2886/211.1-2. GALA Queer Archives and Kewpie Collection.

and many of her answers contradict others. Lewis expresses his frustration—"see, that's your problem with time again"—with Kewpie's resistance to her photographs being fixed in historical time and space.[60] She is asked to describe two photographs of herself, for example, dressed in a camel skirt suit with fur-trimmed collar, hat, handbag, and heels, holding a cigarette in one hand and a drink in the other (figs. 17a and 17b). She is posed, in both images, as though she is climbing up a ladder, with one hand on her hip, and is glancing back at the camera. In the second image, Patti stands behind Kewpie, echoing her pose.[61] Kewpie says both photographs depict "Kayna (Mrs Salie) in her garage."[62] Perhaps instances like this suggest that for Kewpie her photographs didn't function as—or, functioned in ways other than as—historical documents.

If visibility is ultimately about recognition, then Kewpie arguably uses photography and oral testimony to achieve visibility on her own terms, and it would follow that it is in photographs and in moments in audio recordings—not in a historically real space they represent—that she is free. Perhaps, then, she created and curated this archive of photographs, in which she and her sisters are adored, and free, and safe, so that such a space could exist. Now, as this once-private archive is increasingly publicly circulated as documentary evidence, Kewpie is remembered in terms of the adoration, and freedom, and safety it depicts. While being interviewed in 1996, she makes a comment that seems to exactly predict this ongoing process:

> If you kick the bucket now, or tomorrow, or next year. . . they talk the best parts of you. But while you around, they also have a little crossword puzzle

too, in your life. It is like a crossword puzzle, then. But when you—you've kicked the bucket, you have been the best gay around that you can ever think of. People will have stories like . . . like Cinderella was. Then you come out of a *noveltjie* [little story].[63]

In the present that it anticipates, Kewpie's wry description of "the best parts" being transformed into a fairy tale sounds as both a caution against accepting narrative as historical fact and a celebration of the "fantastic" capacity of "re-collection."

The Kewpie Photographic Collection is vast and complex, and any narrative produced from it necessarily "re-collects" it. If, as I have argued, Kewpie uses photography to rewrite District Six, then we might say that this process is extended by those who continue to write narratives of District Six by reading her photographs as documentary evidence. We might say that the 2018 *Kewpie* exhibition honors Kewpie in precisely this way. But, I have tried to demonstrate, these narratives fail to take seriously the artistic and political merit of the collection. They present the latter's "best parts" as evidence that Kewpie and her sisters were not just accepted but celebrated by the wider community, and thereby erase strategies Kewpie uses to navigate oppressions that continue to structure our present. I have offered, here, an alternative reading of the Kewpie Photographic Collection, with the aim of indicating a different way we might consider it to be "moving": not in the sense in which we might describe as "moving" the fairy tale of Cinderella being given permission by her fairy godmother to go to the ball where she can be a star but, rather, in the sense that it is a space Kewpie creates herself in which she can be a star and move, however ephemerally, beyond her inadequate present.

## Notes

I am especially grateful to Linda Chernis, Keval Harie, Genevieve Louw, and Karin Tan at GALA, as well as Tina Smith at the District Six Museum, for their sustained support of and generous engagement with this project. My research on the Kewpie Photographic Collection is supported by the inaugural Stuart Hall Doctoral Studentship, in association with Merton College, the Oxford Research Centre in the Humanities (TORCH), and the Stuart Hall Foundation. Research trips have been funded by additional grants from TORCH, Merton College, and the English Faculty at the University of Oxford.

1.  GALA continues to be known by this acronym even though in 2007 its name changed, to reflect its increasing focus on educational and community work, to Gay and Lesbian Memory in Action (GALA, n.d.).

2.  Kewpie Photographic Collection, AM2886/130.1–130.16, Gay and Lesbian Memory in Action, Johannesburg, South Africa (hereafter GALA).

3.  At the time of writing, fifty-four photographs from the collection are available via Digital Transgender Archives (www.digitaltransgenderarchive.net/col/b5644r52v), and thirty-two via the Instagram profile @daughter_of_d6.

4.  Kewpie, interview by Jack Lewis, January 12, 1996, Achmat-Lewis Collection, AM2790, GALA; and Kewpie, interview by Mark Gevisser, December 4, 1998, Oral Histories Collection, AM2709, GALA.

5.  Kewpie, Gevisser interview.

6.  Kewpie, Lewis interview; Kewpie, Gevisser interview.

7.  Kewpie, Lewis interview.

8.  For more detailed histories of District Six, see Jeppie and Soudien 1990 and Bickford-Smith 1995.

9.  For further discussion of pre-apartheid racial categories, see Bickford-Smith 1995. For discussion of changes in "race names persons came to be known by" as an aspect of the "psycho-political arsenal" of apartheid, see Ratele 2009.

10. Although Dhianaraj Chetty ([1994] 2012) states she moved to Kensington in 1954, when she would have been thirteen years old, Kewpie recalls living in at least three houses after her parents moved away from District Six when she was seventeen. The collection includes photographs, which appear to have been taken in the 1970s, showing these houses and Kewpie traveling from the district to work in Kensington.

11. For further discussion of forced removals to and from Kensington/Windermere, see Field 2001.

12. The collection evidences engagement with a remarkably broad range of photographic practices. Images were captured by professional photographers working in studios, on streets, and for newspapers; by a friend's husband who worked as a photographer; by Kewpie herself and her friends, neighbors, and acquaintances; and, a few, in photo booths.

13. Kewpie, Lewis interview.

14. Kewpie, Lewis interview; Kewpie, Gevisser interview.

15. Kewpie, Lewis interview.

16. Kewpie, Lewis interview.

17. Kewpie, Lewis interview.

18. Kewpie, Lewis interview.

19. Kewpie, Lewis interview; Kewpie, Gevisser interview.

20. Kewpie, Gevisser interview.

21. Kewpie, Lewis interview.

22. Kewpie, Gevisser interview.

23. Their inventor, Missourian Rose O'Neill ([1916] 2015: i), described the Kewpie characters—derived from Cupid—as "a sort of little round fairy whose one idea is

to teach people to be merry and kind at the same time." While there is no record of Kewpie referring to herself by the first name she was given at birth, she chose a variation on it for a hair salon she managed in Kensington: Yugene's Hairtique. In captions she usually refers to herself as Kewpie; less often, as Capucine or Miss Capucine; and occasionally, using her legal surname, Miss Fritz.

24. Kewpie, Lewis interview; Kewpie, Gevisser interview.

25. Bailey's African History Archives, Johannesburg, holds forty years of material from all editions of *Drum* and *Golden City Post*.

26. The tone of the coverage brings to mind Butler's ([1993] 2011: 86) description of the "ritualistic release" provided for "a heterosexual economy that must constantly police its own boundaries against queerness" by Hollywood films that act as a "displaced production and resolution of homosexual panic," as well as Matthew Krouse's ([1994] 2012) memoir detailing the time he spent employed as a visible marker of what was to be reviled: as a drag queen entertaining South African Defence Force troops.

27. Kewpie, Gevisser interview.

28. Kewpie, Gevisser interview.

29. For further discussion of the construction of authenticity in *A Star Is Born*, see Dyer 1991.

30. Kewpie, Lewis interview.

31. Kewpie, Lewis interview.

32. District Six Museum, *Kewpie: Daughter of District Six*, exhibition curated by Tina Smith and Jenny Marsden, Cape Town, 2018. The Kewpie Photographic Collection includes only a handful of photographs in which Kewpie's naturally brown hair is not bleached blonde, all of which were taken during her childhood and teenage years.

33. The formal study of hairdressing at this time was reserved for those classified "White."

34. Kewpie, Lewis interview.

35. For examples of such descriptions, see Visser 2003: 127; Tucker 2009: 77, 85; Munro 2012: 114; Botha 2014: 67; Davids 2017: 112; and Lease 2017: 138. More recently, Gevisser has written that "there has always been an openness to sexual and gender diversity within the creole community, assigned the term 'coloured' by the apartheid state, particularly in and around Cape Town" (Lease and Gevisser 2017: 157). For alternative conceptualizations of experiences, cultures, and identities intersecting with the category "Coloured," see, e.g., Erasmus 2001, Farred 2000, and Adhikari 2005.

36. Discussing this joke at length, Mohamed Adhikari (2006: 147) explains it "hinges on the audience's awareness of the status of Jan van Riebeeck, the commander of the first Dutch settlement established at the Cape in 1652, as the 'founding father' of white South Africa."

37. Although "Coloured" has classified people who are, as Grant Farred (2000: 7) puts it, "completely grounded" in South Africa, it has done so in terms of race as opposed

to ethnicity. For criticism of both the construction of District Six as ethnic homeland and claims to autochthonous (most notably Khoi) identities as a form of forgetting, see Wicomb 1998. Although Adhikari (2005: 183) suggests much of this work has been driven by an academic elite and has failed to resonate with most people formerly classified "Coloured," the process criticized by Richard Rive (1990) as "mythologizing" and "romanticizing," District Six has, Crain Soudien (2001) argues, successfully taken hold in popular consciousness.

38. Discussing "available documentary and oral evidence" from the 1940s and 1950s, Shamil Jeppie (1990: 80) comments that "the voices of 'moffies' are never heard; they are always spoken about (derisively), represented, judged, but never allowed the privilege of discourse."

39. The collection is referenced by Andrew Tucker (2009: 74–75) and Graeme Reid (2013: 18), for example, with the latter stating it "attests to the integration of·moffies within the wider community." Tucker (2009: 75) also reproduces short excerpts from audio recordings featuring Kewpie held at GALA as evidence of "the ease and freedom with which queer life was able to flourish." Brenna M. Munro (2012: 61) and Martin P. Botha (2014: 67) reference *A Normal Daughter* (Lewis 2000) as evidence of "thriving 'moffie' life" and that "gay life flourished," respectively. Bryce Lease (2017: 138) similarly describes the film showing that "District Six was a queer space that allowed for a multiplicity of alternative lives."

40. Kewpie, Lewis interview; Kewpie, Gevisser interview.

41. Kewpie, Lewis interview; Kewpie, Gevisser interview.

42. Kewpie, Gevisser interview.

43. Kewpie, Lewis interview.

44. Kewpie, Lewis interview.

45. Kewpie, Lewis interview; Kewpie, Gevisser interview.

46. Kewpie Photographic Collection, AM2886/98.2–4, GALA.

47. Kewpie Photographic Collection, AM2886/98.4, GALA.

48. Kewpie, Lewis interview.

49. Kewpie Photographic Collection, AM2886/131.4, AM2886/51.4, AM2886/129.8, GALA.

50. Kewpie Photographic Collection, AM2886/131.7, GALA.

51. Kewpie Photographic Collection, AM2886/130.2, GALA.

52. Kewpie, Lewis interview.

53. I draw this statement from a body of theory produced in both academic and nonacademic spaces and distilled by such scholars as madison moore (2018), whose theorization of fabulousness I draw on in my usage of *fabulous* and who reminds us that those forced to the margins are actually, always, the center.

54. Flyer for *A Normal Daughter: The Life and Times of Kewpie of District Six*, 2000, AM2886/C6, GALA.

55. District Six Museum, *Kewpie: Daughter of District Six.*

56. District Six Museum, *Kewpie: Daughter of District Six.*
57. The girls are nowhere to be seen in the work of Cloete Breytenbach (Barrow [1970] 2003), Jansje Wissema (Small 1986), Bryan Heseltine (Newbury 2013), or George Hallett, Clarence Coulson, Wilfred Paulse, Gavin Jantjes, or Jackie Heyns as seen in Hallet and McKenzie 2007—even though Jackie Heyns photographed some of the girls for a few of the *Golden City Post* articles discussed earlier. In a similar vein, Munro (2012: 105) notes that most literary "antiapartheid memorializations," which aim to "reconfigure the urban cultures of the past as a possible model for a future nation," excise "the lively queer public cultures that had been a part of these urban formations," while Nadia Davids (2017: 112) asks "why queer culture—one of the most significant aspects of District Six cultural life—was largely absent in the Museum's exhibition spaces."
58. District Six Museum, *Kewpie: Daughter of District Six.*
59. Kewpie, Gevisser interview.
60. Kewpie, Lewis interview.
61. Kewpie Photographic Collection, AM2886/211.1–2.
62. All photographs in the collection are catalogued at GALA with descriptions given by Kewpie, including this one.
63. Kewpie, Lewis interview.

## References

Adhikari, Mohamed. 2005. *Not White Enough, Not Black Enough: Racial Identity in the South African Coloured Community.* Athens: Ohio University Press.

Adhikari, Mohamed. 2006. "'God Made the White Man, God Made the Black Man . . .': Popular Racial Stereotyping of Coloured People in Apartheid South Africa." *South African Historical Journal* 55, no. 1: 142–64.

Barrow, Brian. (1970) 2003. *The Spirit of District Six.* With photographs by Cloete Breytenbach. Cape Town: Human and Rousseau.

Bickford-Smith, Vivian. 1995. *Ethnic Pride and Racial Prejudice in Victorian Cape Town: Group Identity and Social Practice, 1975–1902.* Cambridge: Cambridge University Press.

Botha, Martin P. 2014. "Queering African Film Aesthetics: A Survey from the 1950s to 2003: Portrayal of Homosexuality in International Films." In *Critical Approaches to African Cinema Discourse*, edited by Nwachukwu Frank Ukadike, 63–86. New York: Lexington.

Bourdieu, Pierre. 1990. *Photography: A Middle-Brow Art*, translated by Shaun Whiteside. Cambridge: Polity Press.

Butler, Judith. (1993) 2011. *Bodies That Matter: On the Discursive Limits of "Sex."* London: Routledge.

Chetty, Dhianaraj. (1994) 2012. "A Drag at Madame Costello's: Cape *Moffie* Life and the

Popular Press in the 1950s and 1960s." In *Defiant Desire: Gay and Lesbian Lives in South Africa*, edited by Mark Gevisser and Edwin Cameron, 115–27. Abingdon, UK: Routledge.

Davids, Nadia. 2017. "'Sequins, Self, and Struggle': An Introduction to the Special Issue." In "Sequins, Self, and Struggle." Special issue, *Safundi* 18, no. 2: 109–16.

Dyer, Richard. 1991. "*A Star Is Born* and the Construction of Authenticity." In *Stardom: Industry of Desire*, edited by Christine Gledhill, 132–41. London: Routledge.

Erasmus, Zimitri. 2001. "Introduction: Re-imagining Coloured Identities in Post-apartheid South Africa." In *Coloured by History, Shaped by Place: New Perspectives on Coloured Identities in Cape Town*, edited by Zimitri Erasmus, 13–28. Cape Town and Moroelana: Kwela Books and South African History Online.

Fallowell, Duncan, and April Ashley. 1982. *April Ashley's Odyssey*. London: Jonathan Cape.

Farred, Grant. 2000. *Midfielder's Moment: Coloured* Literature and Culture in Contemporary South Africa. Boulder, CO: Westview Press.

*Female Mimics*. 1965. "Capucine." *Female Mimics* 1, no. 6: 27–37.

Field, Sean. 2001. "Remembering Experience, Interpreting Memory: Life Stories from Windermere." *African Studies* 60, no. 1: 119–33.

GALA. n.d. "History of GALA." gala.co.za/about/history/ (accessed December 3, 2018).

Gevisser, Mark. (1994) 2012. "A Different Fight for Freedom." In *Defiant Desire: Gay and Lesbian Lives in South Africa*, edited by Mark Gevisser and Edwin Cameron, 14–86. Abingdon, UK: Routledge.

Gevisser, Mark, and Edwin Cameron. (1994) 2012. "Defiant Desire: An Introduction." In *Defiant Desire: Gay and Lesbian Lives in South Africa*, edited by Mark Gevisser and Edwin Cameron, 3–13. Abingdon, UK: Routledge, 2012.

Hallett, George, and Peter McKenzie. 2007. *District Six Revisited*. With photographs by George Hallett, Clarence Coulson, Jackie Heyns, Wilfred Paulse, and Gavin Jantjes. Johannesburg: Wits University Press.

Isaacs, Gordon, and Brian McKendrick. 1992. *Male Homosexuality in South Africa: Culture, Crisis, and Identity Formation*. Oxford: Oxford University Press.

Jeppie, Shamil. 1990. "Popular Culture and Carnival in Cape Town." In Jeppie and Soudien 1990: 67–87.

Jeppie, Shamil, and Crain Soudien, eds. 1990. *The Struggle for District Six: Past and Present*. Cape Town: Buchu Books.

Krouse, Matthew. (1994) 2012. "The Arista Sisters, September 1984: A Personal Account of Army Drag." In *Defiant Desire: Gay and Lesbian Lives in South Africa*, edited by Mark Gevisser and Edwin Cameron, 209–18. Abingdon, UK: Routledge.

Layne, Valmont, and Ciraj Rassool. 2001. "Memory Rooms: Oral History in the District Six Museum." In *Recalling Community in Cape Town: Creating and Curating the District Six Museum*, edited by Ciraj Rassool and Sandra Prosalendis, 146–53. Cape Town: District Six Museum Foundation.

Leap, William. 2002. "Strangers on a Train: Sexual Citizenship and the Politics of Trans-
    portation in Apartheid Cape Town." In *Queer Globalizations: Citizenship and the
    Afterlife of Colonialism*, edited by Arnaldo Cruz-Malavé and Martin Manalansan IV,
    219–35. New York: New York University Press.

Lease, Bryce. 2017. "Dragging Rights, Queering Publics: Realness, Self-Fashioning,
    and the Miss Gay Western Cape Pageant." In "Sequins, Self, and Struggle." Special
    issue, *Safundi* 18, no. 2: 131–46.

Lease, Bryce, and Mark Gevisser. 2017. "LGBTQ Rights in South Africa." In "Sequins,
    Self, and Struggle." Special issue, *Safundi* 18, no. 2: 156–60.

Lewis, Jack, dir., and prod. 2000. *A Normal Daughter: The Life and Times of Kewpie of
    District Six*. Narrated by Kewpie. South Africa: Idol Pictures, 2000. DVD. 56 min.

Livermon, Xavier. 2012. "Queer(y)ing Freedom: Black Queer Visibilities in Postapartheid
    South Africa." *GLQ* 18, no. 2–3: 297–324.

moore, madison. 2018. *Fabulous: The Rise of the Beautiful Eccentric*. New Haven, CT:
    Yale University Press.

Muñoz, José Esteban. 1999. *Disidentifications: Queers of Color and the Performance of
    Politics*. Minneapolis: University of Minnesota Press.

Munro, Brenna M. 2012. *South Africa and the Dream of Love to Come: Queer Sexuality
    and the Struggle for Freedom*. Minneapolis: University of Minnesota Press.

Newbury, Darren. 2013. *People Apart: 1950s Cape Town Revisited*. With photographs by
    Bryan Heseltine. London: Black Dog.

O'Connell, Siona. 2015. "Injury, Illumination, and Freedom: Thinking about the After-
    lives of Apartheid through the Family Albums of District Six, Cape Town." *Interna-
    tional Journal of Transitional Justice* 9, no. 2: 297–315.

O'Neill, Rose. (1916) 2015. *The Kewpie Primer*. With text and music by Elisabeth V.
    Quinn. London: Forgotten Books.

Pacey, Bett. 2014. "The Emergence and Recognition of Moffies as Popular Entertainers in
    the Cape Minstrel Carnival." *South African Theatre Journal* 27, no. 2: 111–24.

Prosser, Jay. 1998. *Second Skins: The Body Narratives of Transsexuality*. New York:
    Columbia University Press.

Rabie, Francois, and Elmien Lesch. 2009. "'I Am like a Woman': Constructions of Sexu-
    ality among Gay Men in a Low-Income South African Community." *Culture, Health,
    and Sexuality* 11, no. 7: 717–29.

Ratele, Kopano. 2009. "Apartheid, Anti-apartheid, and Post-apartheid Sexualities." In
    *The Prize and the Price: Shaping Sexualities in South Africa*, edited by Melissa
    Steyn and Mikki van Zyl, 290–305. Cape Town: HSRC Press.

Reid, Graeme. 2013. *How to Be a Real Gay: Gay Identities in Small-Town South Africa*.
    Scottsville: University of KwaZulu-Natal Press.

Rive, Richard. 1990. "District Six: Fact and Fiction." In Jeppie and Soudien 1990:
    110–16.

Small, Adam. 1986. *District Six*. Philippolis: Fontein Books.

Soudien, Crain. 2001. "Holding on to the Past: Working with the 'Myth' of District Six." In *Recalling Community in Cape Town: Creating and Curating the District Six Museum*, edited by Ciraj Rassool and Sandra Prosalendis, 95–105. Cape Town: District Six Museum Foundation.

Soudien, Crain, and Lalou Meltzer. 2001. "District Six: Representation and Struggle." In *Recalling Community in Cape Town: Creating and Curating the District Six Museum*, edited by Ciraj Rassool and Sandra Prosalendis, 66–73. Cape Town: District Six Museum Foundation.

Tan, Karin. 2018. "Kewpie: Daughter of District Six—Opening Night, Dialogue, Heritage Day Parade, and Public Artworks." GALA, October 3. gala.co.za/2018/10/03 /kewpiedaughter-of-district-six-opening-night-dialogue-heritage-day-parade-and -public-artworks/.

Tucker, Andrew. 2009. *Queer Visibilities: Space, Identity, and Interaction in Cape Town*. Oxford: Wiley Blackwell.

Visser, Gustav. 2003. "Gay Men, Leisure Space, and South African Cities: The Case of Cape Town." *Geoforum* 34, no. 1: 123–37.

Wicomb, Zoë. 1998. "Shame and Identity: The Case of the Coloured in South Africa." In *Writing South Africa*, edited by Derek Attridge and Rosemary Jolly, 91–107. Cambridge: Cambridge University Press.

Worby, Eric, and Shireen Ally. 2013. "The Disappointment of Nostalgia: Conceptualising Cultures of Memory in Contemporary South Africa." *Social Dynamics* 39, no. 3: 457–80.

Zagria. 2016. "Capucine (193?–) Performer." *A Gender Variance Who's Who*, February 16. zagria.blogspot.com/2016/02/capucine-193-performer.html#.XYIipJMzaT9.

# (UN)COMPLICATING MWANGA'S SEXUALITY IN NAKISANZE SEGAWA'S *THE TRIANGLE*

Edgar Fred Nabutanyi

*N*akisanze Segawa's *Triangle* (2016) is a historical novel cum political thriller that fictionalizes the circumstances that led to the religious wars that engulfed the central Ugandan kingdom of Buganda toward the close of the nineteenth century. Deploying an omniscient narrator, complemented with the interior reflections and observations of the novel's key characters, Nagawa and Kalinda, the novel chronicles the troubled history of the reign of a seventeen-year-old Mwanga as he negotiates the political and religious intrigue at his court. Divided into books 1 and 2, the novel plots the major political events of Mwanga's reign (1884–97) that included the execution of forty-five pages who refused to denounce their Christian faith, his dethronement and replacement with his brothers Kiwewa and Kalema, exile unto Lake Victoria's islands teeming with Arab slave traders, the hard trek to the neighboring kingdom of Nkole in search of sanctuary, and the triumphant return after the pragmatic unity of the Catholics and Protestants that led to the oust of the Islam-supported Kalema.

The fictionalized political content of the novel references material about this personality available in the Ugandan archive, as gestured to by Segawa's (2016: 367–69) own acknowledgments and bibliography.[1] This archive curates three distinctly and deliberately simplified images of Mwanga in Ugandan history. While Mwanga's personalities, as the noble savage, patriot, and pedophile (Hoad 2007; Rao 2015), in these archives are simplified stereotypes because of his sexuality, Segawa's fictional re-imagination of this historical figure provides an alternative personality. Granted, Mwanga's actions and inactions at the end of the nineteenth century are significantly woven into and intermeshed with the

*GLQ* 26:3
DOI 10.1215/10642684-8311786
© 2020 by Duke University Press

political tale of contemporary Uganda. The religious wars, the Uganda Martyrs, and the 1900 Buganda agreement—events on which modern Buganda and Uganda are built—justify a political reading of the novel and its protagonist. However, Segawa's novel juxtaposes the political with the personal to suggest how fiction can sidestep the public to humanize a personality whose character has been demonized in the combustive Ugandan sexuality debates.

Segawa effectively deploys a love triangle motif to weave a love story among Nagawa, Sekitto, Kalinda, and Mwanga to offer an alternative reading of this historical figure, because the combustive nature of Ugandan discourse on homosexuality makes fiction a safe space for engaging with this topic. This is because fiction has the potential to sidestep homophobic surveillance and rhetoric in the depicted society. Fiction empowers Segawa to foreground the thoughts, concerns, and musings of Mwanga's young wife Nagawa and his male lover Kalinda, who as his subjects and lovers would otherwise be gagged, to salvage his persona from a metaphor of sexual depravation frequently mobilized in support of Ugandan homophobia. Segawa's novel does more than confirm that this historical figure engaged in same-sexuality. It deploys the love triangle motif to offer readers an alternative description of Mwanga's personality to one that circulates in the Ugandan public sphere. The account of Mwanga that Segawa's fictionalization brings to life is unencumbered by his nonnormative sexual liaisons with men. Even in his relationship with Sekitto, whose interpretation can easily slide into politicized labels of abuse, pedophilia, and predation, fiction elegantly shows how Sekitto's decision to commit suicide rather than continue as Mwanga's lover reinforces the humanity of this historical figure. Fiction erects a flawed Mwanga who abuses his powers over his subjects such as Sekitto to derive sexual pleasure without considering the consequences of his actions on such individuals. However, Segawa's narrative does not also gloss over the deceptive, shrewd, cruel, and irrational aspects of his character.

## Ugandan Queer Fiction: An Exploration

In this article, I am cognizant of the complexly layered nature of the term *queer sexuality* (Ahmed 2006; Warner 1999). Thus, I use the term to mean any sexual orientation that is antithetical to heterosexuality. Here, my use of *queer sexuality* dovetails into Taiwo Adetunji Osinubi's (2015: 163) observation that *queer sexuality* is "not simply [about] same-sex desiring individuals, but also . . . as possibilities of situational non-conformity or improvisation variously incarnated in fluctuating psycho-social fields of sexual desire or performances within models of sex-gender systems." Osinubi provides a broad definition of *queer* that includes any sexual desire that is antiheterosexual or sexual practices that defy the normative. Osinubi's definition of *queer* references the homosexual as a historical figure imagined differently in the African literary public sphere. For example, leading scholars of this figure in African literature, such as Marc Epprecht (2008) and Neville Hoad (2007), have argued that African fiction visualizes homosexual characters that appear in nationalist texts such as Wole Soyinka's *Interpreters* (1965) as symbols of Western perversion, and homosexuality as a sexual practice introduced by Europeans to exploit and effeminate African society. This reading of the homosexual figure in African fiction justifies the homophobic claim that homosexuality is "un-African." This perhaps explains plot lines in African fiction that construct homosexuality as something that exists outside real Africa—what happens to men in cities, in prisons, and at the hands of foreigners (Epprecht 2008).

The recurrent trope of homosexuality as what exists outside "real Africa" that threads through colonial and postcolonial African literature (Epprecht 2008; Hoad 2007) has been queried by scholars such as Stella Nyanzi. Nyanzi (2013: 952) argues that it is myopic to imagine "a homogeneous Africanness and pedestrian oblivion to pluralities within African sexualities." Nyanzi and Karamagi (2015: 24) also note "the impractical impossibility of generalizing any social unit within Uganda as homogeneously homophobic or universally opposed to same-sex practices." In the above passages, Nyanzi not only underlines the pluralities of African sexualities but also disavows the generalization of homophobia to Africa. Her point is that multiple African sexualities are inevitably imagined and represented differently in the public sphere. The scholarship that disputes the homogenization of African sexuality counters a system of governance that excludes the homosexual in African colonial and postcolonial imaginaries. This contestation is highlighted in the works of African writers such as K. Sello Duiker, Chinelo Okparanta, and Binyavanga Wainaina, who deploy their art to reconfigure debates on homosexuality in a manner that rationalizes and destigmatizes this subject. Ugandan writers such as Jennifer Nansubuga Makumbi, Nakisanze Segawa, Monica Arac de Nyeko, and Beatrice Lamwaka have joined into an Africa-wide conversation about same-sexuality initiated by a cohort of the continent's writers listed above to interrogate the common homophobic rhetoric and offer an alternative image of homosexuals.

African fictional writers cited above are comparable to scholars such as Sylvia Tamale (2007, 2009, 2011), Rahul Rao (2015), Neville Hoad (2007), Kevin Ward (2015), Lydia Boyd (2013), and Stella Nyanzi (2013) who have variously used their work to distill important insights about homosexuality. In this article, on the one hand, I explore how fiction can offer alternative interpretation of this sexual practice; on the other hand, I focus on how Segawa's *Triangle* sidesteps the notoriety of a historical personality to humanize his character. Segawa's text disrupts three Ugandan narratives that politicize Mwanga's character in identity politics. These archives, broadly categorized as colonial/Christian missionary, early postindependence, and contemporary state/Christian Right, foreground Mwanga's sexuality to depict him as a noble savage, a patriot, or a pedophile.

For example, Rahul Rao refers to the work of J. F. Faupel (1965) and J. P. Thooren (1941) to underline how the Ugandan colonial/Christian missionary archive deploys an assortment of derogatory/demonic adjectives, such as "abominable vices, unnatural passions, works of Sodom, shameful proposals, unnatural lust and evil purposes" (Rao 2015: 2), to erect a simplified characterization of Mwanga. It is important to note that the demonization of Mwanga serves the missionary/colonial savior narrative that it is the colonial administrators and Christian missionaries that saved Ugandans from a pedophilic "monster." It is interesting that the same register is used by the late postcolonial record as signposted in President Yoweri Kaguta Museveni's 1986 and 2010 speeches at the Ugandan Martyrs' celebrations and Pastor Martin Ssempa's 2005 *New Vision* article. Both Museveni and Ssempa use their speeches and articles to castigate this historical figure. By conflating homosexuality to Mwanga's execution of the forty-five pages who are alleged to have rejected his sexual advances, Museveni and Ssempa mobilize Mwanga's sexuality to justify criminalization of a sexual practice. The third version of the documentation of this historical figure brands Mwanga a patriot who resisted colonialism. This view of Mwanga, rarely centralized in Ugandan sexuality debates, gained currency immediately after independence in the 1960s but was later silenced perhaps by Buganda royalty and a powerful Christian lobby (Rao 2015; Hoad 2007).

Besides the brief lionization in the 1960s, Mwanga's image that Segawa uses fiction to humanize has been largely disparaged in support of homophobia in the Ugandan colonial/Christian missionary and late postcolonial archives. This denigration, handwritten in the simplified images attached to Mwanga because of his sexuality, authorizes his exclusion from the Ugandan polity. Segawa's portrayal of a historical figure who symbolizes homosexuality in the Ugandan popular imaginary raises several questions. What archive is Segawa working with? Do the different archives that document Mwanga by obsessing with his sexuality offer different insights into the persona of this historical personage? What political rhetoric has his character and sexuality been mobilized to serve? What are the underlying intention and purpose of each archive's either demonization or lionization of Mwanga? Although it is not the intention of this article to exhaustively answer the above questions, I argue that these questions remind us of Michel-Rolph Trouillot's thesis: to "be interested in memory is to have an interest in the meaning with which the past is invested by the present rather than the reconstruction of the past with its meaning intact" (quoted in Rao 2015: 4). The essence of Trouillot's argument is that history and memory are tools of powerful constituencies seeking to entrench their ideological points of view. The colonial and late postcolonial actors demonize Mwanga because his characterizations as a noble savage and as a pedophile who executed young Christians who rejected his "unnatural vices" serve their political narrative of excluding and criminalizing homosexuality.[2]

## The Image of Mwanga in Debates about Sexuality in Uganda

The archives that authorize Mwanga's vilification in colonial and postcolonial moments in Ugandan sexuality debates collocate the Christian missionary and colonial/postcolonial government documents (but curiously elide the voice of the Baganda) in the construction of Mwanga as a pervert. While the claim by these archives that he was introduced to this practice by Arabs seeks to justify the argument that homosexuality is un-African, the foregrounding of the execution of the pages underscores the significance of the savior narrative in this archive. It can be argued that Mwanga's unorthodox sexuality is a tool in colonial narrative of "saving the native" from "unnatural" sexual mores. It is also a narrative that justifies an imposition of a dual sexual and/or gender system that aligns proper sexuality with monogamous marriage. This is reflected in the codification of "proper marriage" in both Ugandan customary and penal code edicts that outlaw same-sexuality in Uganda. It is unsurprising that the postcolonial archive of Museveni and Ssempa deploys the same logic and register in using Mwanga to recodify exclusion and criminalization of a sexual practice.

These archives disregard the notion that same-sexuality could have been part and parcel of the norms and customs of Buganda. This perhaps suggests that, when the norms that governed the kingdom came into conflict with Christianity mores, Mwanga become an easy scapegoat. Here, I am reminded of Osinubi's (2016) claim that the colonial encounter established sexual commons that sought to order the social body through strictures placed on the sexual body. Osinubi's point applies to Mwanga's sexuality, which has been demonized to serve a political purpose in Ugandan discourses. I argue that it is not Mwanga's execution of the Christian pages that is important; rather, that the execution posed a direct existential threat to Christian missionary and colonial incursions into Uganda that best explains Mwanga's demonization. This is what Kevin Ward (2013) and Rahul Rao

(2015) have called "homosexuality denialism" (Rao 2015: 1). By *homosexual deni-alism*, Rao gestures to a complex and paradoxical Ugandan register deployed in homosexuality debates. On the one hand, this register claims that homosexuality is un-Uganda, and on the other hand, it justifies enacting laws to criminalize what does not exist. Mwanga's sexuality has become a convenient tool that explains this Ugandan discursive exceptionalism of protecting a Ugandan way of life and Ugandans from sexual corruption and contamination from the West.

Rao's and Hoad's arguments about the construction of Mwanga as a sym-bol in Ugandan public discourses on sexuality are contested in his fictionalization as a same-sex–desiring personality in Segawa's *Triangle* (2016) and Makumbi's *Kintu* (2014). These novels question Museveni's 1986 and 2010 speeches in which he "implicitly [linked] Mwanga with the tyranny of Amin and Obote II . . . [and] invoked the martyrs as symbols of resistance, self-sacrifice and struggle for human rights" (Rao 2015: 7). Rao also reports the 2005 utterances of Ugandan pastor Ssempa in the Ugandan media, in which he "characterized Mwanga as a devi-ant homosexual who used his demigod status to appease his voracious appetite for sodomy by engaging in these unmentionable acts with his pages at court" (7). Museveni and Ssempa deliberately link Mwanga's sexuality to his political actions, such as the execution of the pages to justify state- and church-sponsored homopho-bia. Museveni's and Ssempa's demonization of Mwanga's homosexuality underlines how an alliance between the Ugandan state, church, and an American right-wing evangelist Christianity can politicize sexual acts. For Museveni and Ssempa, who receive financial support from imperial US and American right-wing evangelist Christianity, it is important to demonize Mwanga as a sexual deviant.

However, by absolving Mwanga from Sekitto's suicide, as elaborated in the later sections of this article, Segawa's novel delinks Mwanga's political actions from his sexuality.[3] Rather than engage with the sexuality politics encapsulated in Makumbi's statement that "it is not homosexuality that Europe brought, it was homophobia" (Underwood 2017), Segawa's novel depicts Mwanga as a flawed per-son who happened to desire intimacy with other men. This point is comparable to Hoad's (2007) and Sylvia Nannyonga-Tamusuza's (Rao 2005) analysis of homosex-uality among the Baganda. These scholars explain the complexity that surrounds same-sex desire in Buganda. Hoad observes that homosexuality might have "served ritual, religious, initiatory or fealty-producing functions may have been re-coded . . . as sex" (quoted in Rao 2015: 3). Relatedly, Nannyonga-Tamusuza argues that "conceptions of gender were intertwined with political power and space . . . what appeared to the missionaries as same-sex conduct might not have been understood in this way by the Baganda" (quoted in Rao 2015: 3). The essence of Hoad's and

Nannyonga-Tamusuza's observations about same-sex desire in Buganda is that this practice was complicated and required a level of nuance in its interpretation.

In a society where both men and women expressed fealty to the Kabaka by calling him their husband (Hoad 2007), any interaction between the Kabaka and his subjects was simultaneously metaphorical and corporeal. Without clear boundaries between the metaphorical and the corporeal, any interaction between the Kabaka and, for example, the pages he executed was more complicated than is simplistically framed in Ugandan debates on homosexuality. While Hoad and Nannyonga-Tamusuza do not contest Sylvia Tamale's claim that "it was an open secret . . . that Kabaka Mwanga was gay" (quoted in Rao 2015: 12), the important question that their reading of Mwanga's sexual orientation raises is not whether Mwanga was "gay" or "bisexual" in a normative sense but, rather, how his sexual activities with other men are to be interpreted. For example, in a society where the Kabaka was accorded enormous power over his subjects, is it not possible that he could abuse those powers to derive sexual pleasure from his subjects? Is it not also plausible that his victims could justify satiating his sexual desires as an obligation? By separating his sexual relationships from his politics, Segawa's novel manages to humanize this political figure whose sexuality has often been conflated with his political actions to demonize him.

## Humanizing Mwanga in *The Triangle*

The novel deploys multiperspectival narrative techniques to unravel the complex personality of this historical figure beyond his engagement in same-sexuality. Her depiction of Mwanga using subtle and nuanced tropes reminds us of Hoad's (2007) and Epprecht's (2008) insights into the representation of homosexuality in African fiction. Acknowledging the existence of a huge archive of African fiction that features same-sex–desiring characters, Epprecht (2008) unearths three recurrent tropes in African homosexual fiction: the representation of same-sexuality as an existential threat to the African way of life and as an external (Western) corruption, and recently, gay characters as sexuality warriors liberating themselves from homophobia to claim their agency and sexuality (Epprecht 2008). In describing these tropes, Epprecht focuses on the politicized images of homosexuals (pervert, sexuality warrior, or metaphor of the decadent West) that emerge from African fiction. While it is persuasive to read *The Triangle* through the lens of Epprecht's postulations, I find it interesting to treat it as a counternarrative that rehabilitates a flawed human being.

I argue that Segawa joins an African gay writing tradition generally, and

Ugandan fiction that foregrounds same-sexuality in their texts specifically, to offer an alternative image of Mwanga to one that has circulated in the Ugandan archive in the last 140 years.[4] Segawa employs a multiperspectival focalization—the omniscient narrator fused with first-person accounts by Mwanga's male lover, Kalinda, and his wife, Nagawa—to confirm that Mwanga engaged in homosexuality and that his sexuality can be delinked from the political actions that he was forced to perform to restore his power and save his kingdom in the last half of the nineteenth century, such as executing the forty-five pages. For example, the Ugandan state and church have conveniently claimed that he executed the forty-five Christian pages because they rejected his homosexual advances, rather than foreground the realpolitik justification as to why a seventeen-year-old Kabaka besieged by a cabal at his court that had eroded his power might have been persuaded to take drastic actions to regain his power and save his kingdom. Although *The Triangle* is a political novel that explores the political questions of late nineteenth century Buganda, its section that chronicles Mwanga's unorthodox sexuality helps enact a counternarrative of Mwanga and homosexuality beyond the common stereotypes that circulate in Ugandan public discourses. This places Segawa's novel among pioneering Ugandan texts that depict Mwanga as a flawed husband and lover. Although Segawa succeeds in humanizing Mwanga, she does not whitewash his shortcomings either. She shows how he often abused his power in his relations with men such as Sekitto.

Available analyses of the text include reviews by Abigail Arunga (2016) and Joel B. Ntwatwa (2016). While Arunga focuses on Segawa's fictionalization of Mwanga and the events of the religious war in the late 1890s, Ntwatwa concentrates on the content and craftsmanship of the novel. Arunga's thesis is that Segawa reclaims a Ugandan personality whose character has been distorted for political expediency by providing an alternative perspective to official historical characterization of Mwanga. The Mwanga that emerges in the early section of Segawa's novel debunks his recurrent image that foregrounds his sexuality to demonize him. Ntwatwa compares *The Triangle* to Jennifer Nansubuga Makumbi's *Kintu* and finds it wanting in terms of elegance of writing. However, he commends Segawa for her destabilization of recorded official Buganda history of the late 1890s. It is true that, by showing readers Mwanga from multiple perspectives, Segawa recalibrates the complexity of his personality. Here, Segawa's depiction of Mwanga echoes Arac de Nyeko's portrayal of Sanyu and Anyango in "Jambula Tree" (2006) and Lamwaka's characterization of Grace and Lala in "Pillar of Love" (2012) as same-sex–loving women trying to make sense of their relationships, oblivious of the politics and rhetoric of homophobia surrounding them. For these Ugandan writers, fiction acts as a safe place to tell stories about queer persons that are very ordinary, such as falling in love and being found out. This representation of homosexuality in fiction remarkably contrasts with its depiction in the Ugandan tabloid press, which foregrounds sensational and voyeuristic images of homosexuals.[5]

Segawa's multiperspectival focalization of Mwanga's character reminds us of Andy Carolin's (2015: 49) postulation that fiction is "an alternative archive of marginalized voices and experiences." Although Carolin's comment is about Afrikaner disavowal of same-sex desire that is often recuperated in fiction, I find his argument applicable to Segawa's writing in *The Triangle*. I extend Carolin's foregrounding of fiction's illocutionary power, namely, its ability to give a marginalized subject a voice for self-enunciation, to Segawa's *The Triangle* to argue that fiction can also rehabilitate a much maligned historical personality because of its ability to circumnavigate the "official sites of memorization [that] either erase or radically desexualize the histories of sexual minorities" (Carolin 2015: 49). By sidestepping "official sites of memorization," fiction allows Segawa to ask and answer the question, Who was Mwanga?

The multiperspectival focalization anchored on the omniscient narrator who collocates Nagawa's and Kalinda's views about Mwanga's character provides Segawa with the textual tools to comprehensively reimagine the attributes of this historical figure. Mwanga's beautiful wife Nagawa and his gay lover Kalinda are significant nodes in the double love-triangle motif on which the sexuality theme of the novel is anchored. They also provide a critical and personalized lens through which Mwanga's character emerges. These textual signposts perceptibly disclose the character of Mwanga by acting as normalizing valences of same-sex desire. For example, Nagawa's competition with the pages—Kalinda and Sekitto—for Mwanga's erotic attention normalizes his sexuality. Similarly, Kalinda, who oscillates between bouts of jealousy and tenderness in his engagement with Mwanga, regularizes Mwanga's nonconventional sexuality. This is because Kalinda and Nagawa react as quintessentially spurned lovers. In general, *The Triangle* is a love story that chronicles Africans having complex interior lives contrary to the prevalent caricatured representations of these subjects.

The snapshot of Mwanga that Kalinda and Nagawa paint and that is curated by the omniscient narrator reveals Mwanga as more than a man who sought sexual pleasure nonnormatively. Many attributes of Mwanga emerge from the entirety of the novel. He is portrayed as a shrewd, cruel, and deceptive leader in regards to his political actions. However, in the first section of the novel, which centers on his unconventional sexuality, he is depicted as charismatic, lovable, and well intentioned, as well as a selfish, inconsiderate, and uncaring lover. The two mediators of Mwanga's character provide different insights into his character. For example, when Segawa voyeuristically lets readers accompany Kalinda into Mwanga's private quarters—Muzibu—to eavesdrop on the lovemaking between Mwanga and Sekitto, she uses this encounter to cement the fact that Mwanga engaged in same-sexuality and that he is an egoistic and treacherous character who often abused his power to satisfy his sexual cravings.

Does the fact that Mwanga engages in same-sex relationships make him the devil that the Ugandan archives make him out to be? While Segawa's depiction of Sekitto's reaction to Mwanga's sexual attention lends credence to Mwanga's demonization, the picture of this man drawn by Kalinda and Nagawa is that of a flawed lover. Although Segawa's depiction of Sekitto as scared and possibly traumatized by Mwanga's sexual advances raises several questions, she still humanizes Mwanga. Some of the questions that the episode raises include whether the sexual act was in fact rape. Is this a case of Mwanga abusing his powers as a Kabaka to derive sexual pleasure from his subjects? Does this make Mwanga both a sexual predator and an uncaring sadist who does not care about the pain he inflicts in pursuit of and/or on those from whom he extracts his nonnormative sexual pleasure? Rather than label Mwanga a sadistic sexual predator, this episode in the novel offers two possible humanizing explanations of Mwanga's character: that he is a mere mortal who takes advantage of the enormous powers of the Kabakaship to satisfy his sexual desires, and that his subjects cannot refuse him because they have been nurtured to believe it is their obligation to satisfy his every whim.

Here, consider the exchange between the leader of the English missionaries in Buganda, Rev. Clement, and another priest before the execution of the pages at Namugongo. Rev. Clement is surprised that an unbaptized Sekitto is among the Christians sentenced to death. The reverend's question, "Why was he among the Christians going to Namugongo?" (Segawa 2016: 158), is a very important revelation about the exploitative and abusive character and enormous power of Mwanga. One reading of Rev. Clement's musing is that, by joining the Christians going to Namugongo, Sekitto has chosen to die rather than continue as Mwanga's sexual partner. Sekitto's suicide reminds us of the recurrent trope of suicide as protest utilized by marginalized people to escape their predicament, as famously theorized by Gayatri Chakravorty Spivak in "Can the Subaltern Speak?" (1998) and artistically rendered by Toni Morrison in *Beloved* (1987). Without a foreseeable escape from Mwanga's desires, and perhaps unable to refuse Mwanga's sexual commands, Sekitto is left no alternative but death. That it is in death that Sekitto can escape Mwanga's sexual demands on him underlines both the enormous powers of the

Kabaka and how a flawed Mwanga abuses such powers to extract sexual pleasure from his subjects.

While Sekitto prefers death to sexual intercourse with Mwanga, whom he cannot reject, given Mwanga's demigod status as a Kabaka, Nagawa—Mwanga's second wife—offers us insight into another side of Mwanga's personality. Nagawa uses interiority to sidestep the patriarchal framework that mutes her to comment on Mwanga's complex sexual desires (Nnaemeka 1995; Osinubi 2015). These discursive strategies empower Nagawa to covertly disclose not only Mwanga's sexuality but also how his preference of the company of his pages frustrates and torments her own sexual desires. The case in point is her musing that "this time she wanted the Kabaka to come to her home alone. But chances were he might again come with that page Kalinda, who would, like a dog, wait for his master outside her house while Mwanga made quick thrusts inside her, and then put on his clothes and walk out" (Segawa 2016: 16). Later in the text, she wonders why "Mwanga was spending a lot of time in the company of those pages" (20). Nagawa's fear and anxiety are palpable in the two passages above. She is not only anxious that Mwanga will not come to her bed but also perplexed by a husband who prefers the company of his pages to his beautiful wife. Given that, in the traditional Ganda society of the late 1890s, Nagawa would never criticize or question her husband, let alone her Kabaka, Segawa's focus on Nagawa's interiority provides her with a voice that expresses her discomfort and suffering, on the one hand, and censure of her husband's unorthodox sexual desires, on the other.

It is unsurprising that Nagawa anxiously waits for Mwanga to sleep with her, because bearing children would entrench her position and power in the kingdom. Mwanga's failure to impregnate her, because he spends more time with his male lovers, is a source of psychological anguish. Perhaps Nagawa would not have worried so much about Mwanga's affairs if she had children in this evidently unhappy marriage, or if she was competing for Mwanga's sexual attention with other women. Her description of their lovemaking as "quick thrusts inside her" (Segawa 2016: 16) while one of Mwanga's male lovers waits outside accentuates Nagawa's frustration, devaluation, and vulnerability. Her description of Kalinda as a dog (16) and lashing out at Sekitto when he brings the Kabaka's message that Mwanga would not visit her hut that evening are because of her sense of shame and humiliation due to Mwanga's sexual orientation. The omniscient narrator notes Nagawa's reaction toward Sekitto thus: "Finally the insult came when she found Sekitto at her doorway; the fair skinned and youngest royal page, whose beauty frightened Nagawa. . . . Then she had felt the color of her own skin turn pale when he informed her about the cancellation of Mwanga's visit" (26). Nagawa's disappointment and anger are palpable in this passage. It is not Mwanga's canceling of the sexual appointment that arouses her fury. It is rather the indelicacy of sending the cancellation by his lover. Segawa invites us to imagine how humiliating it is for Nagawa to be put in this position by an indifferent and insensitive husband.

Kalinda is another character in the love triangle through whose eyes we glean Mwanga's persona, namely, the manipulation of his power to derive sexual pleasure with total disregard to people who are devoted to him. Kalinda is Mwanga's long-time lover who is completely devoted to the Kabaka, as suggested by the following passage: "Tonight the two would celebrate his victory in a way none of the spectators anticipated . . . but even as those numerous thoughts danced in his mind, he wondered whether he wanted to marry" (Segawa 2016: 8). While the first part of the passage underlines the sexual pleasure that Kalinda and Mwanga share, the second section underscores the price that Kalinda is willing to pay to please Mwanga—his readiness to forgo marriage to continue pleasing Mwanga. For someone who had reached marriage age—his father informs him that the family is in the process of arranging a marriage for him (14)—his consideration to forgo marriage to please Mwanga is a huge sacrifice. He is ready to displease his family and attract societal censure and ridicule to please Mwanga.

Kalinda's commitment, devotion, and sacrifice to Mwanga and the pain he suffers in the service of Mwanga's nonconventional sexual desires are incontestable. Unfortunately, the exploitative side of Mwanga is revealed when despite Kalinda's devotion he is "treated like some old wrinkled wife" (Segawa 2016: 79). Although several passages in the novel capture Kalinda's torment, the following two stand out: "Pain crowded his thoughts, anger tore his chest apart. He felt his body weaken and his lungs tighten" (51). Kalinda confesses that, on discovering "who the Kabaka's new *kasawe* was, even after acknowledging that the Kabaka was at liberty to decide who his next *kasawe* would be, Kalinda's heart still yearned for Mwanga's dreams . . . some form of yearning, of wanting to touch Mwanga, as if Mwanga controlled his happiness" (79). What is significant about these passages is Kalinda's oscillation between nostalgic anguish and pragmatic resilience.

The unexpected transformation of Kalinda's fortunes because of his replacement by Sekitto as Mwanga's lover would ordinarily arouse bitterness and resentment. For a man whose "eyes lit up and his heart got filled with bliss as he walked towards Muzibu the next evening" (Segawa 2016: 50), it would be devastating to be easily replaced as he is. This would perhaps arouse outrage comparable to Nagawa's hostility toward him and Sekitto. That Kalinda goes out of his way to protect Mwanga's reputation underlines Mwanga's power over and the goodwill of his subjects to his welfare. For example, Kalinda talks to Sekitto and makes him "promise that he would not tell anyone about Mwanga's interests [a promise that makes Kalinda] confident that [Mwanga's] secret was safe" (83). Devoid of historical and political context, Mwanga is revealed in *The Triangle* as an ordinary flawed person who is unaware of how the power of his office makes it impossible for his subjects to reject his sexual advances because they have been drilled to satisfy his desires and keep his sexuality a secret.

## Conclusion

My thesis in this article is that Segawa depoliticizes Mwanga's same-sexuality to reconstruct his persona by showcasing him from multiple perspectives. Her portrayal of Mwanga abstains from the common tropes associated with the appropriation of his image in Ugandan discourses in the last 140 years. This is because her novel attempts to cure the propagandist framing that often reduces Mwanga to a simplistic label of a sexual degenerate. Although the novel confirms Mwanga's homosexuality as a historical fact, it succeeds in disconnecting it from the colonial/Christian missionary and postcolonial Ugandan archives that have used his sexuality to demonize queer sexuality in the country. In writing *The Triangle*, by inserting same-sex desire in its first section and by deploying a multiperspectival focalization, Segawa succeeds in providing an alternative portrait of Mwanga. Her novel debunks the politicized and demonized image of this historical person that circulates in politicized debates of homosexuality in the country.

Thus, it can be argued that Segawa, in writing *The Triangle* and humanizing Mwanga's persona, becomes what Wale Adebanwi (2014) has called a "writer-social thinker." The above characterization of Segawa's intellectual project in *The Triangle* is plausible because her work's construction of a same-sex–loving Kabaka and the plot of his interactions with Nagawa, Kalinda, and Sekitto bestow unto her the Adebanwian vision of a public intellectual who uses her fiction to unearth complex versions of a historical personality's character at a particular moment in the country's history. She rehabilitates someone who has been unfairly labeled a sexual degenerate to symbolize politicized and historicized homophobia in the depicted country. This reminds us of Chimamanda Ngozi Adichie's observation in her Harvard commencement lecture that historical figures are flawed persons like anyone else (see Bolotnikova 2018). Segawa's innovative narrative register coheres with a historical fiction motif to portray Mwanga as a flawed leader, lover, and husband and not a demonic predator that a politicized reading of his persona has placed in the Ugandan public sphere.

**Notes**

I extend my thanks to the Makerere University's Directorate of Research and Graduate Training (DRGT), which funded the research published in this article under its Mak-sida Postdoctoral Scholarships Grant 337.

1.  It is important to note that, having ascended to power at a tender age of seventeen, the youthful and inexperienced Mwanga was no match for the entrenched palace intrigue and privilege of the Ganda elite, as well as the threat of colonialism at the time. Lacking the deftness and astuteness of his father, Muteesa I, Mwanga inevitability resorted to violence and cruelty, as has been variously documented in Ugandan precolonial and post-independence records. While Segawa's novel historically reimagines how these political and existential events that account for the creation of modern Uganda played out in late nineteenth-century Buganda under Mwanga, my focused reading here explores how fiction allows her to humanize this historical figure.

2.  It is important to note that this cohort of Ugandan writers has been accused of writing about homosexuality for mercenary intent, namely, to attain literary recognition from Western literary curating agencies. It is often pointed out that they conveniently place homosexuality plots and characters at the start of their novels and never return to this subject matter. While this can justify the claim that they exploit homosexuality for their own gain, the impact of their creative reimagining of this topic in Ugandan public sphere cannot be underestimated. For example, it may be true that Segawa's insertion of Mwanga's same-sex desire in the opening section of her novel is motivated by an appeal to a literary trend. However, what is significant is that her recuperation and complication of Mwanga place his character beyond the simplified stereotype of a sexual pervert and predator that have long circulated in Ugandan public discourses.

3.  The Uganda Martyrs are an important institution in the Ugandan public imaginary, commemorating the June 3, 1886, execution, on the orders of Kabaka Mwanga, of forty-five Christian pages from his court who had defied his order to renounce their Christian faith. Affirmed at "Blessed" by Pope Benedict in 1920 and canonized by Pope Paul IV on October 18, 1964, the twenty-two Catholics and twenty-three Protestants have evolved into an important symbol of Christian courage in the country, which is celebrated every June 3.

4.  It is prudent to argue that a Ugandan homosexual writing tradition exists, because of the work of such writers as Makumbi (2014), Segawa (2016), Arac de Nyeko (2006), and Lamwaka (2016). These writers have used the recurrent absence/presence motif as a fluent register to distill important insights about homosexuality. Their deployment of articulated silence(s) is a useful technique in unraveling same-sex desire without sensational voyeurism it courts in Ugandan public discourses on this topic.

5.  The Ugandan tabloid newspapers such as *Redpepper* have since 2006 periodically

and sensationally published names and pictures of Ugandans that it accuses of being gay. For example, in August 2006 *Redpepper* published first names and occupations of Ugandans whom it alleged were homosexuals, followed by the September 2006 publication of the names of thirteen Ugandan lesbians. In February 2013 the tabloid printed the identity of people it claimed were recruiting children into homosexuality, and its February 2014 front page showed pictures and names of two hundred people it claimed were homosexuals. *Redpepper*'s sensational and voyeuristic reporting gives the impression that society is besieged by a sexual orientation that poses an existential threat to the nation.

## References

Adebanwi, Wale. 2014. "The Writer as a Social Thinker." *Journal of Contemporary African Studies* 32, no. 4: 405–20.

Ahmed, Sara. 2006. *Queer Phenomenology: Orientations, Objects, Others*. Durham, NC: Duke University Press.

Arac de Nyeko, Monica. 2006. "Jambula Tree." In *African Love Stories: An Anthology*, edited by Ama Ata Aidoo, 164–77. Cape Town: Lynne Rienner.

Arunga, Abigail. 2016. "Book Review: *The Triangle* by Nakisanze Segawa." *Daily Nation*, October 14.

Bolotnikova, Marina N. 2018. "Commencement: Above All Else, Do Not Lie." *Harvard Magazine*, May 23. www.harvardmagazine.com/2018/05/commencement-class-day -chimamanda-adichie.

Boyd, Lydia. 2013. "The Problem with Freedom: Homosexuality and Human Rights in Uganda." *Anthropological Quarterly* 86, no. 3: 697–724.

Carolin, Andy. 2015. "A Novel Archive of Intimacy: Sex and the Struggle in Gerald Kraak's Ice in the Lungs." *Journal of Literary Studies* 31, no. 3: 49–66.

Epprecht, Marc. 2008. *Heterosexual Africa? The History of an Idea from the Age of Exploration into the Age of AIDS*. Athens: Ohio University Press.

Hoad, Neville. 2007. *African Intimacies: Race, Homosexuality, and Globalization*. Minneapolis: University of Minnesota Press.

Lamwaka, Beatrice. 2016. "Pillar of Love." In *Butterfly Dreams*, 21–30. Kampala: Lakalatwe.

Makumbi, Jennifer Nansubuga. 2014. *Kintu*. Nairobi: Kwani Trust.

Nnaemeka, Obioma. 1995. "Feminism, Rebellious Women, and Cultural Boundaries: Rereading Flora Nwapa and Her Compatriots." *Research in African Literatures* 26, no. 2: 80–113.

Ntwatwa, Joel B. 2016. "Should We Use Kintu as a Yardstick for Ugandan Literature?" *Nevender* (blog), December 14. www.nevender.com>should-we-use-kintu-as-a -yardtick-for-ugandan-literature.

Nyanzi, Stella. 2013. "Dismantling Reified African Culture through Localized Homo-sexualities in Uganda." *Culture, Health, and Sexuality* 15, no. 8: 952–67.

Nyanzi, Stella, and Andrew Karamagi. 2015. "The Socio-political Dynamics of the Anti-Homosexuality Legislation in Uganda." *Agenda* 29, no. 1: 24–38.

Osinubi, Taiwo Adetunji. 2015. "Abolition, Law, and the Osu Marriage Novel." *Cambridge Journal of Postcolonial Literary Inquiry* 2, no. 1: 53–71.

Osinubi, Taiwo Adetunji. 2016. "Queer Prolepsis and the Sexual Common: An Introduc-tion." *Research in African Literatures* 47, no. 2: vii–xxiii.

Rao, Rahul. 2015. "Re-membering Mwanga: Same-Sex Intimacy, Memory, and Belonging in Postcolonial Uganda." *Journal of Eastern African Studies* 9, no. 1: 1–19.

Segawa, Nakisanze. 2016. *The Triangle*. Kampala: Mattville.

Tamale, Sylvia. 2007. "Out of the Closet: Unveiling Sexuality Discourses in Uganda." In *Africa after Gender?*, edited by Catherine M. Cole, Takyiwa Manuh, and Stephen F. Miescher, 17–29. Bloomington: Indiana University Press.

Tamale, Sylvia. 2009. "A Human Rights Impact Assessment of the Ugandan Anti-homosexuality Bill 2009." *Equal Rights Review* 4: 49–57.

Tamale, Sylvia. 2011. Introduction to *African Sexuality: A Reader*, edited by Sylvia Tamale, 1–9. Cape Town: Pambuzuka.

Underwood, Alexia. 2017. "Interview with Jennifer Nansubuga Makumbi." *Los Angeles Review of Books*, August 3.

Ward, Kevin. 2013. "The Role of the Anglican and Catholic Churches in Uganda in Pub-lic Discourses on Homosexuality and Ethics." *Journal of Eastern African Studies* 9, no. 1: 127–44.

Warner, Michael. 1999. *The Trouble with Normal: Sex, Politics, and the Ethics of Queer Life*. Cambridge, MA: Harvard University Press.

# THROUGH THE LENS OF MODERNITY

## Reflections on the (Colonial) Cultural Archive of Sexuality and Gender in South Africa

Phoebe Kisubi Mbasalaki

*I*n 2016 the nongovermental organization (NGO) OUT LGBT Well-Being published a research report on hate crimes on the LGBTQI community in South Africa. This research was part of the Love Not Hate campaign to measure levels of discrimination against LGBTQI people in South Africa. One of the indicators in this research was knowledge of murder victims, which showed a significant proportion (41 percent) knew of someone who had been murdered due to their sexual orientation. Moreover, this research indicates that 88 percent of those who experienced hate crimes did not report these incidents. Indeed, very few lesbian murders have gone through the court process and prosecution in South Africa. I read these murders of lesbian women, as well as the various forms of physical and structural violence toward African same-sex intimacies, in South Africa as the "customary" of sexuality in its hegemonic sense, one that has normalized and privileged heterosexuality while othering any practices outside of this through the language of violence. I also connect these murders and all forms of physical and structural violence against those who fall outside heterosexual normativity to Keguro Macharia's (2015: 140) framing of "an archive of disposability," in other words, disposable "bodies that don't matter," as a way of reiterating this hegemonic customary.

The hegemonic customary is in firm juxtaposition with the judicial economy, where the latter is offered as a way out in instances of violation or discrimination. I have been thinking a lot around the language of violence that is ever present in modernity. When the language of violence is used for othering based on race, gender, sexuality, religion, or disability, we actively seek out the law as a means of

*GLQ* 26:3
DOI 10.1215/10642684-8311800
© 2020 by Duke University Press

social justice and policies as solutions (Gqola 2015). This is the language we know and speak, the point of call we go to—this is the status quo. My point here is not to discredit the law and the possibilities it offers, or victories of social and judicial justice; my point is, shouldn't we (re)think other ways, given that the judicial system is heavily indebted to the invention of the customary? By using the word *customary*, I am reiterating the connection to judicial shortcomings and marginality along structural grammars of difference (Hoad 2016).

Moreover, the judicial system, which is entangled within the customary, is rooted in histories of hierarchization. For instance, the law as it stands is very patriarchal in implementation, where the perpetrator is innocent until proven guilty—it is the survivor who has to work hard to prove the crime happened, something we repeatedly witness, for example, in rape cases (Bérard 2016; Henderson 1991; Aboh 2018; Abrahams 1997), but more so with lesbian rape cases (Gqola 2015; Motsei 2007). Why, then, do we put most of our faith in a system that fails many of us, and not think outside the box—a queering of the customary, if you like?

I offer just two examples here, by no means exhaustive of my activism for social justice, to demonstrate the difficulty of working outside the hegemonic customary. In 2014, with hope, I attended several protests calling for justice for the four women who identified as lesbians who were murdered because of their sexuality. Many of these protests were organized through NGOs on the front lines of sexual rights and citizenship. Only one court case materialized out of the four murders, yet again through NGO intervention. On September 5, 2019, I protested together with tens of thousands of comrades, marching to the South African Parliament in Cape Town, hopeful for a significant transformation in gender-based violence in South Africa following the gruesome rape and murder of one of our students at the University of Cape Town (Thom 2019). This mass mobilization died down within a couple of weeks and things went back to normal (perverse forms of physical and structural violence along the grammars of race, gender, and sexuality without collective rage/mobilizing), without notable significant changes in the judicial economy—the hegemonic customary.

NGOs that champion sexual rights and citizenship have played a crucial role in trying to interrogate the customary. For instance, one of the very first organizing bodies, the National Coalition for Gay and Lesbian Equality, played a pivotal role in lobbying for the equality clause and the inclusion of sexual orientation in the postapartheid constitution. Some, such as Jacklyn Cock (2003), argue that the constitutional lobbying effort took a deliberately conservative approach that was characterized as elitist, unrepresentative, and male dominated, as well as predominantly white. To this, Natalie Oswin (2007: 666) adds that the National Coalition for Gay and Lesbian Equality represented by the Equality Project was able to successfully challenge homophobic legislation by creating the figure of the "black, poor, gay and lesbian," who was imagined to be the putative beneficiary of the organization's lobbying efforts. Yet as we know, in contemporary South Africa, the "black, poor, gay and lesbian" is far from accessing these rights in their entirety—i.e., economic, social, health, judicial, and the list goes on, all reflected in the hegemonic customary.

I therefore find myself conflicted, in my own work as activist as well as that of NGOs on the front lines of social and judicial justice. There is definitely some progress on the grounds of sexual rights and citizenship, for instance, the South African constitution's clause on sexual orientation and the laws/policies that emanated from these efforts (Government of South Africa 1996). Yet African same-sex intimacies bear the brunt of physical and structural violence—the hegemonic customary. And so I am reminded of José Esteban Muñoz's (2009: 9) *Cruising Utopia*, where he compares possibilities and potentialities, saying that "unlike a possibility, a thing that simply might happen, a potentiality is a certain mode of nonbeing that is eminent, a thing that is present but not actually existing in the present tense." I despair because I see social and judicial justice as a potentiality for the future, not something we will get to fully experience as possibility for the present. In this potentiality we can, for instance, see full implementation of a nonbiased law for all hate crimes, or NGOs championing sexual rights that are self-sufficient and free from explicit and implicit dynamics that go with donor funding and the global North/South hierarchies. Potentiality therefore suggests futurity, which could be the case regarding the constitution or laws meeting their mandate, and judicial justice to all those relegated to the margins along structural grammars of race, class, gender, sexuality, and ableism.

But what is the alternative, when the hegemonic customary that speaks the language of violence offers us a judicial customary that predominantly speaks the language of the constitution, human rights, laws, and policies from which only a few benefit? The answer is an inherited system of coloniality, marred in a number of historical processes, including the Atlantic slave trade and the European colonization of Africa, Asia, and Latin America (Oyewumi 2000; Mignolo and Wanamaker 2015). We know sexual labor was central to the colonial project, which was essential to the making of the dual sex/gender system, the sexual division of space and labor, and the normalization of rape (Gqola 2015; Abrahams 2003; Tamale 2011; McClintock 1995). For instance, Yvette Abrahams (2003: 17) articulates how "sexual violence which almost functioned as a rite of passage for young settler men, says something about the extent to which institutionalised rape was embedded in settler culture." Abrahams adds that "by the century, this perception was so pervasive that a court reversed a death sentence for rape passed on a white man, upon evidence being brought that the victim was not white, but in fact Khoekhoe" (17). This history of the judicial system working for a few filters into the present. Here I am reminded of Maria Lugones (2010), who posits that the civilizing mission used hierarchical gender dichotomy as a judgment, especially because turning the colonized into human beings was not a colonial goal. In other words, the civilizing mission was not for equality but, rather, for hierarchization through othering—"dehumanisation that fits them for classification, the process of subjectification, the attempt to turn the colonized into less than human beings" (745). This is what stipulates the judicial economy, and thus the modern is entangled with the hegemonic customary.

With regards to modernity, I draw on Walter D. Mignolo and William H. Wanamaker's (2015: 2) conceptualization of the colonial matrix of power, in which "coloniality is constitutive and not derivate of modernity." They add that the discourse of modernity is "tied up with the logic of coloniality, which circumscribes what it takes to advance modernity within all the *domains* used to categorize and classify the modern world: political, economic, religious, epistemic, aesthetic, ethnic/racial, sexual/gender subjective" (3). This, then, is what makes the customary, in its traditional/hegemonic sense.

Queering the customary calls for engaging with an intersectional decolonial approach to interrogate the race and colonial dynamics inextricably linked to sexuality. Decoloniality through intersectional prisms therefore opens up other ways of reimagining African sexuality, as made intelligible by African same-sex intimacies within the locus of colonial difference, that is, ways of being within modernity/coloniality (Mignolo 2000).[1] To expedite this approach, we can draw on what Sandeep Bakshi, Suhraiya Jivraj, and Slivia Posocco (2016: 1) refer to as "querying the workings of neo-colonial epistemic categories, systems of classification and taxonomies that classify people." This entails "queering coloniality and the epistemic categories that classify people according to their body configuration—skin colour and biological molecular composition for the regeneration of the species—[it] means to disobey and delink" (1). Reexistence requires that "you de-link from the rules imposed on you . . . and therefore you re-exist affirming yourself as a human being" (Mignolo 2016: viii). Concretely, this means drawing attention to the (colonial) cultural archive of gender and sexuality while at the same time addressing persisting misrepresentations and knowledge production that originate within former colonial trajectories, particularly in relation to African sexuality. The (colonial) cultural archive of gender and sexuality discussed here has been central to many present-day taboos, laws, attitudes, knowledges, and scholarship surrounding sexuality in Africa, a context in which African sexual subjectivities have been negotiated and shaped in very specific ways (Tamale 2011).

In this article, I offer a conceptual and decolonial methodological lens that enables us to see what is hidden from our understanding of race and sexuality in relation to normative heterosexuality in a postcolony like South Africa. Like Lugones (2010), I note the fact that gender and sexuality are marred within modernity and the logic of coloniality. I connect this to the construction and production of binarized (and polarized) hetero/homo categories and the privileging of heterosexuality. This forms part of the hegemonic customary, and I argue that this construction and production lies at the crux of the disconnect between the progressive South African constitution and the lived realities that African same-sex intimacies in South African experience. I then interrogate how NGOs like Hivos, which have been central in advocating for sexual rights and service provision, are steeped in a neoliberal economy of modernity and therefore do not radically decenter or delink from the colonial matrix of power that shapes the (colonial) archive of gender and sexuality. Finally, I offer three examples of African same-sex intimacies that are working at the locus of colonial difference through grassroots encounters. These examples that queer the customary mostly work to decenter the hegemonic customary—the (colonial) cultural archive of gender and sexuality. Through infrapolitics, they are reclaiming what has been distorted by the customary as African same-sex intimacies. The first example presents what has been made intelligible by Black women in same-sex intimacies in South Africa in the form of sexual language and desire. The second example decenters the rigid construction and understanding of what bodies produce prescribed gender in its binary form and offer a complex gender matrix among gay men in Ermelo, Mpumalanga, South Africa. The third example offers strategies of existence of Black women in same-sex relationships under the hegemonic customary of constrained structural circumstances of unemployment in South Africa. These speak to what a queering of the customary is, at a political, societal level.

## Clearing the Discursive Space / Modernity Unplugged

Many scholars, such as Anne McClintock (1995; also see Arnfred 2004a; Arnfred 2004b; Finley 2011; Lewis 2011; Smith 2006; Tamale 2011), have articulated how sexuality was central to the colonial project. In understanding the crystallization of heterosexuality and the homo/hetero binary, I am guided by Gloria D. Wekker's

(2016) work, particularly her groundbreaking text based on an ethnography of whiteness, Dutchness, and the metropole. Her book *White Innocence* presents key paradoxes of the disavowal of four hundred years of colonial history from Dutch national consciousness, claiming no traces of it in the contemporary, especially with reference to racial oppression and the structural inequalities imbued in the logic of colonialism. I am particularly interested in a notion Wekker surgically articulates: the colonial cultural archive. For Wekker, the content of the cultural archive overlaps with the colonial archive as a "repository of memory," as well as "principles and practices of governance" (Ann L. Stoler, quoted in Wekker 2016: 19) "in the heads and hearts of the people in the metropole, but its content is also silently cemented in policies, in organisational rules, in popular and sexual cultures, and in common-sense everyday knowledge, and all of this is based on four hundred years of imperial rule" (19). Wekker notes how knowledges in different domains have traveled between colonies and metropoles, where she foregrounds the cultural archive as "memories, the knowledge, the affect with regards to race that were deposited within metropolitan populations and the power relations embedded within them" (Wekker 2016: 19). She further notes how it helps to conceptualize the cultural archive along similar lines with Pierre Bourdieu's (1997) notion of *habitus*, where the past is entangled in the present, in the way people have been socialized into it, and it has become naturalized into the unconscious. There is a historical dimension that is structured by and into dispositions that can be systematically observed as practices. For Wekker (2016: 19), the cultural archive in the Dutch context "influences race as a fundamental organising grammar (and how it intersects with class, gender, sexuality etc.) as it is in societies organised by racial dominance." Drawing on Wekker's framing, I connect the cultural archive of gender and sexuality in Africa as an organizing grammar that is heterosexist in nature as influenced by the colonial past.

Noting that sexuality was central to the colonial project, it is only fair to interrogate African sexuality by paying close attention to colonialism, especially because the colonial encounter often defined African sexuality as that of "natural beings" in relation to reproduction. The assumption was that "Africans could not possibly display homoerotic desires or agencies, as these were associated with sophisticated human desires and erotics" (Lewis 2011: 208)—an idea that extended all the way from colonial administration to ethnographic scholarship. This kind of essentialized framing of African sexuality thrived alongside another—that of the marking of same-sex acts as "unnatural acts" that legitimized the colonial project. For the latter, Neville W. Hoad (2007) presents this framing through a discussion of King Mwanga, the last precolonial king of the Buganda

Kingdom in Uganda in the late 1880s. He argues that the production of "the homosexual" as a figure was inescapably linked to the consolidation of colonial power. Working through archival material about King Mwanga, Hoad clinically examines how bodily practices came to be understood as sexual. He convincingly argues that the sexual itself is a deeply ideological category that was extremely productive during colonial modernity: "Bodily practices signified as sexual acts or acts signifying as sexual may have been instrumental in the instigation of colonial rule and were certainly an important part of its implementation" (7).[2]

The above two narratives in discussion, side by side, produced a contradictory framing of African sexuality—that which actually distinguished sex from gender and sexuality. Lugones (2010) noted how sexuality was made a stand-alone in the characterization of the colonized—a crucial point that we need to pay attention to in the study of historicity and meaning of the relationship between sex and gender. This is an important distinction for that epoch when sex/sexuality was a conflation of gender, yet the distinction was clearly made for the colonies. The distinction was based on a contradictory frame of sexuality where, on the one hand, African sexuality was deemed "closer to nature" and therefore had to be heterosexual, while on the other, the appraisal of "unnatural same-sex acts" was steeped within the moralistic order of the time. This, then, became the basis of the (colonial) cultural archive of sexuality and gender, one that privileges heterosexuality. This (colonial) cultural archive of gender and sexuality persists in the contemporary, without many radical shifts.

Crucial stamps and remnants of this cultural archive of gender and sexuality include the alienation of homosexuality from Africanness, situated within the overwhelming trope and fiction that perceives same-sex relationships as un-African, as well as the perverse myth that Africans are homophobic (Ekine and Abbas 2013). I argue that this (colonial) cultural archive of gender and sexuality lies at the crux of the disconnect between the so-called progressive South African constitution and the lived realities of Black people and people of color in same-sex relationships. The numerous accounts (scholarly or otherwise) bring to our attention the lack of access faced by many people of color in same-sex relationships, as well as the high levels of violence and homophobia, unemployment, and lack of access to social, health, and judicial services especially as these relate to Black women in same-sex relationships. I connect this to Xavier Livermon (2012: 302), who draws on what "the literary scholar Brenna Munro calls 'democratic modernity' where a 'threat' rests on the racialization of the queer body as white and the sexualization of the black body as straight."[3] He further notes that "adding a racial analysis to a queer analysis reveals how the white body is emblematic of human rights protections used to position South Africa as a progressive queer-friendly tourist destination (for white queer tourists), while the black body remains the threat to African culture and tradition" (302).

Livermon highlights three elements central to my arguments here on the framings of the (colonial) cultural archive of gender and sexuality. First of all, whiteness is not only a model but also emblematic of most protections. Sylvia Wynter (2003) offers us a clear framing of this logic of modernity emblematic of man (patriarchy and masculinity) as human. "He is one who classifies as white racially and sexually (usually as heterosexual), and therefore his imagination of the world is the normative (yet unmarked) representation of the world" (Mignolo 2016: vii). In other words, when an intersectional dimension is added to take into account grammars of differentiation, he is the ideal citizen with full rights, in line with Wekker's (2016) notion of race as a fundamental grammar of organizing social realities. Second, Livermon's quote also highlights the contemporary global neoliberal order of human rights that has been central to the struggles of same-sex relationships, but more on this later. And third, Livermon's quote demonstrates that the conceptualization of what is deemed African tradition and culture is steeped in the (colonial) cultural archive of gender and sexuality, one that privileges heterosexuality. This is the singular sexuality narrative that Marc Epprecht (2008) refers to in his book *Heterosexual Africa?*, in which he explores the historical processes by which a singular, heterosexual African identity was constructed by anthropologists, ethno-psychologists, colonial officials, the African elite, and most recently, health care workers seeking to address the HIV/AIDS pandemic.

The (colonial) cultural archive of gender and sexuality in South Africa is therefore firmly embedded within this contradictory frame in discussion here, shaped by four hundred years of colonialism and fifty years of apartheid in South Africa. Whereas, on the one hand, it is made up of a singular sexuality narrative that privileges heterosexuality, on the other, it is made up of the polarized hetero/homo binary that also privileges heterosexuality. And by extension, it has produced a rigid binary construction and understanding of gender and race (hooks 2013), where whiteness in entanglement with heterosexuality is emblematic of rights and protection. It is therefore in this construction that we see the language of violence enacted on those who fall outside the normative or privileged status. This forms the "kind of perverted logic" that Frantz Fanon (1963: 210) refers to, where "it turns to the past of the oppressed people, and distorts, disfigures and destroys it," in this case with reference to race, gender, and sexuality. This language of violence has been ongoing for centuries and is therefore firmly established and perverse. It is in this construction that I situate the hegemonic customary of perverse forms of violence, including experiences of everyday heterosexism and homophobia, violence and murder, high levels of unemployment, and lack of access to justice, social, and health services for Black people in same-sex relationships.

However, despite this construction of the (colonial) cultural archive of gender and sexuality that has sidelined those that fall outside the normative, historically there has always been some level of visibility of people in same-sex intimacies on the African continent. But perhaps contemporarily, NGOs that champion sexual rights and citizenship have played a notable role in this visibility, for South Africa in particular, the Triangle Project in Cape Town and Forum for Empowerment of Women in Johannesburg. However, I am interested in international NGOs, especially Dutch international NGOs, that fund and address sexual rights and citizenship, given the history of Dutch colonialism and apartheid in South Africa. In looking at Hivos and some of its work on sexual rights and citizenship,[4] I query whether this work is entangled in the (colonial) cultural archive of gender and sexuality.

## NGO World, Neoliberalism, and the (Colonial) Cultural Archive

One could argue that Dutch philanthropy has manifested through NGOs as well as in various other forms. According to its website, Hivos was founded in 1968, inspired by humanists and based on secular values, as true cooperation presumes respect for differing beliefs. A quick browse through the Hivos website's section on "What We Do" shows many images of people of color, with the main focus on women's empowerment, sexual rights and diversity, freedom and accountability, sustainable food, and renewable energy. This way, Hivos "does" gender, sexuality, governance, food security, and renewable energy in the global South: Africa, North Africa and the Middle East, Asia, and Latin America. According to the South African annual report for Hivos (2015: 3), the organization spent "years of supporting South Africans in the struggle against apartheid." Although a country office was only registered in 2006 as an NGO, the support in the struggle mentioned by this report (without details) has to be acknowledged: it is one of the first sentences in this report. However, what is clear is Hivos's current focus; the then director's opening note in the 2015 report states that "Hivos SA remains relevant and continues to contribute to strengthen civil society voice in processes to deepen democracy, realise human rights for all and ensure effective delivery" (3). This quote emphasizes the fact that (international) NGOs like Hivos are firmly embedded within democratic processes and play a crucial role in implementing the constitution and laws/policies. Indeed, NGOs like Hivos are on the front lines of funding for service delivery and ensuring human rights for all citizens. However, given that the hegemonic customary is rooted in histories of dehumanization and marginality, "human rights for all" is a rather ambitious and perhaps a disreputable statement. Where is the unmaking of these histories reflected in such a statement where the ideal citizen and beneficiary of human rights classifies as white racially and sexually (usually as heterosexual)?

NGOs like Hivos have indeed championed the rights-based approach framed within South Africa's neoliberal constitution.[5] But a central question we can ask here is, How far have NGOs like Hivos gone in challenging the (colonial) archive of gender and sexuality? Is it fair to raise this question, especially because NGOs like Hivos have been at the forefront of promoting rights and highlighting the struggles of people in same-sex relationships in South Africa? Without a doubt, Hivos is deeply embedded within the development narrative. For example, the first thing that hits you when you open any page of its website is its current slogan: "People Unlimited" (Hivos 2019). This slogan is neatly packed, catchy, and meant to offer a rounded feeling of what Hivos does. It "sells" what Hivos has to offer. For instance, this could mean full access to equality and sexual rights/citizenship of same-sex communities in South Africa. When this slogan is interrogated in the context of South Africa, given the history of Dutch colonialism and apartheid, where do the blind spots lie? What does a slogan like this, from an international NGO based in the Netherlands, given its history with South Africa, obscure or leave unsaid? Noting that the (colonial) cultural archive of gender and sexuality is historically marred with the language of violence, could these complexities in South Africa ever be fully addressed by such a slogan? Where do dynamics of grammars of differentiation along race, class, gender, and sexuality lie? Perhaps a slogan like this plays within the normative development discourse, where it may gloss over the layers of meanings and experiences that manifest in the day-to-day lives of African individuals in same-sex intimacies who bear the brunt of physical and structural violence.

Hivos works through four main approaches: giving grants to partner community-based organizations (CBOs); facilitating partnerships, networks, and movements; capacity development through technical support; and knowledge development through research. This implies that their groundwork is mostly through funding programs of partner CBOs. Indeed, working with or through CBOs is a strategy that could work well. It offers an opportunity to partner (as stipulated in Hivos's report) with CBOs and therefore engage with some grassroots groundwork. Take, for instance, their partner CBO Buwa, Theta, Speak, based in Philippi Township in Cape Town. This CBO works with arts-based approaches such as plays, storytelling, music, dialogues, and poetry to engage with and empower youth to combat homophobia, domestic violence, and hate crimes in Philippi (Hivos 2015). This is certainly innovative work in conscientization. However, where Hivos falls short in being transformative is in its approach, which is firmly embedded within the rights-based approach as well as the global North donor–global South recipient narrative. With histories of colonialism entangled in this donor-recipient relationship, what form of partnership manifests, and which dimensions of power are reinscribed along racialized grammars? The report clearly stipulates this relationship with the CBO as a partnership, and therefore what is crucially left uninterrogated is how Hivos "does" race or racialized histories that are firmly embedded in this partnership. Recalling both Hivos's slogan and the quote by Hivos's former director on realizing human rights for all, how does this partnership with the CBO radically decenter the language of violence embedded in the (colonial) archive of gender and sexuality?

Critical development scholars such as Aturo Escobar (1995) have brought to the fore the fact that the development discourse is governed by the same colonial principles: "Development has successfully deployed a regime of government over the Third World, a space for subject peoples that ensures certain control over it" (10). For instance, the implicit self-representation of the West, in relation to the "other," is silent on whiteness; it neither acknowledges nor interrogates it. But how can the other ever measure up to whiteness? This self-representation assumes the benchmark against which the other is measured—in this case, sexuality, where the benchmark on sexual citizenship is modeled on the Dutch one, with a heavily encoded implicit narrative of the developed Dutch expertise on sexual rights being appropriated to the "developing" southern African context. This way, modernity is synonymous with whiteness, that is, the perpetuation of the idea of Western/white superiority on sexual citizenship, in this case, which makes development a mission that is unattainable and continuously reasserted as a failed project. Yet the lack of critical reflection on whiteness and modernity also becomes a reinscription of the colonial past.

The global neoliberal discourse in which Hivos exists and functions is one framed within universal human rights. Decolonial scholars have pointed out how universalisms, such as universal human rights, stem from the colonial project. Moreover, universalisms obscure and mask nuances of hierarchization and therefore end up maintaining these same hierarchies of privilege and oppression. I situate the template that frames gender and sexuality deployed by NGOs like Hivos within the global discourse of universalism. This, therefore, connotes a universal understanding of gender and sexuality when the language of human rights is implemented, for instance, by Hivos in the Netherlands and South Africa in a similar framing, yet the histories and contexts of these two countries are very different. As this template is steeped in the (colonial) archive of gender and sexuality, when race and heterosexuality are not radically challenged, the status quo is maintained.

This is not in any way to negate or discredit the great work Hivos has done and is still doing with regard to sexual rights and citizenship of people in same-sex relationships in South Africa but, rather, to add to the ongoing conversation on the disconnect between constitutional and legal rights of people in same-sex relationships and their lived experiences. This is important to highlight here, given that international NGOs like Hivos are on the front lines—perhaps a rethinking of approach would work toward addressing the crux of this contradiction, by taking a critical look at how to challenge the narrative of whiteness and, by extension, modernity, in which the hegemonic customary is imbricated.

## Toward Decolonized Sexualities

Having framed the (colonial) cultural archive of gender and sexuality, as rooted in modernity and entangled in the neoliberal narrative in which NGOs like Hivos that have championed sexual rights are heavily embedded, perhaps with a decolonial framing, we can envision multiple narratives that contest this (colonial) cultural archive. I situate these contestations through everyday experiences that produce plural knowledge that is nuanced and recognizes the vastness of African sexuality, in this way delinking it from the colonial matrix of power (Mignolo 2007). This is not in any way a new or different form of existence but, rather, something that has been within and among us. In the discussion that follows, I offer three examples that in a way decenter the (colonial) cultural archive of gender and sexuality in the everyday lived experiences of African same-sex intimacies. These examples are by no means exhaustive; rather, they offer what I read as queering the customary.

Decolonized sexualities working at the helm of colonial difference could be hard to recognize and articulate mostly because of, first, the overconsuming modernity/colonial matrix of power in which we are all calibrated and imbricated, and second, grassroots resistance/reexistence that tends to be invisible especially in relation to coloniality. How, then, do we get to the point of the nonmodern (Lugones 2010)? For Lugones, nonmodern would be "knowledges, relations, and values, and ecological, economic, and spiritual practices (that) are logically constituted to be at odds with a dichotomous, hierarchical, "categorical" logic" (743). This has to lie the locus of colonial difference (Mignolo 2000), not necessarily counter to the modern machinery of the nation/state or public politics but, rather, at an infrapolitical or grassroots level. Here I draw on James C. Scott's (1990) notion of infrapolitics, or everyday resistance, which can be articulated as variously quiet, dispersed, disguised, or otherwise seemingly invisible (Vinthagen and Johansson 2013). Everyday resistance is about how people act in their everyday lives in ways that might undermine hegemonic power structures. Therefore, such forms of resistance are not easily recognized, as are public or otherwise collective resistance, such as rebellions and demonstrations. What matters is how people are acting and not what their intentions might be. In other words, whether or not these acts or behaviors are consciously performed is not important. Rather, what counts is that they challenge and disrupt the status quo.[6]

A decolonial encounter would therefore be at a grassroots/infrapolitical level "from and at the colonial difference, with a strong emphasis on ground, on hierarchized, incarnate intersubjectivity" (Lugones 2010: 746). Concretely, in what I call everyday resistance or infrapolitics in relation to everyday experiences of heterosexisms and homophobia. Robin D. G. Kelley (1997) argues that scholars should take a more expansive look at what is considered labor, particularly with respect to Black communities, and specifically with regard to the question of what forms of creative expression can be considered labor. Elsewhere (Mbasalaki 2019), I work with the notion of cultural labor; in Mbasalaki 2019 I argue that Black women in intimate same-sex relationships in South Africa "articulate deficits, claim resources, and seek inclusion in national narratives" (Maxwell and Miller 2006: 263). This cultural labor is at the core of infrapolitics, where I found Black women in same-sex intimacies resisting hegemonies of heterosexuality, masculinity, and religion while, at the same time, creating spaces of belonging. This way, Black women in same-sex relationships were able to articulate slippages in heterosexist frames by undertaking cultural labor. And in doing so, they were able to simultaneously resist and create spaces of belonging (van Zyl 2015). Black women in same-sex relationships thus draw on available resources, for instance, to articulate female masculinities, as well as to facilitate their inclusion into spaces that are often the primary drivers of homophobia. This is what I refer to as the *queering of the customary*, where the (colonial) cultural archive of gender and sexuality is disrupted.

The first disruption of this archive I locate in the work of Zethu Matebeni (2011). In her work, Matebeni articulates the sexual intimacy of Black lesbians who have their own language attached to sexual acts—such as 50/50 and 100 percent, this way offering a plural narrative on sexual desire that displaces heterosexual privilege rooted in the (colonial) cultural archive of gender and sexuality. I read these sexual arrangements as infrapolitical delinking from the rules imposed—in this case, heteronormative rules—and creating one's own rules communally to reexist, as witnessed in the local lingual, sexual acts and sexual arrangements made intelligible by Black township lesbian women. This is celebrated and specific to Black township women in same-sex relationships and is presented in Matebeni's (2011) PhD thesis based on her interviews with Black lesbian women in the townships of Johannesburg, in which she also provides an insight into localized sexual arrangements. She posits how "the 50/50 notion implies a series of negotiations between partners about how sex should take place between them; who penetrates whom and how; and how pleasure is achieved for each partner" (270). I take this a step further by reading these negotiations/doxa as infrapolitical—counterscripts to prevailing heteronormativity as henceforth delinking to reexist. Indeed, it may be that the notion of 50/50 is used generally in South African society, but the way in which specific rules relating to lesbian sex are applied to it differ from the general rules that play out in mainstream society, affirming resistance to heterosexism—the customary—through daily lived experiences and sexual intimacies of black lesbians.

The second example of queering the customary I draw from is Graeme Reid's (2005) ethnography on the marking of gendered identities among gay men, who refer to themselves as "ladies" and "gents" in the small town of Ermelo in Mpumalanga Province. I locate these expressions in a complex gender matrix that decenters the (colonial) archive of gender and sexuality that is prescriptive of what bodies express certain genders. Lugones (2007: 202) recommends that "understanding the place of gender in precolonial societies is also essential to understanding the extent and importance of the gender system in disintegrating communal relations, egalitarian relations, ritual thinking, collective decision making and authority, and economies." On this both Oyeronke Oyewumi (1997) and Ifi Amadiume (1987) have laid out precolonial scenarios where gender was not an organizing principle, rather comprising a complex matrix of gender(s) where women were not necessarily in subjugated positions and were part of the economic and governing structures. When a decolonial lens of revealing underlying assumptions (Smith 1999) is added to gendered expressions of "ladies" and "gents" in Reid's (2005) study, it exposes the singular narrative of the gender binary in modernity/the contemporary that is rooted in the (colonial) cultural archive of gender, and this way, changes the "terms of the conversations" (Mignolo and Wannamaker 2015) that dictate and prescribe which bodies should produce masculinities and femininities, bringing to light a complex gender system. I therefore read Reid's ethnography as part of this complex gender system, where he demonstrates what it means to be a "gent" or a "lady" among gay men, where ideas about gender were developed in everyday practices as well as through ritual performances such as an engagement. He articulates how "for 'ladies' and 'gents' in Ermelo, sexual difference is not determined by who you are but by what you do," and therefore "a 'lady' is a lady, not because of biological signifiers, but because of everyday social practices and performances" (218). And "similarly, a 'gent' is a gent based on a set of social relationships and practices, and not because of a fixed biological essence" (218). By undertaking cultural labor, these performances of masculinity and femininity therefore not only are infrapolitical but also contribute the masculine and feminine capital of a complex gender matrix that queers the customary.

My third example draws from my doctoral research, where I connect everyday existence to NGO work (Mbasalaki 2018). It has been established that the state, framed within the hegemonic customary, marred in structural violence, has failed miserably in providing full participation and access to economic and other opportunities, which remain meager for people of color in same-sex intimacies in South Africa. The survey I conducted of Black women in same-sex intimacies ($n = 209$) revealed high (51 percent) unemployment (Mbasalaki 2018). With dire conditions, life was really difficult for some women in same-sex intimacies—not knowing where food for the next day was going to come from, how to get transport from one place to another, or where to get money to purchase airtime (telephone credit) to communicate.

However, through their own networks, alternative support systems were established to get through life on a day-to-day basis—a queering of the customary. The sense of community I got from the women was quintessentially "I am because we are"—the basis of *ubuntu*, perhaps a queered *ubuntu*.[7] The supportive nature of this sense of community and belonging was both emotional and material: helping each other out with money to take a taxi to go for an interview or to buy airtime (telephone credit) to make phone calls about job inquiries, finding accommodation for those who have nowhere to stay, and so on. These actions may be largely invisible, yet they work within the ubuntu framework to support and shoulder one another. In this case, ubuntu is working within the frameworks of everyday resistance, as a set of hidden transcripts that counter the hegemonic customary of structural discrimination and inequalities. The LGBTQI NGOs were also sharing some of the burden by mentoring and linking women in same-sex relations to possible opportunities, such as assistance with how to compile a resume, as well as advocating for recognition through the human rights framework. I am inclined to agree with A. R. Wilson (2009), who contends that sexual citizenship is interesting because it did, and still does, purchase power within a liberal democratic tradition. Human rights discourse is interesting for similar reasons. Although human rights do not form part of daily lived experience, this discourse may be a valuable resource in certain instances, such as in the context of LGBTQI NGOs in South Africa, which are firmly rooted within neoliberal discourse. Here, human rights have a form of purchasing power, as referred to by Wilson, in advocating for labor rights. However, when it comes to employability of Black lesbian women, these rights are limited because of the perverse (colonial) cultural archive of gender and sexuality that privileges heterosexuality. Therefore, in addressing citizenship and rights, I am cautious and mindful of the fact that feminist theorists have pointed out that the formal inclusion of subjects into citizenship does not necessarily deliver substantive citizenship or social justice (Gouws 2005).

## Conclusion

This article has brought to light what decolonial scholars have emphasized: coloniality is not an affair of the past but a matter of the geopolitics of knowledge and knowledge production. When the language of violence in its various physical and structural forms—along the grammars of race, gender, class, sexuality, and ableism—is one with the hegemonic customary, the judicial customary offered through the constitution and human rights becomes limited. Working within the human rights framework as the main template offered to counter this hegemonic customary only masks the incompetence within this frame. If these constitutional and judicial systems work only for some (mostly those who classify as white racially and as heterosexual), they are not fully decentering the (colonial) cultural archive of gender and sexuality and therefore not good enough. It is in this context that we see lesbian murders and hate crimes in South Africa; something has to shift radically to disrupt this. This is not to say that human rights don't serve a purpose—they do. But perhaps, given the complex histories that filter into the present, a rethinking of approach could be useful in this shared world. And perhaps plural rather than rigid binary spaces that disrupt the (colonial) archive of gender and sexuality could be "where restitution of subaltern knowledge . . . [takes] place and where border thinking" (Mignolo 2000: ix) and "doing" emerges, thus offering an epistemic reconstitution of African same-sex intimacies, a queering of the customary.

## Notes

1.  I mostly work with terms *same-sex relationships* and *intimacies* (interchangeably) due to their all-encompassing nature. This is especially so because same-sex practices are understood differently across different historical and cultural contexts and are thus not necessarily labeled and contextualized as homosexual, gay, or lesbian. Therefore, to focus on relationships and intimacies brings the historical (dis)continuities of same-sex sexual cultures to the fore. Moreover, the term *intimacy* opens up horizons for the intimate sexual encounters beyond relationships tapping into same-sex sexual desire and pleasure.

2.  Religion—in this case Judeo-Christianity—plays a crucial role here, as is illustrated by the encounter between Christianity and King Mwanga's "unnatural desires," discussed here to further ratify the hetero/homo binary.

3.  Although the label *queer* comes from Livermon's text, I do note that *queer* is a contested term.

4.  Hivos is a Dutch-based international NGO that works within the framework of development. It was founded as a humanitarian organization in the Netherlands in the 1960s but has since opened up in several countries in the global South. According to its website, Hivos seeks new and creative solutions to persistent global problems, solutions created by people taking their lives into their own hands. See www.hivos.org /what-we-do/our-focus-areas/.

5.  The Hivos (2015: 21) report states as its organizational goals the following: "Our objective is to 'create larger opportunities for sexual minorities in Southern Africa to enjoy the freedom to live their lives in their own way and to be accepted by and have full participation in society'. Our key thematic areas include: sexual health and rights, advocacy for rights and policy change, amplifying civic voices and public participation, knowledge development and exchange, safety and security, movement building and collaborative efforts."

6.  For Scott (1990), subaltern forms of resistance produce "hidden transcripts" that critique or challenge power in its intersectional predicament, thus escaping and contrasting with the dominant "public transcripts" of power relations. "Infra-political acts thus operate insidiously, beneath the threshold of political detectability" (Marche 2012: 6), which "makes them all the more reliable vehicles of resistance" (6) as subaltern people lay claim to their dignity, either by upholding or, paradoxically, by challenging internal group cohesions, thereby reinforcing their sense of community, dignity, and empowerment.

7.  *Ubuntu* comes from the Bantu languages of sub-Saharan Africa, all of which refer to a person with a word suffixed by the vowel *tu*, *thu*, *to*, or *du* (Oduor 2014). Christian B. N. Gade (2011) offers a historical analysis, showing that the term *ubuntu* has been appearing in written sources since 1846. *Ubuntu* was mostly defined as a human

quality prior to the 1960s, although all these accounts were written by people of European descent. Gade's historical analysis notes Alexis Kagame—a Rwandese historian, philosopher, and Catholic priest—as the first African to publish a text on ubuntu as liberality. Later on, African religious philosopher John S. Mbiti (1969) coined the maxim "I am because we are" as an appeal to ubuntu. He further elaborates that "ubuntu is expressed in isiZulu, isiXhosa and other Nguni African languages as a maxim of 'a person is a person through persons'" (141). Dani W. Nabudere (2005) denotes that ubuntu involves an individual being an individual in a community, belonging within that social, moral, and political framework. Further, Nabudere adds, in his or her existence or being, *umuntu* (a person) strives to create conditions for existence with other beings. Ubuntu is fluid, dynamic, and believed to be rooted in historically continuous processes, making it greatly symbolic in the act of memory. According to Charles Villa-Vicencio (2009: 121), ubuntu "remembers past generations and ancestors, drawing on the memory of the lived experiences to success and failure. Like any ethical idea, it must adapt in order to survive."

## References

Aboh, Augustine B. 2018. "Between Limited Laws and Conservative Patriarchal System: Why the Indian Security and Justice System Is Less Effective to Prevent Gender-Based Violence against Women and Girls." *Global Media Journal* 16, no. 31: 143–53.

Abrahams, Yvette. 1997. "The Great Long National Insult: Science, Sexuality, and the Khoisan in the Eighteenth and Early Nineteenth Century." *Agenda: Empowering Women for Gender Equity* 13, no. 32: 34–48.

Abrahams, Yvette. 2003. "Colonialism, Dysfunction, and Disjuncture: Sarah Bartmann's Resistance (Remix)." *Agenda: Empowering Women for Gender Equity* 17, no. 58: 12–26.

Amadiume, Ifi. 1987. *Male Daughters, Female Husbands: Gender and Sex in an African Society.* London: Zen.

Arnfred, Signe. 2004a. "African Sexuality/Sexuality in Africa: Tales and Silences." In *Re-thinking Sexualities in Africa*, edited by Signe Arnfred, 59–76. Stockholm: Almqvist and Wiksell Tryckeri.

Arnfred, Signe. 2004b. "Re-thinking Sexualities in Africa: Introduction." In *Re-thinking Sexualities in Africa*, edited by Signe Arnfred, 7–29. Stockholm: Almqvist and Wiksell Tryckeri.

Bakshi, Sandeep, Suhraiya Jivraj, and Slivia Posocco. 2016. Introduction to *Decolonizing Sexualities: Transnational Perspectives Critical Interventions*, edited by Sandeep Bakshi, Suhraiya Jivraj, and Slivia Posocco, 1–16. Oxford: Counterpress.

Bérard, Jean. 2016. "Can a Patriarchal World Be Corrected by a Criminal Law? Feminist

Struggles, Penal Justice, and Legal Reform in France (1970–1980)." *Laws* 5, no. 12: 1–14.

Bourdieu, Pierre. 1997. *Outline of a Theory of Practice*. Cambridge: Cambridge University Press.

Cock, Jacklyn. 2003. "Engendering Gay and Lesbian Rights: The Equality Clause in the South African Constitution." *Women's Studies International Forum* 26, no. 1: 35–45.

Ekine, Sokari, and Hakima Abbas. 2013. *Queer African Reader*. Dakar: Pambazuka Press.

Epprecht, Marc. 2008. *Heterosexual Africa? The History of an Idea from the Age of Exploration to the Age of AIDS*. Athens: Ohio University Press.

Escobar, Aturo. 1995. *Encountering Development: The Making and Unmaking of the Third World*. Princeton, NJ: Princeton University Press.

Fanon, Frantz. 1963. *The Wretched of the Earth*. New York: Grove Press.

Finley, Chris. 2011. "Decolonizing the Queer Native Body (and Recovering the Native Bull-Dyke): Bringing 'Sexy Back' and Out of Native Studies' Closet." In *Queer Indigenous Studies: Critical Interventions in Theory, Politics, and Literature*, edited by Qwo-Li Driskill, Chris Finley, Brian Joseph Gilley, and Scott Lauria Morgensen, 31–42. Tucson: University Press of Arizona.

Gade, Christian B.N. 2011. "The Historical Development of the Written Discourses on Ubuntu." *South African Journal of Philosophy* 30, no. 3: 303–9.

Gouws, Amanda. 2005. *(Un)thinking Citizenship: Feminist Debates in Contemporary South Africa*. Burlington, VT: Ashgate.

Government of South Africa. 1996. "The Constitution of the Republic of South Africa." Pretoria: Government of South Africa.

Gqola, Pumla. D. 2015. *Rape: A South African Nightmare*. Johannesburg: Jacana Media.

Henderson, Lynne. 1991. "Law's Patriarchy" *Law and Society Review* 25, no. 2: 411–44.

Hivos. 2015. "Hivos in South Africa: A Report on the Activities of Hivos Country Office South Africa 2015." The Hague: Hivos.

Hivos. 2019. www.hivos.org (last accessed January 19, 2020).

Hoad, Neville W. 2007. *African Intimacies: Race, Homosexuality, and Globalization*. Minneapolis: University of Minnesota Press.

Hoad, Neville W. 2016. "Queer Customs against the Law." *Research in African Literatures* 47, no. 2: 1–19.

hooks, bell. 2013. *Writing beyond Race: Living Theory and Practice*. New York: Routledge.

Kelley, Robin D. G. 1997. *Yo' Mama's Disfunktional! Fighting the Culture Wars in Urban America*. Boston: Beacon.

Lewis, Desire. 2011. "Representing African Sexualities." In *African Sexualities: A Reader*, edited by Sylvia Tamale, 199–216. Cape Town: Pambazuka Press.

Livermon, Xavier. 2012. "Queer(y)ing Freedom: Black Queer Visibilities in Postapartheid South Africa." *GLQ* 18, no. 2–3: 298–324.

Lugones, Maria. 2007. "Heterosexualism and the Colonial/Modern Gender System." *Hypatia* 22, no. 1: 186–209.

Lugones, Maria. 2010. "Towards a Decolonial Feminism." *Hypatia* 25, no. 4: 742–59.

Macharia, Keguro. 2015. "Archive and Method in Queer African Studies." *Agenda* 29, no. 1: 140–46.

Marche, Guillaume. 2012. "Why Infrapolitics Matters." *Revue francaise d'etudes americaines* 1, no. 131: 3–18.

Matebeni, Zethu. 2011. "Exploring Black Lesbian Sexualities and Identities in Johannesburg." PhD thesis, University of Witwatersrand.

Maxwell, Richard, and Toby Miller. 2006. "The Cultural Labor Issue." *Social Semiotics* 15, no. 3: 261–66.

Mbasalaki, Phoebe K. 2018. "Decolonised Sexualities: The Lived Experiences of Black Township Women Who Love Women in South Africa." PhD thesis, Utrecht University.

Mbasalaki, Phoebe K. 2019. "Women Who Love Women: Negotiation of African Traditions and Kinship." In *Routledge Handbook of Queer African Studies*, edited by S. N. Nyeck, 37–48. London: Routledge.

Mbiti, John S. 1969. *African Religions and Philosophy*. Oxford: Heinemann.

McClintock, Ann. 1995. *Imperial Leather: Race, Gender, and Sexuality in the Colonial Context*. New York: Routledge.

Mignolo, Walter D. 2000. *Local Histories / Global Designs: Coloniality, Subaltern Knowledges, and Border Thinking*. Princeton, NJ: Princeton University Press.

Mignolo, Walter D. 2007. "Delinking." *Cultural Studies* 21, no. 2–3: 449–514.

Mignolo, Walter D. 2016. "Foreword: Decolonial Body-Geo-Politics at Large." In *Decolonizing Sexualities: Transnational Perspectives Critical Interventions*, edited by Sandeep Bakshi, Suhraiya Jivraj, and Slivia Posocco, vii–xxii. Oxford: Counterpress.

Mignolo, Walter D., and William H. Wanamaker. 2015. "Global Coloniality and the World Disorder: Decoloniality after Decolonization and Dewesternization after the Cold War." Paper prepared for the World Public Forum, "Dialogue of Civilizations," Rhodes, Greece. October 9.

Motsei, Mmatshilo. 2007. *The Kanga and the Kangaroo Court: Reflections on the Rape Trial of Jacob Zuma*. Johannesburg: Jacana Books.

Muñoz, José Esteban. 2009. *Cruising Utopia: The Then and There of Queer Futurity*. New York: New York University Press.

Nabudere, Dani W. 2005. "Ubuntu Philosophy: Memory and Reconciliation." Texas Scholar Works. repositories.lib.utexas.edu/bitstream/handle/2152/4521/3621.pdf.

Oduor, Reginald. M. 2014. "Book Review: A Critical Review of Leonard Praeg's *A Report on Ubuntu*." *Thought and Practice: A Journal of the Philosophical Association of Kenya* 6, no. 2: 75–90.

Oswin, Natalie. 2007. "Producing Homonormativity in Neoliberal South Africa: Recognition, Redistribution, and the Equality Project." *Signs* 32, no. 3: 649–69.

OUT LGBT Well-Being. 2016. *Hate Crimes against Lesbian Gay Bisexual and Transgender (LGBT) People in South Africa, 2016.* Pretoria: OUT LGBT Well-Being.

Oyewumi, Oyeronke. 1997. *The Invention of Women: Making an African Sense of Western Gender Discourses.* Minneapolis: University of Minnesota Press.

Oyewumi, Oyeronke. 2000. "Family Bonds/Conceptual Binds: African Notes on Feminist Epistemologies." *Signs: Journal of Women in Culture and Society* 25, no. 4: 1093–98.

Reid, Graeme, 2005. "'A Man Is a Man Completely and a Wife Is a Wife Completely': Gender Classification and Performance amongst 'Ladies' and 'Gents' in Ermelo, Mpumalanga." In *Men Behaving Differently: South African Men since 1994*, edited by G. Reid and Liz Walker, 1–20. Cape Town: Double Storey.

Scott, James. C. 1990. *Domination and the Arts of Resistance: Hidden Transcripts.* New Haven, CT: Yale University Press.

Smith, Andrea. 2006. "Heteropatriarchy and the Three Pillars of White Supremacy: Rethinking Women of Color Organizing." In *Color of Violence: The INCITE! Anthology*, edited by INCITE! Women of Color Against Violence, chap. 6. Boston: South End Press.

Smith, Linda T. 1999. *Decolonizing Methodologies: Research and Indigenous Peoples.* London: Zed.

Tamale, Sylvia. 2011. "Researching and Theorizing Sexualities in Africa." In *African Sexualities: A Reader*, edited by Sylvia Tamale, 11–36. Cape Town: Pambazuka Press.

Thom, Anso. 2019. "One Voice at the Cape Town Protest: 'No More, No F**king More!'" *Daily Maverick*, September 5. www.dailymaverick.co.za/article/2019-09-05-one -voice-at-the-cape-town-protest-no-more-no-fking-more.

van Zyl, M. 2015. *A Sexual Politics of Belonging: Same-Sex Marriages in Post-apartheid South Africa.* Johannesburg: ResearchGate.

Villa-Vicencio, Charles. 2009. *Walk with Us and Listen: Political Reconciliation in Africa.* Washington, DC: Georgetown University Press.

Vinthagen, Stellen, and Anna Johansson. 2013. "'Everyday Resistance': Exploration of a Concept and Its Theories." *Resistance Studies Magazine* 1, no. 1: 1–45.

Wekker, Gloria D. 2016. *White Innocence: Paradoxes of Colonialism and Race.* London: Routledge.

Wilson, A. R. 2009. "The 'Neat Concept' of Sexual Citizenship: A Cautionary Tale for Human Rights Discourse." *Contemporary Politics* 15, no. 1: 73–85.

Wynter, Sylvia. 2003. "Unsettling the Coloniality of Being/Power/Truth/Freedom: Towards the Human, After Man, Its Overrepresentation—An Argument." *New Centennial Review* 3, no. 3: 257–337.

# "FAKE GAYS" IN QUEER AFRICA

## NGOs, Metrics, and Modes of (Queer) Theory

Cal (Crystal) Biruk

In a conference room in a lakeside district of northern Malawi, twelve peer educators (PEs) sit in plastic chairs around a table waiting for a training, led by the staff members of a Malawian-led LGBTI rights nongovernmental organization (NGO), to begin.[1] In front of each is a bottle of water, a memo notebook, and a pen. The room is quiet as they pass around and sign a piece of paper to confirm they have received their per diem (about US$25) as participants in two-day workshops that prepare them for work in the field: recruiting men who have sex with men (MSM) and referring them to hospitals for health care, distributing safer-sex materials (condoms and lubricants), and facilitating conversations about sexuality, gender, and human rights. After attendees receive backpacks to carry their materials and booklets of referral forms, the meeting begins with a prayer, followed by icebreakers. The morning is spent discussing the duties, expectations, and proper comportment for PEs, who receive a small monthly incentive payment in exchange for their volunteering. After lunch, participants engage in breakout sessions where each group role-plays scenarios that might be encountered in the field (a young MSM with sores on his genitals, a truck driver who sleeps with men on his journeys, an MSM who has been beaten at a bar, etc.), practicing empathy and counseling skills and studying forms that track the numbers and nature of each encounter for donors. Late afternoon, we break for tea and samosas. Following this, each group reconvenes, using markers and flip charts as needed in discussions. After a long day, we part ways.

The next morning, some attendees report to NGO staff members that "fake gays" have infiltrated the space in the interest of obtaining per diems, and staff are left with the awkward task of sussing out the "truth"

*GLQ* 26:3

DOI 10.1215/10642684-8311814

© 2020 by Duke University Press

of potential interlopers' sexual identifications. The possibility that these
so-called fake gays might embed themselves as spies to feed information
or names to those opposed to the NGO's "gay agenda" in a homophobic
context is not far-fetched.

This scene, a composite recreated from notes on trainings and workshops led by
a Malawian LGBTI-rights NGO between 2013 and 2019, is a window onto NGO
worlds, ritualized spaces within the global health-human rights nexus in one corner of Africa. The trappings of the workshop form are evident: bottles of water, tea
breaks, role-playing, memo books, flip charts, and icebreakers. The sign-in sheet,
on which attendees attest to receipt of a donor-set per diem, betrays the rhythms of
monitoring and evaluation, an audit culture. Documents like this, sent to Northern
donors by periodic deadlines, capture such data as number of attendees, number
of condoms distributed, and number of people sensitized. The workshop, however,
is disrupted by a specter that takes shape on the second day: the fake gay who,
allegedly, insincerely mimics a marginalized sexual orientation to acquire money.
This mythologized figure is a kind of queer hologram in whom we glimpse the
coproduction of value, authenticity, and sexual selves amid circuits of resource
distribution in the global South.

This scene embeds dynamics documented by scholars of the politics of
development and aid in Africa, wherein outsiders' agendas and projects—and the
resources they import—reformulate moral economies and identity-based claims
on the ground. NGOs like the one mentioned here, meanwhile, are cast as complicit in normalizing projects: they spread homonationalism, sap radical agendas
by institutionalizing liberal human rights frameworks, produce entrepreneurial subjects, reinforce social hierarchies, bolster state projects, and smuggle in
Euro-American logics of sexual modernity (Kamat 2004; Englund 2006; Bernal
and Grewal 2014; Patternote 2016).[2] As Neville Hoad (2015: 30) puts it: "The
social movement politics of the LGBT movement diluted into rights-based claims
as it went international and as it institutionalized in neoliberal form in the North
Atlantic world." Anthropologists document how NGOs in the global South employ
confessional technologies that produce "usable" subjects and identities (such as
"gay" and "MSM") as they respond to the whims of funders in an international aid
economy (Nguyen 2010: 35–60; Moore 2016). Others document the failure of the
"globally dominant identity category" MSM to capture the experience of individuals whose queer identities and practices exceed biomedicalized nominalization
(Boellstorff 2011: 288). NGOs appear in critical scholarship largely as patently
unqueer places where radical politics go to die, useful only perhaps for observ-

ing the "excesses of gay imperialism" (Otu 2017). They are, so the story goes, inauthentic containers of practices, nominalizations, and activists that bear little if any resemblance to the more authentic queer lives happening outside their walls (Dave 2012).

My work with a Malawian-led LGBTI-rights NGO indicates that many of these trends hold true.[3] But, inspired by Naisargi N. Dave's (2012: 14) focus on the "inventiveness of queer politics" in lesbian and feminist activist spaces enabled and constrained by NGOization in India, I read against the grain of dominant renderings of NGOs in the literature to depict how normalizing technologies of audit culture in postcolonial geographies of aid might proliferate, rather than sap, queer emergences and potentials. Ethnographically tracking idioms and practices of "faking" in NGO worlds, I show how performative transnational mediations dismissed as accoutrements of neoliberalism or normalization (documentation, metrics, flows of funding and resources, e.g.) intersect queer projects on the ground. In line with the interest of this special issue, I suggest that, much as the customary (a thing that, on the surface, appears most unqueer) can become queer, so too can the clunky apparatus of LGBTI rights become a queer resource, as a site of multiplying possibilities and emergences.

The repertoire of practices that constitute faking, I argue, are modes of theory and queer iterations of the customary that ask us to sit with and learn from the contradictions inherent in queer becomings enabled, rather than foreclosed, by the "Gay International" or the global ga(y)ze (Altman 1997; Massad 2008).[4] Throughout, this article models what ethnography—attentiveness to relations and transactions in social worlds—brings to the text-centric and US-centric field of queer studies; yet, I hope to disabuse readers of the notion that ethnography necessarily entails a methodology of comparative study of cultural particularity of sexual or gender difference or in merely providing cultural "context." With Hoad (2016: 14), I ask: How are customary practices (here, in the global health-LGBTI rights apparatus) affected when they are queerly inhabited? Rather than exposing "faking" as duplicity or insincerity, I argue that normalizing practices (rooted in logics of standardization, quantification, and replicability) and faking are co-constitutive. Tracking the discursive itineraries of faking and the fake gay in political speech, public discourse, everyday NGO spaces, and queer studies itself, I expose the instability of moralized dichotomies nested beneath real/fake (such as good/bad, white/black, North/South, moral/immoral, true/false). Throughout, I show how faking might act as a mode of (queer) theory and world making that destabilizes metrics and technologies we use to arbitrate authenticity, and foreground how these categories gain meaning within racialized geographies and economies.

## Culture, the Customary, and Ritual

One of my efforts in this article is to move beyond a conflation of custom or the customary with tradition, ethnic identity, or ritual. I read NGO spaces as customary forms, framing ritualized and repetitive practices—trainings and recording numerical data as part of monitoring and evaluation exercises, for example—as customary enactments. These practices betray a normalizing imperative to create forms of equivalence between the North and South. For an NGO to receive funds to cover the costs of their yearly activities, for example, it must meticulously convert work on the ground into portable metrical forms such as indicators, reports and sign-in sheets. This documentary labor of recording names, counting attendees, and measuring progress aims toward *normative* targets, such as training X number of LGBTI people on human rights or on safe sex or on how to "come out" to family members, often detracting from more "political" work (Crewe 2014).

 NGO practices serve socially significant functions such as making a person legible through their citation of acronyms or categories like LGBTQI, often through activities that assume Euro-American notions of self as an autonomous thing to be confessed, named, or worked on, in notable contrast to scholarly renderings of African personhood as a state of becoming rather than being, and as ongoing achievement (Menkiti 1984; Comaroff and Comaroff 2001). In his study of conflict resolution workshops in the Middle East, Nikolas Kosmatopoulos (2014: 554) theorizes the workshop form common to NGO spaces as an "assemblage of particular technomoral arrangements that aim at organizing (and finally disciplining) the ways that bodies behave, move, and express feelings, opinions and attitudes."

 Custom and the customary are inflected with a sense of repetition, of attaining solidity and stability through being done again and again, recalling Judith Butler's ([1990] 2006: 152) suggestion that gender "ought not to be conceived as a noun or a substance or a static cultural marker, but rather as an incessant and repeated action of some sort." From Butler and from symbolic anthropologists whose fetish is custom and ritual, we learn that people are who they are not because of internal essence; they become legible through performative iterations of saying and doing that stabilize tokens like "man" or "woman." NGO worlds, embedded in larger aid economies and audit infrastructures, are spaces dense with categories, symbols, and ritualized scripts that become the fodder of repetitive and normative performances, confessions, and embodiments.

 In NGO worlds, ritualized workshops and trainings compel attendees to repeatedly name that which they "genuinely" are, yet the success of such performances is delimited by the rigid yet ever-elongating alphabet soup of LGBTQI (and other acronyms and categories), artifice from which attendees piece together or profess selves. In his classic works on ritual, Victor Turner ([1969] 2017: 183) observed that cultural rites like initiation ceremonies are "bound up with cyclical repetitive systems of multiplex social relations," identifying an "intimate bond of relationship between an institutionalized and only slowly changing structure" and the individuals who come to relate to and recognize one another through terms and roles bequeathed them by the "pedagogics of liminality" (105). In NGO spaces, these pedagogics take the form of icebreakers, role-playing, lectures, call-and-response activities, and artistic exercises that invite participants to reflect on gender, sexuality, and LGBTI rights. These objects and lessons act as Turnerian "blazes" (as in blazing a trail) that help attendees find their way as they proceed into, if only temporarily, the structured world of compulsory identification that aims to initiate them into roles, subjectivities, and forms of personhood proscribed by identitarian categories (see also Reid 2006).

Ethnographic study of canonical sites of cultural reproduction or social pedagogy—rites, traditions, rituals—indicates that, for a ritual to produce new kinds of people (e.g., wife or confirmand), "happy" or "felicitous" conditions must be met: ritual speech or activities must manifest in the right place, at the right time, and among the right authorities or audiences (Austin 1962). For Turner, customs are sites where norms become most visible as they seek reaffirmation. Yet, even as customs and rituals are where people learn and/or rekindle their intimacy with norms, they are sites of ambivalence and danger because of the risk that ritual subjects might invert or subvert their normalizing thrust, or perhaps "fake it."[5] It is the subjunctive mood and the aspect of potentiality in performative iterations that cite norms—their inherent asymptotic nature, ambivalence, and slippage—that make custom and the customary queer (Turner [1969] 2017; Bhabha 1984).

Queer readings of the potential in the performative, the possibility that people might inauthentically inhabit a category such as MSM that aspires to "real" isomorphism with their identity as an expression of subversion, however, are often inattentive to how recognition, sincerity, authenticity, and realness are themselves metrics constituted by racialized (post)colonial geographies of aid.[6] The monitoring and evaluation mechanisms gestured at above (performance assessments and evaluations, reports, and sign-in sheets) have their origins in racialized logics of suspicion and surveillance, emergent from long anxieties about "giving Africans money" evident in widely circulating tropes of African fakery, including "corruption," scammers, or tricksters (Ferguson 2015). Yet, metrics, categories, and indicators are ontologically queer in their failure to fit people perfectly and their susceptibility to manipulation by those who might inhabit them (Biruk 2020);

MSM, for example, counts among its inhabitants self-identified gay men, men who identify as *mathanyula*, self-identified MSM, male sex workers, beach boys, self-identified trans women, straight men, and people who identify as none of the above, even as its tidy token form pulverizes all of this internal diversity.[7] The customary structures and rhythms of accountability and audit culture normalize and standardize technologies of quantification that classify and count, yet they also produce queer potentials.

Custom and the customary are important analytics in queer studies, particularly in a body of work, indebted to ethnographic and archival data, that examines how vernacular queer or queer-adjacent identities and practices manifest in other places, troubling assumptions of queerness as un-African and highlighting fluid relations between gender, economy, sex, and social arrangements (Amadiume 1987; Moodie 1988; Epprecht 2004). Scholars show how forms of resource distribution and intervention associated with public health and LGBTI rights harden categories like gay, MSM, or trans that misalign with local frames for identification or personhood (Valentine 2007; Lorway, Reza-Paul, and Pasha 2009; Currier 2012; Thomann 2016) and trace how capitalism and neoliberalism reshape queer bodies, erotic labor, kinship, and the customary itself (Kempadoo 2001; Manalansan 2010; Meiu 2017). Finally, scholars challenge the assumption of monolithic or psychologized cultural (customary) homophobia in Africa (Murray 2009; Awondo, Geschiere, and Reid 2012).

Yet, a relatively narrow conception of custom, the customary, and culture as particularity pitted against grand narratives of gender and sexuality runs through discussions of queer Africa. Some suggest that scholars have operationalized queer African culture and customs in order to make claims that "we" (queers) have always been here and to dispel myths of heterosexual Africa, often reproducing the idea that tradition is "authentically and unproblematically African" while same-sex sexuality is its "constitutive outside" (Livermon 2015: 16; see also Hoad 2006; Epprecht 2008; Macharia 2015). Underlying this quest for African queers and queerness, historically undertaken by white scholars, is an impulse to "discover" the "sexual alterity of cultural others" (Dave 2012: 15), with the assumption that alterity is found in initiation ceremonies, in ethnic articulations of desire or kinship, or in religious spaces rather than, say, in NGOs. NGOs are presumed tainted and made un-African (thus, inauthentic) by practices, transactions, and forms of value associated with modernity and capitalism.

Eschewing definitions of the customary that presume its association with narrowly defined notions of what we imagine when we hear the word *culture* then, this article mobilizes the queer (in the) customary as analytic to track the emer-

gence and transformations of faking in NGO worlds. I first elaborate on the meanings and implications of the phrase *gay-for-pay*, or (allegedly) faking marginalized
sexual orientations to access funds from foreign donors, foregrounding how homosexuality paradoxically came to be linked in the public imagination to money and
insincerity. Then I analyze vignettes from work with an LGBTI-rights NGO, tracking the genre of faking and its performative entailments. I conclude with reflections on what ethnographic study of relations, transactions, and histories unfolding
in one African context might bring to queer studies, following recent provocations
to look beyond Euro-American sites canonized in queer studies' methodology and
theoretical scaffolding (Arondekar and Patel 2016; Currier and Migraine-George
2016).

## Gay-for-Pay/Fake Gays

While Western nations' commitments to tolerance are cast in rhetoric of universal
human and sexual rights, the enduring particularity of African culture and custom, so the story goes, makes homophobia an intractable problem; homophobia has
become a stand-in for Africa itself, and "sexual orientation minority rights have
become a vector for making civilizational distinctions" (Hoad 2015: 35). Enlisting LGBTI people, activists, human rights bodies, governments, and epidemiolo-
gists, the "gay issue"—inextricably entangled with the new "scramble for Africa"
manifested by global health in the era of AIDS (Crane 2013) is a political site of
competing interests.[8] The arc of dominant stories, especially in the media, about
queer Africa tends to cast it as a "heart of homophobic darkness" on which rescue
narratives rooted in heroic Whiteness might play out (Otu 2017).[9] Scholars have
observed anxious rhetorical policing of the meanings of culture and Africanness
amid the rise of NGOs, LGBTI rights organizations, and social movements. Others,
meanwhile, have critiqued the politics of conditional aid, arguing that it reinforces
the argument that homosexuality is a Western import and distracts attention from
intersectional and structural oppressions that affect all Africans (Abbas 2012;
Kabwila 2013).

The phrase *gay-for-pay* gains meaning in a body of media accounts and
political speech in Malawi, one of the poorest and most aid-dependent countries
in the world. Malawi is ranked 171 out of 189 countries on the Human Development Index, and its mostly rural population engages in small-scale farming and
depends on rain-fed agriculture to grow maize. Subsistence farming is complemented by growing small cash crops (e.g., tobacco and cotton), casual agricultural
labor, and informal trading. Malawi's aid dependence produces entire sectors of

(mostly temporary) jobs (drivers, enumerators, stipended volunteers, etc.); formal and permanent employment is difficult to come by. The LGBTI-identified people I know find some measure of "work" as beneficiaries of the NGO (e.g., as PEs, enumerators, or research assistants); most also engage in inconsistent piecework, such as selling secondhand clothing or mobile phone air time. Some of the gay-for-pay arguments rehearsed across media and political and public forums since the mid-2000s include that donors are forcing Malawians to adopt homosexuality, that donors should keep their money while Malawi lives in impoverished dignity, and that people involved in promoting rights of sexual minorities are hunting for donor money. Each of these tropes links being gay to monetary gain, and they become idioms through which actors reflect on anxieties around Malawi's economic dependency on donors, erosion of national autonomy, and changing social norms.[10]

Linkages between the moralized issue of gay rights and flows of material resources became explicit in the wake of a well-publicized "gay" traditional engagement ceremony (*chinkhoswe*). A queer couple was arrested in December 2009 and later stood trial for "unnatural offence(s)" under Malawi's colonial-era penal code (for detailed discussion of the *chinkhoswe* and the penal code, see Biruk 2014 and Currier 2019). In mid-2011, amid citizen unrest and protests against rising fuel prices and shortages, then-president Bingu wa Mutharika aimed to bolster his political legitimacy via manipulation of "custom," taking up the rhetoric of national self-reliance and framing homosexuality as un-African (Chanika, Lwanda, and Muula 2013; Biruk 2014; Currier 2019). Malawi, this rhetoric insisted, should stand strong in its "custom and traditions" rather than "beg for money" from donors. His turn to "custom" reflects how culture, custom, and tradition are remade in relation to contemporary events, to development, humanitarian, colonial, settler-colonial, and state agendas, global markets, and to actions of institutions (Chanock 1985; Mamdani 2000; Povinelli 2002; Kogacioglu 2004; Comaroff and Comaroff 2009). T. J. Tallie (2013: 170), for example, furthers understanding of the queer-in-the-customary by showing how European settlers in Natal cast Zulu polygamy as "queer" even as it remained ostensibly heterosexual in practice, thus inventing and shoring up the construction of a "proper" bourgeois, nuclear family unit that underpins sexual modernity.

Scholars who examine homophobic discourse in Africa have documented (and employed in their analyses) tropes of Westernization, imperialism, neocolonialism, neoliberalism, and modernity. When the gay issue first began to appear in Malawian national newspapers (albeit infrequently) around the mid-2000s, NGOs were the subjects of much ire, already being accused of having "run out of ideas." As one letter to the editor put it, "Having felt they [NGOs] exhausted their objectives and to avoid closing down their organizations, they are running wild, championing useless and unheard of motions or causes that are in direct conflict with not only our culture but also biblical precepts" (*Nation* 2005b). Another writer suggested that NGOs should "find a better way of spending donor money" (*Nation* 2005a). In 2007, a Malawian human rights activist registered her disapproval of LGBTI rights in Malawi, suggesting that people who support such causes copy foreign ideologies for monetary gains (they "want to be funded [by donors]"), and imploring leaders not to "sell our nation" (*Nation* 2007).

NGOs thus have long been accused of brokering ideas that are not deeply held but, rather, emerge from their desire for money. Journalists and media, for example, have described gay rights as a "carrot" used to entice NGOs to do donors' bidding (*Daily Times* 2011a), and government officials often accuse NGOs of "milking donors" (*Daily Times* 2011b) by pretending to support gays, which, according to government, do not exist in Malawi. In their supposed insincerity (faking), NGOs are, like LGBTI Malawians, accused of being gay-for-pay. They allegedly subvert the norms of Malawian society by advocating for and benefiting from causes inimical to heterosexuality, gender expectations, or heteronormativity; worse, they are "masquerading" as human rights bodies (a term frequently used to indict NGOs by then President Mutharika during the 2011 crisis). Yet, neither "real gays" nor fake gays are intelligible forms without attention to colonial and postcolonial entanglements between North and South, self, and other. It is the circuits of knowledge and resources that link North and South—networks that mime imperial geographies—that act as felicitous conditions, pace Austin (1962), that produce the contrast between real and fake.

Following on this notion of NGOs "making up" issues that are not pressing, or even invented, media stories often construct gays as fictions, exotic specimens, or figments of the imagination. Newspapers printed stories that query whether any gays or lesbians actually exist in Malawi, as in a 2005 article titled "Any Malawians Who Are Gays?" that calls on them to come out in the open (Mapondera 2005). A number of stories aimed to unmask the mysterious bodies and practices of gays, as in one Malawian columnist's retelling of his personal experience riding an elevator with a "homo" in South Africa and seeing with his own eyes his "large behind," feminine ways, and nonerotic interactions with women. He speculated that this man likely "made friends with some foreigner who was visiting the country [SA] on some official engagements" and suggested that "all that remains is for the young man to land in a foreign country" (Drycleaner 2006). Being "gay," here, becomes a ticket to a "foreign country"; this potential migration signals a future transformation from poor to rich through embodying gayness. The narrator

codes the homo as a nonwhite South African taking on or performing (faking) a foreign sexual identity to gain access to social and economic mobility. Notably, South
Africa's economically powerful position in southern Africa connotes it as a kind of
foreign paradise to which Malawians seek to migrate (recalling Malawi's long place
as a labor reserve for South Africa). Yet, the recounting of a Malawian's encounter
with a "homo" while in South Africa reveals tacit assumptions that cohere in the
category homo, inflecting it as not only un-Malawian, but as un-African (specifically, as White, through its proximity to global power structures, "foreigners," and
"foreign countries"). (In this article, I borrow Jemima Pierre's [2012: 72] definition
of *Whiteness* as "ideology, trope and cultural practice," distinguished from actual
phenotypically white bodies).

Common to these stories are tropes of gays as fake (as in, Do they even
exist in Malawi?) and gays as intimate with or influenced by foreigners (referred
to as *azungu* in Malawi's dominant language, Chichewa). The link between foreign influence and sexual identity or practice is a conversion narrative that frames
material benefit as coming through proximity to Whiteness. This narrative, however, implicitly cites what others refer to as customary patterns of provider love
in Malawi, where sexual intimacy and material dependence entangle in gendered
ways (Swidler and Watkins 2007; Hunter 2010; Mojola 2014). Giving and receiving gifts or money in or through intimacy, then, is customary when engaged in by
a Malawian man and a Malawian woman but a queer aberration between two men;
notably, the nature of material exchange in intimate relationships is more deeply
moralized when the provider is a foreigner and the recipient a Black African man
(as in the scene above). *Whiteness*, as enacted in such stories, is a metonym for the
reality of Malawi's racialized position in global political and cultural economies
vis-à-vis the global North, citing here not only phenotype but also legacies of racial
capitalism that manifest in who can travel willingly and who is stuck in place or
forcibly relocated (Pierre 2012: 69–100; Redfield 2012). Whiteness stands in as
the complex mediation and that which is simultaneously disavowed and desired,
a "discourse of race that is articulated through practices that . . . reflect global
economic, political and cultural hierarchies" (Pierre 2012: 72); queerness, meanwhile, becomes the "constitutive outside of blackness" (Livermon 2012: 299).

Being gay-for-pay, then, implies persons—supposed NGO beneficiaries—
faking their sexual identity. This faking is framed as copying or mimicry, as in the
suggestion that "Malawians look back and take a stock of their cultural traditions
and values by looking at what has been lost and *what has been copied*" (Tsitsi
2005; my italics) and in former President Mutharika's claim that citizens were
"aping" Western culture. When famous couple Steven Monjeza and Tiwonge Chim-

balanga Kachepa (Auntie Tiwo of the engagement ceremony) broke up and the former moved in with a cisgender woman, headlines reinforced Malawians' sense that gays were gay-for-pay (BBC News 2010). This bolstered Malawians' sense that gays are fake and that the NGO's provision of legal aid and support to the couple furthered assumptions that they were being "paid" because they were gay. Similarly, when Malawi's "first lesbian" came out of the closet in a newspaper interview, rumors circulated that she was a hoax and was being paid by NGOs so they could generate donor interest (*Nyasatimes* 2013; Ntilo 2013).

Amid public perceptions that NGOs encourage or influence people to fake marginalized sexual identities, the NGO has faced accusations that it recruits people to a gay lifestyle and that its staff members are gays themselves. It is in the interest of proving that gays were "real" that they began their evidence-based advocacy work, where evidence of high HIV prevalence might shift policy but also prove that gay people exist in Malawi. For example, a research study that highlighted MSM's HIV risk was summarized under the headline: "Homosexuality in Malawi Real—Research" (Mpaka 2007). As the NGO's gender officer suggested at a meeting with policy makers, activists, and NGOs, "Our data has made this space. Without [that data] we wouldn't be here." Data, then, serves a performative function in making gays (and NGOs) "real."

Rising interest in the vulnerability and epidemiological significance of "key populations" like MSM in countries where homosexuality is illegal or stigmatized has drawn increased funding for vulnerable populations previously left out of official HIV responses. The Global Fund, which recently disbursed to Malawi its largest allocation of funds to any country or organization ever, places "indigenous key-population led" organizations at the core of its global strategy, and its investment in these populations has given organizations working with vulnerable populations leverage in and resources toward overcoming national barriers to service delivery and interventions (Biruk 2019). Between 2019 and 2021, through the Key Populations Investment Fund, US$4 million will be funneled to service delivery, HIV prevention, and research targeting key populations in Malawi.

Donors who provide funds for programming call on the NGO to regularly monitor and report on its activities, counting the numbers of clients served, summarizing activities, and so on, tasks central to regimes of quantification, a kind of "governance by indicators" (Davis et al. 2015). This documentary labor, particularly for an NGO completely reliant on donor funds from more than ten donors in a single year, entails a cascade of metrics that call into being things that can be counted (see also Tichenor 2017). In a dense thicket of categories, resources, and indicators, local sexual and gendered subjectivities are reorganized and reflected upon, and new opportunities and risks have arisen; elsewhere, I describe this as an "economy of harms," a network of social relations that hinge on transactions and obligations that are simultaneously risky and potentially profitable (Biruk and Trapence 2018). The global health–LGBTI rights nexus is a "flexible assemblage of data production, number crunching and scale-up profit sourcing" that aims to standardize and harmonize (Adams 2016: 45). But metrics produce "collateral effects and opportunities" (10) and act as the political and economic infrastructure in which the fake gay becomes meaningful. The next section employs vignettes to illustrate how the fake gay and faking are symptoms of, but also fragment and disrupt, the gaze between donors and Malawian LGBTI-identified persons.

## Queer Metrics: Real Numbers, Fake Gays

How do we assess whether subjects are "really gay" (or really whatever) when "gay" (or whatever) is incentivized? The NGO had to arbitrate this very question when trusted PEs informed staff members that fake gays were attending workshops merely to earn per diems.[11] On some occasions, the NGO enlisted me to meet with women who claimed to be lesbians to determine whether these women actually were lesbian or were trying to infiltrate.[12] This task is rooted in logics of authentic and fixed sexual identity but demonstrates tensions between critical analytics in queer theory that expose the fiction of stable identities and the real possibility that fake gays might embed themselves to feed information to those who oppose the "gay agenda." The workshop form—quintessential artifact of circuits of resource distribution that characterize LGBTI rights networks in the global South—is a space where the boundaries of real/fake or sincere/cunning become blurred, even revealed as fake themselves. It is in this sense that its normalizing imperative embeds the queer customary, which manifests as fake gays gaining meaning by virtue of departure from loosely shared criteria of realness that are felt more than fixed: those accused of being fake gays could be strangers yet unknown to the other attendees, sex workers who were "only in it for the money," persons who weren't "serious" about "the work" (e.g., being a PE), and so on. The play of real and fake is a dance orchestrated by the categories, metrics, and discourse embedded in aid infrastructures and enables, as Ashley Currier (2012) puts it, strategic queer toggling between visibility and invisibility.

For example, depending on a specific donor's interest, a workshop or training held one day might call for ten women who have sex with women (WSW) and ten MSM; the next might require five WSW, five MSM, and ten trans persons. Between workshops, the same individual might undergo a temporary "transformation" from WSW into trans or MSM into trans, to ensure that quotas for attendance, parsed by sexual orientation or gender identity, might be met. Yet, this faking for the purposes of attaining metrics hinged to monetary gain sometimes becomes real, as in numerous cases of lesbian-identified women who came back from trainings on LGBTI rights in South Africa and "suddenly" (according to NGO staff) identified as trans. "They learned that language there [in South Africa]," a Malawian program officer informed me. These newly trans individuals, then, trouble notions of sincerity that assume words or identities express underlying beliefs, intentions, or selves. The trans individuals are somehow fake because signs performatively conjure the self and interiority instead (Keane 2002). Yet, while NGO staff found this transformation surprising, becoming queer—anywhere—is a process of employing semiotic, social, and material resources developed in social relations and transactions, technologies that aid in articulating "inchoate interiority" (Wilf 2011: 463; de Lauretis 1987). As Graeme Reid (2013: 184) puts it, reflecting on his work with Black communities in small-town South Africa, "naming, creating and performing what it mean[s] to be gay remain[s] a work in progress . . . inconclusive and open-ended."

The NGO space is a convenient window through which we can observe intimate pedagogies in action and chart how selves gain coherence or unravel in relation to norms made explicit by technologies of quantification oriented toward targets or quotas (Howe 2013; Romani 2016). In her work on nonnormative systems of sexuality and gender in India, Kira Hall (2005: 131) suggests that sexual and gendered authenticity is better studied as an outcome of sociolinguistic processes rather than orientation preexisting them, a socially achieved act. Likewise, faking, rather than mendacious sham or duplicity, is a genre of queer becoming that interrogates power's demand that things be made real or transparent to knowledge (Morgensen 2016: 608). Becoming trans through travel abroad or being trans one day and cis the next to meet donor-set quotas parsed by identity expose the fakeness inherent in the "horizon of trans" that aims to "domesticate . . . the trans body into the regulatory norms of permanence" (Puar 2017: 56).

MSM PEs, too, necessarily toe the line between real and fake in going about their work in the field. At a June 2017 training, nine new PEs signed a detailed memorandum of understanding to formalize their position as volunteers with the NGO, to learn how to document each encounter they have with an MSM "client" and how to use referral forms to send MSM to district hospitals. Much of the meeting was spent reading the three-page memorandum aloud as a group; emphasis was put on the fact that the monthly "monetary incentive" the PEs receive was *not* a salary but a gesture of thanks for their help. Nonetheless, the PEs referred to their volunteering as *kugwira ntchito*, or labor/working. The staff member also provided specific examples of "corrupt acts" that would result in immediate termination, for example, "We shouldn't hear about you seeing yourself as a shop, charging [money] for a condom [meant to be free]." She explained that they would receive their monthly incentive only if they successfully submitted documentation of all encounters they had with MSM in the field and if they were "finding" enough MSM each month. The PEs grew visibly anxious.

One PE asked, "What if we can't find enough MSM in a month? How many is enough?" She responded ambiguously, suggesting that PEs focus on helping (*kuthandiza*) others rather than worrying about numbers. If they did a good job, she said, it would be obvious. Yet, the PEs expressed worries that "sometimes we can't find enough, or we already know them all." Rather than throwing into question whether PEs recruit fake gays or fabricate data, this anecdote points to the absurdity of audit culture, rooted in metrics that claim to accurately measure what is "really going on." This absurdity intersects in complex ways with economies of harm: PEs are willing to put themselves at risk, through being associated with a "gay" project or carrying "gay" paraphernalia in their communities, for example, in order to earn what they see as a salary (around $13 per month) for labor minimized by reframing small payments as gifts for sincere and passionate ("real") volunteering.

The categories invented by global health and human rights regimes that fetishize indicators and quantification counterfeit, or fraudulently imitate, persons they seek to know. On the referral form the labor of PEs is broken into discrete enumerable data points. These documents are performative: it is their completeness and appearance (are all boxes checked off? Is the writing legible?), rather than their veracity, that determine whether they (and what they document) are deemed successful or not (Cavanaugh 2016; Erikson 2019). Donors in distant offices presume an indexical relation between a dated document and what happened on that date: the document is a mirror of other places and times. In listing a number next to "number of clients reached this month" and in making the document traceable, the PE enters relations of accountability and brings into being a population of "real" gays: actual people met by him on a specific day to whom he distributed information or condoms. The PE enacts his own realness as a sincere "volunteer" entitled to his monthly stipend.

Whereas donors in distant offices focus on the "real data" the documents carry, analyzing how documents function in and through NGO worlds reveals their sleight of hand: whereas the documentation process clearly enumerates and tracks the repetitive and intensive labor of PEs, geographies of aid name PEs as volunteers, inciting them to adhere to a repertoire of moralized practices and behaviors rooted in punctuality, sincerity, deadlines, professionalism, and hygiene (Rogozen-Soltar 2012). Just as the forms they carry convert chaos into order, so too are their bodies and selves fashioned into modern subjects; this becomes the substrate for becoming a real gay through attaining increments of legibility and respectability that might enable one to have all the trappings of, if not actually, a job and to redistribute resources through social and kin networks.

But audit cultures also produce a space beyond the control of enumerating logics. Ethnographic tracing reveals that documents only ever partially represent what they claim to, yet they function to establish the NGO's credibility through compliance with monitoring and evaluation imperatives, ensuring continued flow of monies. In tracking faking as specter inherent in documentary labor, then, I suggest that fake and real are constitutive of each other, following Marlon M. Bailey's (2013: 76) assertion that LGBT members of Detroit's ballroom community "challenge the power and consequences of interpellation by assuming greater agency in the dialectic between subjectification and identification" through valorizing and evaluating a shared schema of criteria for gendered realness. Rather than necessarily narrowing the space available for creativity or negotiation, documents and metrics can become queer resources. Here, I see resonance with Sasha Newell's (2012) analysis of how bluffing operates, not unlike masking rituals, among Ivorian youth who engage in conspicuous consumption of (real, expensive) branded clothing and accessories amid a market flooded with counterfeits. Similar to how Ivorians cobble together "real fake" performances of wealth and style, individuals in NGO worlds piece together selves that are simultaneously "signified and obscured by . . . deceptive surfaces" (141). Faking is a kind of "masking" where iterative performances cite circulating referents (MSM, WSW, trans) that themselves conjure what they aim to count or see. The fake gay thus unravels and reorganizes the dual fictions of identity and coherence, tactically enlisting symbolic and economic resources in the house of mirrors that is economies of aid.

## The Fake Gay as Mode of (Queer) Theory

"What if one were to refuse the instinctive recoil that says 'native informant,' the queer assimilation that gathers yet another term to prove that 'we have always been everywhere,' or the anti-identitarianism that fetishizes 'description' over 'identity'?" I take Keguro Macharia's (2016: 184) questions as provocation to tell other stories about "queer Africa." Macharia succinctly points to troubling threads in queer studies: a valorization of custom and culture as authentically queer and concomitant framing of African experiences of queerness as raw data from "native informants"; the instrumentalization of queer Africa toward the ends of universal claims that might further Western projects of all stripes; and the tendency toward description that assumes that "others" who enthusiastically claim identities deemed "foreign" (MSM, gay, even queer) are necessarily duped or pawns in an imperial queer game. Macharia's queries also indict scholars' resistance to seeing "native" cultural production as "theory" (Christian 1987; Allen 2016: 618).

The work I present here attempts to complicate the general thrust of queer studies when it comes to Africa, which has historically reflected a collecting impulse to document and compare sexualities and genders across the globe (Tamale 2011; Morgensen 2016: 611). As Natalie Oswin (2006: 781) puts it, "Scholar after scholar has ventured out into various fields to return with evidence of existing heterogeneous expressions of queerness." Queer studies and anthropology remain complicit in propagating imagery and representations of the West's alter ego(s), images always inflected by racialized assumptions of gender and sexual difference.

As much as a quest for authentic African queerness betrays a sense that "queer Africa" must be something different from or originary to the "queer West," it also implies that manifestations of queer that do not conform to Western imaginaries of authenticity are fake. Both orientations revive the fantasy of what might be called homo-noble savages and excise postcolonial histories and geographies from analyses of queer Africa. In my close reading of NGO spaces usually dismissed as "boring" or "fake," I hope I have illuminated how queer politics in the global South, as anywhere, is as much a politics of the possible as a politics of purity: "Particular possibilities for acting exist at every moment, and these changing possibilities entail a responsibility to intervene in the world's becoming, to contest and rework what matters and what is excluded from mattering" (Barad 2003: 827). NGOs, crucibles of subjectivity formation crosscut by transnational flows of diverse interests, concepts, agendas, and resources, are one site in which to witness messy queer becomings, that is, "how bodies gain and lose meaning over time, how sex and sexuality become attached to bodies as they move through space, how power circulates and shifts" (Macharia 2015: 144). In viewing the "fake gay" and "faking" as modes of theory, rather than pale apparitions of "real" queer politics, we observe the queer potential of faking as "free radical that . . . attaches to and permanently intensifies or alters the meaning—of almost anything," including the material and conceptual infrastructures of NGO worlds (Sedgwick 2003: 62). Through faking, LGBTI persons might "rewrite the socially constructed meanings shackled to them" through "embodied social choreography that leads to shifts in how they are seen, counted or assessed" in material worlds in constant flux (Cox 2015: 29–30; see also Cabot 2013).

Even amid rampant NGOization, the vast majority of queer Malawians remain outside the orbit of NGO worlds. Yet, reframing NGOs as customary sites helps us think beyond locating queerness in or queering rituals, customs, or practices (such as rites of passage, "traditional" healing, or initiation ceremonies) most typically imagined as customary. Notably, most LGBTI-identified persons I have met through my work with the NGO are powerfully invested in customary cultural forms as sites to be queerly inhabited (most identify as very religious, and most LGBTI-identified men in the NGO's orbit are married to women, meaning they already queerly inhabit a customary form they nonetheless wish could be further queered). The stories and snippets I have offered here stem from the provocation with which I started this article: that NGO worlds produce and are produced by customary practices that become sites of queer potential, pragmatism, and ambivalence. It is my hope that readers come away from this article with the sense that queer is most useful when mobilized as an unsettling analytic for the stories we tell and retell ourselves about "Africa." Nor should we ignore the potential of theorizing to do violence. Kira Hall (2005: 140) observed that "nonnormative sexual and gendered subjects in India [namely, *hijras*] have become particularly vulnerable to . . . [queer] theorizing." The director of the NGO I work with, meanwhile, once termed Malawian MSM "victims of research," called upon to participate in countless studies and projects at minimal to no financial benefit to themselves. *Hijras* and MSM, respectively, are made vulnerable—even as their lives may be capacitated—through their recruitment into postcolonial geographies of knowledge production, whether epidemiological or queer theoretical.

Tracking faking reveals the fallacy of searching for authentic politics, subjectivities, or spaces and the importance of attending to histories, intertexts, and transnational flows. Spending time in NGO worlds made me very aware of the complex personhood of queer Malawians and the "ways in which complicity is sometimes necessary for survival" (Amin 2017: 11). Here, the long tradition of Black/ queer anthropology, which insists on narratives constituted by "and/both, intersections and compounds, hyphens, strokes, parentheses and messy interstices of real life and audacious imagination," should be an inspiration (Allen 2016: 622). The fake gay, an ambivalent, liminal, instable, and playful figure made real by the holography of global health–LGBTI rights audit cultures, deterritorializes dominant Eurocentric and racialized idioms and categories of queer identity and the "Human" that continue to undergird theoretical production in the social sciences and humanities (Wynter 2003). The fake gay and faking do not fit neatly within norms of victimhood or redemption, captivity or freedom that form the lexicon of liberal subjecthood.

In their essay on the intersection of African and queer studies, Ashley Currier and Thérése Migraine-George (2016: 284) suggest that "Whiteness and white supremacy haunt both African studies and queer studies." Given my own ambivalent relationship to African studies as a white queer "Africanist" (that territorial-mastery–inflected eponym), I seek to think and write critically about infrastructures that Whiteness, colonialism, and imperialism birthed and continue to uphold (e.g., foreign aid, NGOs, foreign-led research projects, and African studies itself). I have been interested here in reading NGOs as counterintuitive sites of (queer) customary practices so as to bring to light flows of resources, ideas, and categories that both limit and enable all kinds of queer projects and interests in places like Malawi, without losing sight of postcolonial histories and power asymmetries.

Queer studies might learn from anthropology's attentiveness to everyday relations, transactions, and modes of theory from which people fashion lives and worlds. A robust queer African studies should point out the "limits or liminality of theory" and sit with nuance and complexity, rather than reduce it to raw material for theoretical production (Currier and Migraine-George 2016: 293; Nyeck 2019). Rather than "giving voice to" queer African experiences, seeking to uncover authentic queer Africa, or mobilizing culture as critique of universals (worthy pursuits in their own right), the *fake gay*—an idiom of the contemporary— asks us to take pause in building theory, to pay attention to world-making practices even in the most normative or mundane spaces. The fake gay is a figure that gains meaning only when situated within the infrastructures and practices of African aid economies. Faking is a mode of theory with far-reaching implications for our understandings of the operations of identity, race, authenticity, and desire in a postcolonial world divided all too neatly and convincingly into normalizing categories that nonetheless carry within them queer potential and slippage.

## Notes

1.  This article uses *LGBTI* in alignment with the NGO's self-description and for the sake of consistency. *LGBTI-identified* refers to persons in the NGO's orbit, but the reader should not assume these individuals do not identify in many and complex ways beyond the acronym that names them in NGO spaces.

2.  Saida Hodžić (2014), in a departure from normative critiques of NGOization, deploys the cyborg as a figure that confounds boundaries between NGOs and social movements, where the form of feminist organizing need not determine whether it is progressive.

3.   I write in more depth and specificity about this NGO (Centre for the Development of People, or CEDEP) elsewhere (Biruk and Trapence 2018; Biruk 2019). I refer to the organization in this article merely as *the NGO* to foreground dynamics common to such spaces and organizations within and beyond Malawi, and because NGOs are what link my argument to a larger body of literature in queer studies and anthropology. The NGO was started by Malawians in 2006 and, since then, has been the primary activist organization engaged in advocacy, research, and policy change related to LGBTI issues; its headquarters are in the capital, with satellite offices across Malawi. I have spent two- to four-month increments (2012, 2013, 2014, 2017, and 2019) involved in everyday life at the NGO office, drop-in centers, workshops, trainings, proposal writing sessions, peer education sessions, government and civil society meetings, and so on. I am also a cofounder (with Gift Trapence and Dr. Alister Munthali) of the Key Populations Research Programme based at the Centre for Social Research in Zomba, Malawi. For more on the lives of LGBTI-identified Malawians, see the collections of LGBTI Malawians' life stories in Xaba and Biruk 2016 and Watson 2010.

4.   What I mean by *queer iterations of the customary* is elaborated below, but I use the term in two main senses: as the immanent uncertainty and potential for "repetition with difference" in NGO spaces, practices, and discourse deemed normalizing; and as the co-constitutive nature of queer and customary, whereby we recognize the fiction of replicable homogeneity, equivalence, or singular authority the customary claims.

5.   Think of the slippage in Turner's (1967) proclamation that "ritual is transformative" (95), which presumes that rituals always work to move a person from one socially sanctioned state to another. This assumption of linear progression overlooks that persons live in many social worlds at once, invisibilizing the queer transformations that inhere in the customary, as in the case of Xhosa-speaking gay men in South Africa who undergo customary rites of passage specifically to be seen as "gay men" (Fiereck 2018).

6.   See Ferguson's (2002) critique, still timely, of reading mimicry as "cultural resistance," or parody of the colonizer.

7.   In Chewa, Malawi's national language, *mathanyula* commonly refers to homosexuals. It carries derogatory connotations of animality but has begun to be reclaimed by some LGBTI-identified Malawians.

8.   Elsewhere, I show how anthropologists like myself are likewise entangled and complicit in this nexus. See Biruk 2019.

9.   Work such as Kwame Edwin Otu's, which combines African studies and Black studies frames in analyzing race in postcolonial Africa, is timely provocation for African studies scholars, who have for too long not explicitly considered racial formation(s) in Africa within the context of global White supremacy, often dismissing such efforts by making recourse to notions of the local specificity of race. African studies in the late 1960s, as Jean Allman (2018) reminds us, actively marginalized Black studies and Black scholars, establishing it as a white man's domain; "race" became the

purview of African diaspora studies, and "Africa" the purview of African studies, with consequences for knowledge production in both fields. Relations between donors and African-led organizations are a site par excellence in which we can examine how racialized suspicion and stereotypes justify technologies of control and discipline (e.g., metrics, indicators, performance-based funding) as applied to Africa. Aid economies and structural dependency are by-products of colonization, enslavement, and imperialism that forced racialized others into webs of "development" (Rodney 1972), which manifests in development's persistent racial vernaculars (Pierre 2019).

10. For further discussion of gay-for-pay arguments in southern Africa, see Currier 2012.

11. David A. B. Murray (2015) observed how sexual orientation and gender identity (SOGI) refugees in Canada claim that support groups they attend have been infiltrated by fakers, people from their home country who were not really gay.

12. In line with donor interest, the NGO has expanded its target populations outside MSM to include transgender individuals and women who have sex with women. Lesbians often feel marginalized by donors' hyperfocus on HIV risk, which channels the bulk of resources toward MSM.

## References

Abbas, Hakima. 2012. "Aid, Resistance, and Queer Power." *Pambazuka*, April 5. www .pambazuka.org/governance/aid-resistance-and-queer-power.

Adams, Vincanne. 2016. *Metrics: What Counts in Global Health*. Durham, NC: Duke University Press.

Allen, Jafari. 2016. "One View from a Deterritorialized Realm: How Black/Queer Renarrativizes Anthropological Analysis." *Cultural Anthropology* 31, no. 4: 617–26.

Allman, Jean. 2018. "#HerskovitsMustFall? A Meditation on Whiteness, African Studies, and the Unfinished Business of 1968." Lecture given at the Annual Meeting of the African Studies Association, Atlanta, GA, November 29.

Altman, Dennis. 1997. "Global Gaze/Global Gays." *GLQ* 3, no. 4: 417–36.

Amadiume, Ifi. 1987. *Male Daughters, Female Husbands: Gender and Sex in an African Society*. Chicago: University of Chicago Press.

Amin, Kadji. 2017. *Disturbing Attachments: Genet, Modern Pederasty, and Queer History*. Durham, NC: Duke University Press.

Arondekar, Anjali, and Geeta Patel. 2016. "Area Impossible: Notes toward an Introduction." *GLQ* 22, no. 2: 151–71.

Austin, J. L. 1962. *How to Do Things with Words*. Oxford: Oxford University Press.

Awondo, Patrick, Peter Geschiere, and Graeme Reid. 2012. "Homophobic Africa? Toward a More Nuanced View." *African Studies Review* 55, no. 3: 145–68.

Bailey, Marlon M. 2013. *Butch Queens Up in Pumps: Gender, Performance, and Ballroom Culture in Detroit*. Ann Arbor: University of Michigan Press.

Barad, Karen. 2003. "Posthumanist Performativity: Toward an Understanding of How Matter Comes to Matter." *Signs* 28, no. 3: 801–31.

BBC News. 2010. "One Half of Malawi Gay Couple 'Moves In with a Woman," June 9. www.bbc.com/news/10273459.

Bernal, Victoria, and Inderpal Grewal, eds. 2014. *Theorizing NGOs: States, Feminisms, and Neoliberalism.* Durham, NC: Duke University Press.

Bhabha, Homi. 1984. "Of Mimicry and Man: The Ambivalence of Colonial Discourse." *October* 28: 125–33.

Biruk, Cal. 2014. "Aid for Gays: The Moral and the Material in 'African Homophobia' in Post-2009 Malawi." *Journal of Modern African Studies* 52, no. 3: 447–73.

Biruk, Cal. 2019. "The MSM Category as Bureaucratic Technology: Reflections on Paperwork and Project Time in Performance-Based Aid Economies." *Medicine Anthropology Theory* 6, no. 4: 187–214.

Biruk, Cal. 2020. "Queer Metrics: An Embodied Data Story as Speculative Ethnography." Unpublished manuscript.

Biruk, Cal, and Gift Trapence. 2018. "Community Engagement in an Economy of Harms: Reflections from an LGBTI-Rights NGO in Malawi." *Critical Public Health* 28, no. 3: 340–51.

Boellstorff, Tom. 2011. "But Do Not Identify as Gay: A Proleptic Genealogy of the MSM Category." *Cultural Anthropology* 26, no. 2: 287–312.

Butler, Judith. (1990) 2006. *Gender Trouble: Feminism and the Subversion of Identity.* New York: Routledge.

Cabot, Heath. 2013. "The Social Aesthetics of Eligibility: NGO Aid and Indeterminacy in the Greek Asylum Process." *American Ethnologist* 40, no. 3: 452–66.

Cavanaugh, Jillian R. 2016. "Documenting Subjects: Performativity and Audit Culture in Food Production in Northern Italy." *American Ethnologist* 43, no. 4: 691–703.

Chanika, Emmie, John L. Lwanda, and Adamson Muula. 2013. "Gender, Gays, and Gain: The Sexualised Politics of Donor Aid in Malawi." *Africa Spectrum* 48, no. 1: 89–105.

Chanock, Martin. 1985. *Law, Custom, and Social Order: The Colonial Experience in Malawi and Zambia.* Cambridge: Cambridge University Press.

Christian, Barbara. 1987. "The Race for Theory." *Cultural Critique* 6: 51–63.

Comaroff, John L. and Jean Comaroff. 2001. "On Personhood: An Anthropological Perspective from Africa." *Social Identities* 7, no. 2: 267–83.

Comaroff, John L, and Jean Comaroff. 2009. *Ethnicity, Inc.* Chicago: University of Chicago Press.

Cox, Aimee Meredith. 2015. *Shapeshifters: Black Girls and the Choreography of Citizenship.* Durham, NC: Duke University Press.

Crane, Johanna. 2013. *Scrambling for Africa? AIDS, Expertise, and the Rise of American Global Health Science.* Ithaca, NY: Cornell University Press.

Crewe, Emma. 2014. "Doing Development Differently: Rituals of Hope and Despair in an INGO." *Development in Practice* 24, no. 1: 91–104.

Currier, Ashley. 2012. *Out in Africa: LGBT Organizing in Namibia and South Africa.* Minneapolis: University of Minnesota Press.

Currier, Ashley. 2019. *Politicizing Sex in Contemporary Africa: Homophobia in Malawi.* Cambridge: Cambridge University Press.

Currier, Ashley, and Thérése Migraine-George. 2016. "Queer Studies/African Studies: An (Im)Possible Transaction." *GLQ* 22, no. 2: 281–305.

Dave, Naisargi N. 2012. *Queer Activism in India: A Story in the Anthropology of Ethics.* Durham, NC: Duke University Press.

Davis, Kevin, Angelina Fisher, Benedict Kingsbury, and Sally Engle Merry, eds. 2015. *Governance by Indicators: Global Power through Quantification and Rankings.* Oxford: Oxford University Press.

de Lauretis, Teresa. 1987. *Technologies of Gender: Essays on Theory, Film, and Fiction.* Bloomington: Indiana University Press.

*The Daily Times* (Blantyre, Malawi). 2011a. "Carrot of Gay Rights." April 11.

*The Daily Times* (Blantyre, Malawi). 2011b. "Govt Accuses Activists of Milking Donors." April 20.

The Drycleaner [pseud.]. 2006. "Of Homosexuals, Money, and Handsome Young Men." *Sunday Times* (Blantyre, Malawi), October 29.

Englund, Harri. 2006. *Prisoners of Freedom: Human Rights and the African Poor.* Berkeley: University of California Press.

Epprecht, Marc. 2004. *Hungochani: The History of a Dissident Sexuality in Southern Africa.* Montreal: McGill-Queen's University Press.

Epprecht, Marc. 2008. *Heterosexual Africa? The History of an Idea from the Age of Exploration to the Age of AIDS.* Athens: Ohio University Press.

Erikson, Susan. 2019. "Faking Global Health." *Critical Public Health* 29, no. 4: 508–16.

Ferguson, James G. 2002. "Of Mimicry and Membership: Africans and the 'New World Society.'" *Cultural Anthropology* 17, no. 4: 551–69.

Ferguson, James. 2015. *Give a Man a Fish: Reflections on the New Politics of Distribution.* Durham, NC: Duke University Press.

Fiereck, Kirk. 2018. "Queer Customs, Customarily Queer." *Medicine Anthropology Theory*, February 1. www.medanthrotheory.org/read/10018/queer-customs -customarily-queer.

Hall, Kira. 2005. "Intertextual Sexuality: Parodies of Class, Identity, and Desire in Liminal Delhi." *Journal of Linguistic Anthropology* 15, no. 1: 125–44.

Hoad, Neville. 2006. *African Intimacies: Race, Homosexuality, and Globalization.* Minneapolis: University of Minnesota Press.

Hoad, Neville. 2015. "Back in the Mythology of the Missionary Position: Queer Theory as Neoliberal Symptom and Critique." *Thamyris/Intersecting: Place, Sex, and Race* 30: 29–47.

Hoad, Neville. 2016. "Queer Customs against the Law." *Research in African Literatures* 47, no. 2: 1–19.

Hodžić, Saida. 2014. "Feminist Bastards: Toward a Posthumanist Critique of NGOization." In Bernal and Grewal 2014: 221–47.

Howe, Cymene. 2013. *Intimate Activism: The Struggle for Sexual Rights in Postrevolu-
tionary Nicaragua*. Durham, NC: Duke University Press.

Hunter, Mark. 2010. *Love in the Time of AIDS: Inequality, Gender, and Rights in South
Africa*. Bloomington: Indiana University Press.

Kabwila, Jessie. 2013. "Seeing beyond Colonial Binaries: Unpacking Malawi's Homosexuality Discourse." In *Queer African Reader*, edited by Sokari Ekine and Hakima
Abbas, 376–92. Oxford: Pambazuka Press.

Kamat, Sangeeta. 2004. "The Privatization of Public Interest: Theorizing NGO Discourse
in a Neoliberal Era." *Review of International Political Economy* 11, no. 1: 155–76.

Keane, Webb. 2002. "Sincerity, 'Modernity,' and the Protestants." *Cultural Anthropology*
17, no. 1: 65–92.

Kempadoo, Kamala. 2001. "Freelancers, Temporary Wives, and Beach-Boys: Researching Sex Work in the Caribbean." *Feminist Review* 67, no. 1: 39–62.

Kogacioglu, Dicle. 2004. "The Tradition Effect: Framing Honor Crimes in Turkey." *Differences* 15, no. 2: 119–51.

Kosmatopoulos, Nikolas. 2014. "The Birth of the Workshop: Technomorals, Peace Expertise, and the Care of the Self in the Middle East." *Public Culture* 26, no. 3: 529–58.

Livermon, Xavier. 2012. "Queer(y)ing Freedom: Black Queer Visibilities in Postapartheid
South Africa." *GLQ* 18, nos. 2–3: 297–323.

Livermon, Xavier. 2015. "Usable Traditions: Creating Sexual Autonomy in Postapartheid
South Africa." *Feminist Studies* 41, no. 1: 14–41.

Lorway, Robert, Sushena Reza-Paul, and Akram Pasha. 2009. "On Becoming a Male Sex
Worker in Mysore: Sexual Subjectivity, 'Empowerment,' and Community Based HIV
Prevention Research." *Medical Anthropology Quarterly* 23, no. 2: 142–60.

Macharia, Keguro. 2015. "Archive and Method in Queer African Studies." *Agenda* 1:
140–46.

Macharia, Keguro. 2016. "On Being Area-Studied: A Litany of Complaint." *GLQ* 22, no.
2: 183–89.

Mamdani, Mahmood. 2000. *Beyond Rights Talk and Culture Talk: Comparative Essays on
the Politics of Rights and Culture*. New York: St. Martin's Press.

Manalansan, Martin F. 2010. "Servicing the World: Flexible Filipinos and the Unsecured
Life." In *Political Emotions*, edited by Jen Staiger, Ann Cvetkovich, and Ann Reynolds, 215–28. New York: Routledge.

Mapondera, Godfrey. 2005. "Any Malawians Who Are Gays?" *Sunday Times* (Blantyre,
Malawi), November 27.

Massad, Joseph A. 2008. *Desiring Arabs*. Chicago: University of Chicago Press.

Meiu, George Paul. 2017. *Ethno-erotic Economies: Sexuality, Money, and Belonging in
Kenya*. Chicago: University of Chicago Press.

Menkiti, Ifeanyi. 1984. "Person and Community in African Traditional Thought." In

*African Philosophy: An Introduction*, edited by Richard A. Wright, 171–81. Lanham, MD: University Press of America.

Mojola, Sanyu A. 2014. *Love, Money, and HIV: Becoming a Modern Woman in the Age of AIDS*. Berkeley: University of California Press.

Moodie, T. Dunbar. 1988. "Migrancy and Male Sexuality on the South African Gold Mines." With Vivien Ndatshe and British Sibuye. *Journal of Southern African Studies* 14, no. 2: 228–56.

Moore, Erin. 2016. "Postures of Empowerment: Cultivating Aspirant Feminism in a Ugandan NGO." *Ethos* 44, no. 3: 375–96.

Morgensen, Scott L. 2016. "Encountering Indeterminacy: Colonial Contexts and Queer Imagining." *Cultural Anthropology* 31, no. 4: 607–16.

Mpaka, Charles. 2007. "Homosexuality in Malawi Real—Research." *Daily Times* (Blantyre, Malawi), July 4.

Murray, David A. B., ed. 2009. *Homophobias: Lust and Loathing across Time and Space*. Durham, NC: Duke University Press.

Murray, David A. B. 2015. *Real Queer? Sexual Orientation and Gender Identity Refugees in the Canadian Refugee Apparatus*. Lanham, MD: Rowman and Littlefield.

*Nation* (Blantyre, Malawi). 2005a. "Away with Homosexuality." Letter to the editor, April 2.

*Nation* (Blantyre, Malawi). 2005b. "MHRRC under Fire." Letter to the editor, September 9.

*Nation* (Blantyre, Malawi). 2007. "Vera against Gay Marriages." August 27.

Newell, Sasha. 2012. *The Modernity Bluff: Crime, Consumption, and Citizenship in Cote d'Ivoire*. Chicago: University of Chicago Press.

Nguyen, Vinh-Kim. 2010. *The Republic of Therapy: Triage and Sovereignty in West Africa's Time of AIDS*. Durham, NC: Duke University Press.

Ntilo, Ndi. 2013. "Claimed Lesbian Mercy Kumwenda Is a Hoax." *Face of Malawi*, February 9.

*Nyasatimes*. 2013. "Malawian Woman in Rare Confession: 'I Am a Lesbian'." February 7.

Nyeck, S. N., ed. 2019. *Routledge Handbook of Queer African Studies*. London: Routledge.

Oswin, Natalie. 2006. "Decentering Queer Globalization: Diffusion and the 'Global Gay.'" *Environment and Planning* 24: 777–90.

Otu, Kwame Edwin. 2017. "LGBT Human Rights Expeditions in Homophobic Safaris: Racialized Neoliberalism and Post-traumatic Whiteness in the BBC's *The World's Worst Place to Be Gay*." *Critical Ethnic Studies* 3, no. 2: 126–50.

Patternote, David. 2016. "The NGOization of LGBT Activism: ILGA-Europe and the Treaty of Amsterdam." *Social Movement Studies* 4: 388–402.

Pierre, Jemima. 2012. *The Predicament of Blackness: Postcolonial Ghana and the Politics of Race*. Chicago: University of Chicago Press.

Pierre, Jemima. 2019. "The Racial Vernaculars of Development: A View from West

Africa." *American Anthropologist*. Published ahead of print, December 30. doi:10.1111/aman.13352.

Povinelli, Elizabeth. 2002. *The Cunning of Recognition: Indigenous Alterities and the Making of Australian Multiculturalism*. Durham, NC: Duke University Press.

Puar, Jasbir. 2017. *The Right to Maim*. Durham, NC: Duke University Press.

Redfield, Peter. 2012. "The Unbearable Lightness of Expats: Double Binds of Humanitarian Mobility." *Cultural Anthropology* 27, no. 2: 358–82.

Reid, Graeme. 2006. "How to Become a 'Real Gay': Identity and Terminology in Ermelo, Mpumalanga." *Agenda* 20, no. 67: 137–45.

Reid, Graeme. 2013. *How to Be a Real Gay: Gay Identities in Small-Town South Africa*. Pietermaritzburg, South Africa: University of Kwa-Zulu Natal Press.

Rodney, Walter. 1972. *How Europe Underdeveloped Africa*. London: Bogle-L'Overture Publications.

Rogozen-Soltar, M. H. 2012. "Ambivalent Inclusion: Anti-racism and Racist Gatekeeping in Andalusia's Immigrant NGOs." *Journal of the Royal Anthropological Institute* 18, no. 3: 633–51.

Romani, Sahar. 2016. "Being NGO Girls: Gender, Subjectivities, and Everyday Life in Kolkata." *Gender, Place, and Culture* 23, no. 3: 365–80.

Sedgwick, Eve Kosofsky. 2003. *Touching Feeling: Affect, Pedagogy, Performativity*. Durham, NC: Duke University Press.

Swidler, Ann, and Susan Cotts Watkins. 2007. "Ties of Dependence: AIDS and Transactional Sex in Rural Malawi." *Studies in Family Planning* 38, no. 3: 147–62.

Tallie, T. J. 2013. "Queering Natal: Settler Logics and the Disruptive Challenge of Zulu Polygamy." *GLQ* 19, no. 2: 167–89.

Tamale, Sylvia. 2011. "Researching and Theorizing Sexualities in Africa." In *African Sexualities: A Reader*, edited by Sylvia Tamale, 11–36. Cape Town, South Africa: Pambazuka Press.

Thomann, Matthew. 2016. "HIV Vulnerability and the Erasure of Sexual and Gender Diversity in Abidjan, Cote d'Ivoire." *Global Public Health* 11, no. 7–8: 994–1009.

Tichenor, Marlee. 2017. "Data Performativity, Performing Health Work: Malaria and Labor in Senegal." *Medical Anthropology* 36, no. 5: 436–48.

Tsitsi, Chimwemwe. 2005. "No to Homosexuality." *Nation* (Blantyre, Malawi), March 16.

Turner, Victor. 1967. *The Forest of Symbols: Aspects of Ndembu Ritual*. Ithaca, NY: Cornell University Press.

Turner, Victor (1969) 2017. *The Ritual Process: Structure and Anti-structure*. London: Routledge.

Valentine, David. 2007. *Imagining Transgender: An Ethnography of a Category*. Durham, NC: Duke University Press.

Watson, Patricia, ed. 2010. *Queer Malawi: Untold Stories*. Johannesburg: MaThoko's Books.

Wilf, Eitan. 2011. "Sincerity versus Self-Expression: Modern Creative Agency and the Materiality of Semiotic Forms." *Cultural Anthropology* 26, no. 3: 462–84.

Wynter, Sylvia. 2003. "Unsettling the Coloniality of Being/Power/Truth/Freedom: Towards the Human, after Man, Its Overrepresentation—An Argument." *Centennial Review* 3: 257–337.

Xaba, Makhosazana, and C. Biruk, eds. 2016. *Proudly Malawian: Life Stories from Lesbian and Gender-Nonconforming Individuals*. Johannesburg: MaThoko's Books.

# AFTER PERFORMATIVITY, BEYOND CUSTOM

## The Queerness of Biofinancial Personhood, Citational Sexualities, and Derivative Subjectivity in South Africa

**Kirk Fiereck**

*O*n one particularly chilly, crisp winter morning in early July 2011 I met Themba (a pseudonym) in the waiting room of the Health 4 Men clinic, which was located in the sprawling Baragwanath Hospital campus in Soweto, short for the Southwest Townships of Johannesburg. The population the clinic targets is referred to as "men who have sex with men" (MSM), which originated among global health experts (Boellstorff 2011) as well as community activists. Themba was a young man with a slight build, fashionably dressed with an easy-going yet studied feminine comportment.[1] We were both flipping through a number of LGBTQ+ magazines and newspapers that the staff had put out for visitors. He had asked me about my previous weekend excursions and if I had a chance to explore a bit of Soweto. I told him that I had and that one of the clinic's gay staff members introduced me to his close-knit group of gay male Sowetean friends, one of whom was named Thomas (also a pseudonym). Thomas introduced himself to me as a gay male but was also seen by Themba to be a woman, given my description of Thomas in my retelling of the weekend's activities.

To be sure, Thomas did not identify as a trans woman and did not tell me himself that he was a woman. Rather, I came to an understanding of Thomas as a "gay woman" based on Themba's interpretation of my description of my weekend activities spent with Thomas, the gay clinic staff member, and their group. It was Themba who indicated to me the possibility of being a gay woman in this context. This queer form of personhood does not refer to a lesbian woman or a trans woman, as it does in many Euro-American contexts, and connotes more than

*GLQ* 26:3

DOI 10.1215/10642684-8311829

© 2020 by Duke University Press

one form of personhood, one customary, one constitutional. In South African contexts a gay woman is someone who may be assigned the male sex at birth but who is also—and alternately—assigned to be a woman socially either by themselves or by others, but may not be trans-identified.[2] I have never known gay women to be simultaneously gay men and women at the same time in relation to the same person.

I mentioned to Themba that our group had started our weekend revelry at Meat Meet, a *shebeen* (neighborhood bar), butcher shop, and restaurant specializing in award-winning *braai* (BBQ) in Diepkloof, a township adjacent to Baragwanath within Soweto. I was curious if Themba had heard of it and wanted to see what he thought about my experience with Thomas. I described how, after Meat Meet, our group ended up at another shebeen somewhere around Sebokeng, which seemed to me to be a township of Soweto as it is a thirty-minute drive from Diepkloof. Thomas started talking to one of the Black straight male revelers watching the soccer game on television. Thomas's hairstyle was ornate, with long braids in Black and some braids having green hair woven in, connoting a modern, stylish sensibility. The braids cascaded down to the small of her back, all mostly collected in a ponytail. As they continued their introductions, Thomas changed his gait and comported notably in a feminine register despite her male body and self-described identity, gently moving her long braids out of her face past her cheek while flirting with a potential new beau.[3]

When describing Thomas's subtle yet noticeable transformation that night to Themba in the clinic days later, he chuckled slightly at my incredulity. He found endearing my poorly disguised confusion that someone who identified to me as a gay man would then comport quite starkly as a woman in a different context without donning drag or describing it as a gender-queer performance. The context of the comportment—Thomas's giving themselves to be seen to the desiring gaze of his possible new beau—was important. My other friends referred to the space and Black male gaze I observed in Sebokeng as *straight, less developed*, and *not as liberal* as the more "gay" spaces of Soweto.

Themba referred to the interaction between Thomas and the man in Sebokeng as an "older" mode of engendering queer bodies in South Africa. This mode is well documented (Donham 1998; McLean and Ngcobo 1994) and was spatially located in contemporary public cultures by my research participants as more normalized within rural South African contexts than it was in the urban, aspirational township cultures where I worked. These rural forms of gay womanhood are explored by Graeme Reid (2008, 2013) in his ethnographic research focusing on the experiences and subjectivities of "gay ladies" in rural Mpumalanga Province, which is adjacent to Gauteng, the most populous and primarily urban province, which includes Johannesburg, Pretoria, and their townships.

Similar to gay ladies in Mpumalanga, and from what I could surmise from my research participants, gay women enact a style of comportment and citation where Black gay men present themselves to be seen by Black straight men as women. For now, suffice it to say that across South Africa older ways of doing things among Black South Africans are usually, but not always, cast in the register of heterosexist African traditionalisms, which are overtly or implicitly homophobic. African traditionalists' attempts to monopolize something referred to as *African custom* is expressly not what I refer to as *the customary*. To be sure, such monopolies reflect the colonial form of customary law, which was written by British colonialists throughout the African continent (Mamdani 1996).

Ironically, the idealisms of African ethnotraditionalist sexual personhood and politics capitulate to Euro-American and overwhelmingly white sexual cultures within global capitalisms. Just as these cultures maintain the strict alignment of gender and sex within the heterosexual matrices of neoliberal capital (Berlant and Warner 1998), so do the norms of sexual personhood within countless (South) African traditionalisms. Such ethnonationalist ideologies are products of the seemingly irresolvable contradictions of customary and constitutional law in South Africa. The latter underwrites new regimes of ethnicity (White 2015) and property law (Comaroff and Comaroff 2009), as well as a rapidly growing trade in financial and other derivatives I refer to as *bioderivatives* (Fiereck 2020).

In lieu of ethnic identity underwritten by colonial customary law, a customarily queer reading of Thomas's actions provides a sutured account of customary and liberal personhood. By *liberal personhood* I mean various local yet globally circulating liberal political and economic regimes of legal jurisprudence and constitutional laws and ideologies that produce particular subjectivities. Thomas becoming a woman in the eyes of myself, his admirer, and Themba is expressly not part of traditionalists' all-too-modern construction of African ethnicity, which would classify Thomas as un-African because he also identifies as a gay man. Rather, Thomas is doing what so many people do the world over when (neo)liberalisms, populisms, and ethnonational traditionalisms fail to provide forms and relations of intimacy that are not overdetermined by the predations of capital. Thomas's womanhood and his gay manhood are part of a lateralized, inflected space of cultural practice and meaning making that most other authors in this issue and myself sketch roughly as the *queer customary*. This cultural space is irreducibly one of citation of multiple forms of personhood that coexist in both customary spheres of social improvisation beyond as well as in relation to the rationalizations of customary and constitutional laws. A groundbreaking example of autoethnographic writing identifiable as canonical of the queer customary perspective is the autobiography of Nkunzi Zandile Nkabinde (2008) and their experiences as an *isisangoma*, or traditional healer. What remains to be seen is how—or even if—a rhetoric of bodily and linguistic inflection in the register of the customary can be constitutive of emergent forms of liberatory praxis, queer or otherwise.

I have shown previously how the customary is disjunct from what I describe here as biofinancial personhood and how this disjuncture is instantiated through financialized, which is to say the datafication of, biomedicine (Fiereck 2015), although I did not label these processes in this way at the time. This article is intended to flesh out that ethnographic deconstruction and queering of global bioethics and epidemiological science and to develop another step toward understanding how the hybrid queer personhood of gay women like Thomas in South Africa complicates and critiques Euro-American, which is to say Eurocentric, antinormative queer theory, namely, gender performativity theory. The next two sections develop arguments for critical concepts needed to support the main argument. I then relate those concepts to each other in the final three sections to show how the concepts developed throughout are linked by considerations of citationality and specifically how and why citationality is needed to supplement gender performativity theory in order to understand the disjuncture between biofinancial personhood and the queer customary in South Africa. In doing so, I argue for citational sexualities as a theoretical supplement to think what comes after performativity and how research informants have enacted citational sexualities to point to a potential future beyond custom and (neo)liberal constitutionalisms.

## Citationality: On the Mirror Logics of Ethnography and Derivatives

The opening vignette, like all ethnographic writing, is the retelling of particular sets of experiences, or texts, in the attempt to ground theoretical generalization in real-world circumstances experienced by ethnographers and their research participants and interlocutors. As such, they are all forms of citation. The critical question is whether or not such citational descriptions performatively instantiate the sociocultural worlds they seek to describe. While it is likely true that all human signification is citational, not all citational utterances are performative. For example, when individuals read about gay women, the subject position conjured in the readers' minds might be a lesbian woman or a trans woman. If this happens, the intended performative of *gay woman* that my research participants and I desire to be instantiated fails as it discounts the citational contextual description in the ethnographic vignette above.

Ethnographic writing is in many ways an impossible yet necessary attempt to instantiate performatively one's own or someone else's world. The contexts to which ethnographic inscriptions refer are subject to the failure not of citations— which always cite—but of those citations' ability to performatively conjure particular contexts of meaning for readers or listeners, which is strictly necessary for the success of performatives. No matter how concrete or detailed ethnographic contextualization is, such writing is nonetheless decontextualizing because it cannot represent the richness of everyday embodied experience, and therein lies the irreducible risk of ethnography.

Undoubtedly, ethnographic description allows a deeper understanding of a cultural context, yet it does so by abstracting the experiences and senses of an ethnographer (and their coethnographers, or informants) from the original, intersecting sets of temporalities and geographies.[4] In fact, any sense an ethnographer has of a field informant's experience is already an abstraction of the informant's own sense and context of reference. As the above vignette attempts to describe, my sense of context was radically influenced by Themba's reading of my reading of Thomas's behavior in the shebeen that weekend. In this regard, ethnographic writing is perhaps a kind of antidote to the theoretical speculations of philosophical praxis, as well as speculation of a different kind: that of derivative trading. While ethnography attempts to ground its specular theorizing in real-world experience, philosophical thought and financial speculation are largely unmoored from the real-world experiences of those about whom they speculate, namely, humans and other commodified entities.

The ethnographic scenes presented and explored throughout this article are therefore instances of double abstraction. The double disembedding of human experience embodied within ethnographic writing is, perhaps ironically, mirrored by the double abstractions of financial derivatives themselves, as this value form continues to reshape human sociality within finance capital's own image. Necessary to start is an operational definition of *derivatives*. Simply put, derivatives are contracts about underlying commodities, which themselves embody already abstract social relations. Derivatives, such as credit default swaps, or, as I argue, Facebook user agreements or biomedical research consent forms (Fiereck 2020), produce a further, double layer of abstraction beyond commodified social relations. Derivatives do this by allowing aspects of their underlying commodity to be traded without trading that underlying commodity. This occurs through datafication processes. The underlying commodities of credit default swaps are mortgages, which were made (in)famous during the 2008 global financial crisis. The underlying commodities of Facebook user agreements and biomedical consent forms are human beings and are what I refer to as *bioderivatives*. What all three of these contracts have in common is that they are concerned with trading aspects of the underlying commodities and not the commodities themselves.[5]

Suffice it to say for now, derivatives—as well as their temporal, subjective, and contextual displacements—are neither as arcane nor as irrelevant to the lives of everyday South Africans or anyone else as they might first seem. The narratives I explore of Black LGBTQ-identified South African informants attest to the significance of opaque derivative value forms as opposed to the commodity value form in the lives of those most marginalized by financial and industrial capital. I argue for this significance because derivatives are widely seen to be arcane and relatively unimportant to most human beings and other living entities on the planet, despite the fact that derivatives are the predominant value form where economistic value is produced globally (Dejardins 2017).

Specifically, here I show that these informants exist within overlapping cultural spaces that include global, financial; national and transnational, industrial; and local, customary contexts, and that the financial aspects of informants' everyday lives go largely unremarked or acknowledged as such. Each of these contexts has its particular forms of identification and subjectivation, but ones that are hierarchically organized in relation to the logic of derivative that are the hallmark of global financial cultures, and that have been overlooked by queer and African studies scholarship. As I translate the experiences of informants throughout, I employ the Bakhtinian concept of the chronotope (Bakhtin 1981) to underscore that any combination of particular assemblages of time and space is necessarily accomplished in the register of citation and only secondarily of the performative (Austin 1975; Butler 1999), nor is the performative conceived as only a temporal and not cross-contextual citation (Butler 1993). Citation as I explore it here occurs through the triple process of abstraction, iteration, and the irreducibly dual process of dis/embedding that Jacques Derrida (1995) identified more than three decades ago as the structural condition of possibility of the performative.

I am concerned with two modes of citationality. The first is temporal and has been previously identified by Judith Butler (1993) as part and parcel of the structure of gender performatives. The second is akin to Danai Mupotsa's discussion of conjugality (in this issue). This mode has to do with two or more contemporaneous performativities that belong to overlapping yet distinct cultural contexts or spaces, which intersect within and among persons who straddle contemporary but not coterminous cultural spaces and legibilities of identity and subjectivity. It is this second mode that I am primarily concerned with in this article and how the citations of different modes of identification and subjectivation between the three cultural contexts of financial, industrial, and customary sociality produce queer forms of what I call *biofinancial* personhood.

As other anthropologists have argued, inflecting norms can destabilize them toward progressive ends (Mahmood 2005; Wilder 2015); such practices are potentially just as politically fecund as the antinomy of staunchly antinormative queer politics (Halberstam 2016). For example, Elizabeth A. Povinelli's (2015) analysis of the destabilized figures of queer antinormativity demonstrates that antinormative positions are in flux and are not as universal or timeless as once previously imagined. As Rosalind Morris (1994: 22) argued more than two decades ago, antinormative stances rooted in "the theory of gender as performance . . . may even shore up the absolutist claims" they seek to undermine. The secret normativity of ostensibly queer antinormativity theory and politics is arguably Euro-American forms of personhood. These ideologies of personhood are the silent, yet no less salient, norms of gender performativity theory, which is to say, the norms underwritten by the financialized neoliberal subjectivities that shore up Euro-American intersectional and queer theory. These theories and ideological subjects are produced by and productive of financialized Euro-American capital, given their historical origins within the US neoliberal academy (Halperin 2003; Reed 2013).

## Biofinancial Personhood and Dividuality

Back to Baragwanath Hospital ("Bara") and the Health 4 Men clinic. Bara is on the outskirts of Soweto, an area that consists of twenty-nine townships where Black Africans make up 98.5 percent of the population. Soweto is situated just to the south of the N1 national highway, whereas Bara lies across the N1 bypass from a number of large steppe-shaped golden brown mine dumps that are built up from more than a century of gold mining by Black labor.

Global capitalism includes ostensibly noncapitalist, communist nations, which are arguably state-mediated capitalist economies. In communist capitalism, as in all industrial capitalist societies, labor as commodity is the engine of production of surplus value. In communist capitalism the state distributes this surplus instead of the market (Postone 1993). In this way, the gold mine dumps across the highway from Bara are an ever-present reminder of both the racist monetization of (Black) labor and its displacement by the predominance of bioderivatives that monetize data and information through processes of medical research, which increasingly is housed at Bara because South Africa has the largest HIV epidemic in the world and Bara touts itself as the third-largest hospital in the world. Whereas wage labor is the building block of commoditized mediations of industrial capitalist social relations, (bio)datafied selves are the source of derivativized mediations of biofinancial dividuality globally.

Claims to identity and subjectivity and/or their subversion through the well-known performative *I* instantiate the political category of the *individual* person, such as persons who LGBTQ identify, and link these social identities to their various subjectivities. Such individualism is a hallmark of liberal societies and industrial capitalisms globally. However, individuals may or may not belong to communities in which persons are bound to one another through shared identities. On the other hand, claims to the existence of a global, datafied population grouping through the MSM performative—typically but not always by global health experts—instantiate the political category of the *dividual* person.

Dividual subjectivities are the preeminent aspect of personhood produced through the datafication of individuals in financial capitalisms. However, classic studies by Marilyn Strathern (1988) and Marcel Mauss (1990) demonstrate that dividuation does not have to be abstract and point to possibilities that the abstract and predatory dividualism of persons in financial capitalisms could be redressed through political and social movements. The predominance of abstract dividual, datafied personhood in relation to individual personhood would seem to be a hallmark of neoliberal societies (Foucault 2008) and financial capitalisms (Appadurai 2016). *Biofinance* and *biofinancialization* are terms I coined that describe how specific communities and publics, including humans and nonhumans (Fiereck 2017), are reconceived as globally diffuse, abstract dividual populations made up of sexual behavioral groups, personality types, or ecological entities, rather than only socially embedded individual persons. In this way, it is significant that the clinics are funded and MSM data produced by national and international HIV/AIDS biocapital from USAID in partnership with the South African Department of Health and the Elton John AIDS Foundation. All of these entities are formed in relation to various local late (neo)liberal political and legal regimes enacted through constitutional law.

These clinics were set up to address the abnormally high rates of HIV that gay Black men have been found to have in South Africa.[6] My study on the relation of the customary to biofinancial personhood (Fiereck 2015) drew attention to one epidemiological study that estimated about one-third of the Black, gay-identified MSM population is HIV positive, while only about one-sixth of Black, non-gay-identified MSM are HIV positive (Lane et al. 2009). The only other group in the country that shouldered as heavy an HIV burden was young Black women. The epidemiological similarity between gay-identified Black men and Black women in South Africa is significant because the epidemiological relation (the prevalence estimates of HIV) between gay Black men and Black women is similar, and the relation between gay and nongay men is comparably disparate. I flag it here as a curious kinship, which helps to further contextualize the arguments around citational sexualities and their production by gay women.

The way that dividuality and biofinancial personhood are enacted through the MSM clinics can be best demonstrated by analyzing some of the clinics' MSM logos and other promotional materials. Dotted across the walls of the clinic waiting area of the Bara MSM clinic were sexual health posters. The images alternated between factual information about sexually transmitted infections and promoting condom use. Some others encouraged clinic attendees to get an HIV test and to share the result with their partners. The images on the sexual health marketing posters featured an erect phallus and half- or completely naked barrel-chested Black men. The figures in the images stood confidently on their own as if to portray themselves as the responsible individuals, the desired subjects of HIV prevention discourse and global biocapital who are proactive about reducing their risk for HIV. One image depicted a muscular, masculine couple locked in a loving embrace, depicting the caring dyad that is the putative goal for so much discourse on love, sex, and risk in these neoliberal times in South Africa and beyond.

This approach to HIV prevention reflects a globally diffuse, sex-positive approach to HIV prevention among gay men and MSM. The clinic was clearly invested in its mandate to "improve care, reduce stigma and provide targeted HIV treatment information" to MSM groups. In addition to the Bara clinic, another clinic with similar community outreach programs was operating concurrently in Cape Town during my fieldwork.

Sexual health campaigns targeting MSM are admirably the first of their kind on the African continent. However, the marketing images did not reflect the type of gender presentation of most of the Black gay men and gay women that I encountered during my ongoing field research. More to the point, the types of imagery—particularly the grounding of masculinity in an erect phallus in the Health 4 Men logo—reflect a globally diffuse neoliberal sexual ideology, not the local sexual ideologies that give texture vis-à-vis their customary instantiation in everyday life and social interactions for most South Africans. A hallmark of a liberal sexual ideology is the normative grounding of gender identity in sex, which simultaneously marginalizes Euro-American forms of queer theory, gender transness, and queer political subjectivities. These forms of queer subjectivity, related as they are to transgressive sexuality, are the liberal sexual ideology's legible space of critique. Conversely, there are local, or customary, forms of personhood, critique, and subjectivity that gesture and, most important, cite beyond such (late) liberal ideological legibility, to which I turn now.

## Citational Sexualities

To begin a discussion of citational sexualities it is necessary to contextualize the ground of financial wealth in our neoliberal times by exploring a critical transition in Themba's life narrative and subjectivity. The next time he and I met, Themba was at the clinic for an HIV test result and we were talking about his upbringing. Specifically, he discussed growing up wanting to be a girl.[7] To explain he compared himself to another gay guy in his community, which was one of the poorer, newer neighborhoods in Soweto that were populated primarily by recent arrivals from the rural South African "homelands" around the 1970s and 1980s.

He described himself as "the gay one" because the "other one was gay but too much of a guy." Specifically, he pointed out that he had played with girls growing up. Some of these girls would say to him, "Oh, you want to be a girl," and he would agree, saying "Yes, . . . sometimes I want to be a girl. I want to grow up. I want to be a girl." Older girls in his neighborhood would also underscore his girlhood by complimenting the clothes Themba would wear, telling him he looked "girly" and "stunning" in women's clothing. Reinforcing, positive support like this about his femininity from other girls made Themba feel more like a girl than a boy. At one point growing up, though, he felt that he didn't want to be a girl, and he had eventually been introduced to the idea of being gay. While it is significant that his experience of subjectivity was gendered as female to begin with, despite his male anatomy, it ended up for Themba that he really wanted to be gay. As he told it to me, "At the end of the day you are a guy. You know, every guy, like a straight guy, if they have wet dreams and you're gay, you're also gonna have wet dreams."[8] I argue that this is an instance of citational sexuality. It is significant that Themba decided that aspects of the liberal sexual ideology were more suitable for him. However, this is not to say that customary interpretations of sexual personhood are not still significant for him, since they make up his past personas.

To understand how sexual personhood changed over time, I conducted life history interviews with approximately twenty Black and colored LGBTQ-identified South Africans in order to understand how and why transitions, reverberations, and modulations of sexual subjectivities occur among these individuals. I was interested in the significant features of these shifts. I use multiple notions of change to describe what I refer to above and in other writing as *hybrid queer personhood* (Fiereck 2017, 2018). For many Black and colored South Africans, LGBTQ identities tell only part of their story of sexual personhood. Themba's narrative is exemplary in this regard. The fact is that during their lives many South Africans have experienced sexual subjectivities that index radically different genders, forms of personhood, and sexual ideologies. Sometimes their life trajectories amount to a thoroughgoing paradigm change, or transition of register. Other times they describe more of a frequency modulation, or retuning, in that they transition back and forth between forms of personhood and subjectivity with no clear permanent direction.

In this way, personhood, not identity, is the analytical philosophical-anthropological concept that allows us to understand how the customary in its many local instantiations can specifically mediate sexuality in ways that may be liberatory, not merely antinormative or the result of those quotidian "flexible" pragmatisms that neoliberal societies require of their citizenry (Ong 1999), be they transnational or not. Butler's theory of gender performativity, despite its superficial mention of ethnicity as a mediating factor of gender identity and sexual subjectivity, neglects to identify personhood as a primary analytic category (Butler 1988, 1999). Aside from two mentions of personhood in *Gender Trouble* (Butler 1999), the book does not grapple with how gender performativity differs between radically different cultural contexts that may be chronotypically differentiated. Therein lies the irony of that book's laudable attempts to ground gender performativity theory in the ostensible universality of analytic approaches to linguistic philosophy as well as particularistic theories of ritual in anthropology.

The limitation of this approach is structured by the anthropology of ritual canon in that the canon and gender performativity both presume a singular undifferentiated context where a ritual such as gender takes place and is performatively, iteratively, undone and redone with each gendered practice by a subject. As the narratives of Black South Africans clearly demonstrate, this presumption does not bear out in reality. *Bodies That Matter* (Butler 1993) rightly points out the limits of gender performance theory in that it is primarily a temporal citation of what has come before, but none of the gender citationality arguments in that book consider the structure of the performative in that it might fail if a particular context of the intended performative is not previously known by those who witness or interpret the performative coevally with those who utter it. What, then, of the citational sexualities and the queer customary's relation to what I propose be understood provisionally as derivative subjectivity?

## Derivative Subjectivity

In this section I discuss the relationship between citational sexualities and what I refer to as *derivative subjectivity*, which is produced when subjects become entangled with biofinancial datafication processes and ideologies, such as when people take PrEP to treat the risk of HIV and not HIV itself. I once met Themba with another gay friend of his, and they described how a group of their friends had grown up wanting to be girls and started taking birth control pills or hormone patches to modify their bodies, specifically to grow breasts. Themba specifically had asked his sister to get extra birth control pills for him so he could take them to grow breasts. His other friends would try to get hormone patches from transgender women friends who were accessing the patches from their medical providers. Strikingly similar narratives regarding the radically different relationship—with regard to what I call a *liberal sexual ideology*—between sex and gender in the context of Black gay sexuality in Soweto have been reported historically by anthropologist Donald L. Donham (1998). Donham de/contextualizes the femininity of some of the Black gay-identified members of the Gay and Lesbian Organization of the Witwatersrand (GLOW), which was the first Black lesbian and gay rights organization in South Africa. He specifically describes the funeral of Linda Ngcobo, who was raised as a girl and thought of herself as a woman but also identified as gay and a man.

Despite the similarities, one major difference between existing accounts of figures like Linda and the gay men and women I spent time with is how the anatomical body emerges in Themba's life history as a significant object in the production of gendered subjectivity, personhood, and knowledge. In earlier generations of gay women, such as Linda's, the anatomical body was not the same kind of sexual epistemological object. Linda described this difference in a tactile way:

> On a weekend I went to a shebeen with a lady friend of mine. I was in drag, I often used to do this on the weekends—many *skesanas*[9] do it. We were inside. It seemed as if four boys wanted to rape us, they were *pantsulas* [archetypal macho figure] and they were very rough. One of them proposed my friend and she accepted. The others approached me one by one. The first two I didn't like so I said no! I was attracted by the third one, so said yes to him.
>
> As we left the shebeen, my one said to me: "If you don't have it, I'm going to cut your throat." I could see that he was serious and I knew I must have it or I'm dead. So I asked my friend to say that she was hungry and we stopped at some shops. I went inside and bought a can of pilchards. I

knew that the only thing the *pantsula* was interested in was the hole and the smell. *Pantsulas* don't explore much, they just lift up your dress and go for it. . . .

Sardines are one of the tricks the *skesanas* use. We know that some *pantsulas* like dirty pussy, for these you must use pilchards, but not Glenrick because they smell too bad. Other *pantsulas* like clean pussy, for these you can use sardines. For my *pantsula* I bought pilchards because I could see what kind he was. So before I went to bed I just smeared some pilchards around my anus and my thighs. When he smelled the smell and found the hole he was quite happy. We became lovers for some months after that. (McLean and Ngcobo 1994: 172)

The difference in how the anatomical signifies in Linda's and Themba's narratives turns on the emergence of biotechnology in the form of pharmaceuticals and hormone therapies in the production of sexual and gender identities. I asked Themba some of the reasons that he and his friends wanted to be girls at the time, even though he had since changed his mind and decided that the terms *man* and *gay* were more fitting to describe himself. He said that the existence of homophobic people made him feel that if he was a girl, "nobody's gonna call me gay, nobody's gonna treat me bad, nobody's gonna swear at me when I pass him." He then brought up his friend Sipho whom he and his friends would envy because, as he put it, "she was transgender." When they were all hanging out together in the street or at the mall, people would call out to the group, "Oh! Gays!" Sipho would then remind them that they weren't talking to her because she was a girl. Having narrated Sipho to me as a transgender woman, I was surprised when Themba mentioned that Sipho actually did not consider herself as transgender at all but, rather, saw herself as a woman. As Themba described it, "When maybe we were walking in the mall, people can see me and Simphiwe as guys [and] they can see her as a girl. . . . Yeah, but tjo! She's a girl. Everywhere we go they consider him as a girl and us as guys."[10]

Themba describes a social world for which social identities like gay or transgender are genres of personhood that are distinct from the genres of personhood referenced by being male bodied and wanting to grow up to be a "girl" or actually being a "woman" like Sipho. In fact, as Themba describes, the male anatomies of the girl and woman subject positions do not signify publicly (or necessarily intimately as well as intersubjectively, given Linda's narrative), which is to say normatively, since everyone in the mall and wherever they go see Sipho as a girl and the others as gay men. In other words, multiple forms of sexual personhood are culturally legible in places like Soweto. Such a narrative also expresses that the relation between public and private sexual personas in customary spheres of personhood are not normatively required to be aligned like they are in a liberal ideology of bodily aesthetics and comportment. Instead of grounding gender identity only in the imaginary origin of the anatomical, increasingly biomedicalized body—a sexual, biological essence—and private individualism (liberal ideology), here gender identity is grounded in bodily comportment and normatively constituted through social signification and an individual's maintenance of public personas.

In Themba's description of Sipho, a liberal sexual ideology does not provide a legible genre of sexual personhood for her. She draws instead from a local sphere of cultural meaning. From what I know of Sipho through Themba's citational reference of her, Sipho is Zulu speaking and articulates her gender and sexual identities in relation to cultural ideologies typically associated with Zuluness. Rural versions of these ideologies in South Africa's Mpumalanga Province have been explored in detail by Reid (2013). In that account, the reader is introduced to "gay ladies" or, as I commonly heard them refer to themselves, gay women. I met a number of these individuals in the context of a global clinical trial. About eighty Black gay women and men were enrolled in one of the world's first truly global clinical trials to test the efficacy of the pharmaceutical HIV prevention technology called preexposure prophylaxis, or PrEP.[11]

The goal of the PrEP clinical trial was to find out if taking HIV antiretroviral medications daily would be a viable biomedical risk-hedging strategy to prevent HIV infection. This is also where citational sexualities converge with new forms of subjectivity I submit as derivative. Precisely like citation, financial derivatives—which are economic risk-hedging tools—act very similarly to pharmaceutical risk-hedging tools like the contraceptive pill, PrEP, and hormones (as is the case in Themba's narrative). Both derivatives and preventative pharmaceuticals (which treat risk and not disease) are imbued with value by monetizing the price information and data they retain about commodities. However, the main, critical difference between them is that, unlike financial derivatives, which are based on fluctuations in cows, currencies, or credit default swaps, the underlying commodity for pharmaceutical and other bioderivatives (in this case, based on humans and their data) is us, particularly those of us in clinical trials and who take the medications. It is the data we produce in clinical trials and then use in the real world that is the basis for the value of pharmaceutical derivatives. As such, human bioderivatives are tools of double abstraction and reiteration, because their value is based on the information and data about commodities, which are themselves already abstracted from direct social relations among humans.

Unlike financial derivatives, however, pharmaceutical derivatives have a materiality (in both a Marxist and a philosophical sense). The derivative contract is inscribed and priced with reference to financializing cultures in the idioms of risk and monetized information. Such idioms are the symbolic economies that condition the possibilities of economistic calculation and strategic action in an increasingly uncertain world. Risk management and cost-benefit ratios are the dominant political cultural sieve through which authoritarians currently attempt—but ideally will fail—to bypass with blatantly fascist and racist discourse, the moral economies that provide ethical direction for material and semiotic experiences. Derivatives are (information-based) contracts that serve as priced overlays representing an underlying commodity, such as a currency, a credit default swap, or (your)self-as-data (whether you know it or not, or consent to it or not).

This last aspect has ironically become the predominant experience of what it means to be human to financial capital in late liberalisms globally. The data that we produce in relation to elaborate systems of calculation is what drives global processes of financialization and the derivitivization of sociality (LiPuma 2017). This financial species of capital is radically different from industrial capital in that the basis of value is rationalized information, not human labor-time. In this clinical context, the need of global biofinancial capital for rationalized globally relevant information about the specific treatment populations for PrEP is enabled by the scientificity about sex and ostensibly achieved by the enactment of the MSM category that enumerates data about a global population. What this does is make the incommensurability of different MSM populations commensurable. As I have argued (Fiereck 2015), patching over the incommensurable is an ethical, cultural conundrum, which inadvertently generates new health and other economic inequalities of a specifically financial sort.

While financial derivative contracts are priced according to the volatility of the underlying commodities, pharmaceutical derivatives, on the other hand, use epidemiological risk groups to help calculate the preventative values of treating risk. In other words, biofinancial value is roughly ascertained by asking, for example, How well will the contraceptive pill work versus the pull-out method for women regardless of their socioeconomic or cultural contexts globally? As with derivatives that enumerate price information of commodities, MSM is a risk-based information overlay that represents an underlying, global population of human men, but this also will regularly include gay women, trans women, and many other nonbinary trans-like groups in the context of South Africa, as well as many other national contexts globally. This is good and bad.

The good part is that both biofinancial risk groups and derivatives create connectivity, which translates into the potential for increased political solidarities between disparate groups of MSM globally. The bad part can be seen through the trading of currency-based derivatives, which create unprecedented connectivity (as well as risk and uncertainty) between national economies globally. One only needs to think here of the 2008 global financial meltdown for what could be bad about creating such connectivity. It must be said that the unprecedented connectivity between national populations of MSM and the subpopulations of queers these populations undoubtedly encompass globally will have yet unpredictable effects, ideally for the better. But who is to say?

For instance, the US Food and Drug Administration's approval of PrEP was based on the results of the PrEP global clinical trial, which was based in eleven cities in six countries on four continents. In other words, "MSM" globally are able to take PrEP today only because the men I was working with in this trial in Cape Town were contributing to a form of global data abstraction facilitated by the MSM category. The downside is that epidemiological practice in real time lags shamefully behind epidemiological science. I have argued that the men in this trial whose bodies demonstrated PrEP's efficacy were not guaranteed access to the intervention their bodies authorized to begin with (Fiereck 2015). If it were not for the largesse of philanthropic organizations such as the Elton John Foundation, for one, these men would not have been given access to the intervention, period.

As with financial derivatives, so go pharmaceutical derivatives; the crisis of representation looms large for both. What to make of the suppressed presence of gay women as MSM in global health knowledge production? Given their affinity, both derivatives and pharmaceuticals are highly contested forms of abstraction, reiteration, and dis/embedding, which is to say, citation. This affinity for citation and circulation and their role in global processes of the datafication of literally everything are also why I argue that the form of subjectivity that citational sexualities take is derivative.

## Conclusion

Themba's transition between a customary subjectivity of "girl" to that of "gay" and the overlap between the two that occurred during his shift in forms of personhood, not to mention my ethnographic rendering of these practices, are first and foremost practices of citation, which includes "discourse genres, ideologies of personhood, and institutional regimes of knowledge" (Goodman, Tomlinson, and Richland 2014). This is to say, their narratives are fraught with de/contextualization and *différence*, which troubles theories of gender performativity.

In the case of Themba being a girl, he was always careful to note that his public persona was that he was known as a "girly one" and that his status as a girl in public had limitations that occurred with regard to his private persona and his anatomical body, which is why he approached his sister to ask for birth control pills. By comparing Linda's and Themba's accounts, we can see a political transition to a predominance of liberal forms of sexual personhood and the centrality of the anatomical body, and not the gendered, social body in the context of Black township sexual culture.

This can be mapped in the span of about two decades when looking at a transition of narratives from figures like Linda Ngcobo to Themba and Sipho. Linda was known alternately as a woman (in a customary sense), as gay (in a liberal sense), and as a gay woman (in a citational sense). The first two subject positions, woman and gay, are performative in that they call into being the phenomenon and social worlds of subjectivity that they name and index, respectively. On the other hand, gay woman is a curious and notably queer kinship of subjectivities and social worlds.

I argue this is a form of hybrid queer personhood and should be rendered conceptually as a citational sexuality, not just as two simultaneous and alternately un/successful gender performatives. This is because gay woman coheres only through mutual, simultaneous cross-cultural citation, despite the failure or success of the performatives involved. In other words, for sexuality to be citational it needs to be a hybrid of two (or more) performative subjectivities, one of which must fail to call forth that which it names for some people who are involved with the person trying to cite two radically different socialites. This is also not an example of "performativity as citationality," which Butler (1993: 12–16) discussed in reference to monocultural contexts and between different times in the same social context. Rather, the form of citationality I discuss here derives from work in linguistic anthropology where citationality is used to explain shifts in personhood genres, subjectivity, and knowledge (in this case as they relate to gender and sexuality). In fact, it is precisely where the explanatory force of anthropological theories of citationality begin that the illocutionary force of philosophical performativity meets its limit.

Among most Black South Africans who live or have lived in townships or rural areas, an utterance invoking the figure of a gay woman would be understood as a person who alternately slips in and out of subjectivities depending on the predominance of liberal or customary genres of discourse in a given context or among a group of people. This process goes beyond mere code-switching. The social position of gay women (or lesbian men, for that matter) coheres when individuals abstract, reiterate, and dis/embed multiple genres of personhood, subjectivity, and sexual knowledge. It is precisely this assemblage of practices (abstraction, reiteration, dis/embedding) that underscores the work of citational practices as opposed to performative speech acts. Where only liberal genres of sexual personhood are legible, such subjects would be gay or lesbian and engage in performative speech acts about being gay men or lesbian women. In contexts where customary genres of sexual personhood—many of which might be based on perceived ethnic identity, although this is not necessary—are more readily legible or important, these subjects would likely engage in performative speech acts about being women. In still other contexts, people understand both customary and liberal cultural legibilities and can (de)contextualize between the two on the fly. Here is where the citational sexuality of being a gay woman, or lesbian man, makes perfect sense as a form of citationality and mutual dis/embedding between multiple genres of sexual personhood.

As citational practices these sexualities also expose "the secret ground of normativization in speech act theory" of gender performativity theory (Morris 2007: 359), themselves grounded in John L. Austin's (1975) linguistic philosophy. This secret normativity as it has been developed in relation to and within—but ironically marginalized by—queer theory and studies persists and is located in the fact that little attention has been paid to the preconditions necessary for Austin's "successful" performative. In short, such success depends strictly on the existence of what he refers to as "the total situation" or "the total speech act" (52). Austin's totality is one where all of the precepts, entailments, rights, and responsibilities of the speaker and the receiver are mutually shared. This shared cultural context is strictly necessary so that the infelicities that haunt the successful performative utterance can be considered the exception and not the rule.

Aside from Rosalind Morris's (1994, 1995, 2007) analyses, there has been little work in queer studies regarding the preconditions necessary for Austin's successful performative or Butler's successful transgressive resignification of a gender performative or citation. The implication is that, for both normative and antinormative positions in the queer studies debate to be performative, a shared cultural context is strictly necessary. The normative and antinormative positions in, through, or against queer studies logically work and are given life if and only if one is working in some shared reference of meaning. It is perhaps less surprising, then, that the references to anthropology of ritual research (Geertz 1983; Turner 1974) that looks specifically at one cultural context are those that serve the (unstable) citational ground for gender performativity theory (Butler 1988, 1999). In contexts of globalization we need something more than performativity, because it is unable to address most of the speech acts based on citational communication of people who exist largely betwixt and between two or more cultural contexts in any given social field.

Thus, a supplement is needed. Derrida (1995: 15) reminds us

> that the value of risk or exposure to infelicity, even though, as Austin rec-
> ognizes, it can affect a priori the totality of conventional [speech] acts, is
> not interrogated as an essential predicate or as a *law*. Austin does not pon-
> der the consequences issuing from the fact that a possibility—a possible
> risk—is *always* possible, and is in some sense a necessary possibility. Nor
> whether—once such a necessary possibility of infelicity is recognized—
> infelicity still constitutes an accident. What is a success when the possibil-
> ity of infelicity [échec] continues to constitute its structure?

The presumptions of performativity, and the strict culturalist presumptions of suc-
cessful performatives, are therefore where Derrida locates a critique and the secret normativity of the performative. In the contexts I have just attempted to describe, it is precisely such infelicities that are the rule for performative utterances and ethnographic writing and not the exception. The presumption of performatives is therefore where Derrida locates his critique and specifically where I suggest cross-cultural citationality as a supplement to performativity for queer anthropology and queer studies.

Cross-cultural citationality as a theoretical paradigm for sexual subjectiv-
ity and politics is particularly acute in contexts where multiple and contradictory cultural contexts diffuse in and out of one another, as is the case everywhere in the world where social media operates and citations from one context can contribute to radically different performative effects in faraway contexts via a viral video on a smartphone, or even between global health researchers and research participants in a global clinical trial. South Africa and other postcolonial contexts are precisely the places where contestations between constitutional and customary law are compelling queer reconnections with the customary, not only as law (Fiereck 2017) but, rather, as contingent cultural crucibles (Hoad 2016; Fiereck 2018). Customar-
ily queer citational sexualities like these expose, as a rule, the conditions of infe-
licity and failure that Austin and Butler mistakenly presume to be mere exception.

## Notes

First, I must account for the innumerable debts I have to the many informants, coethnographers, friends, and queer family in South Africa who shared their lives and narratives with me during the past decade. Without Hylton White's generosity of thought introducing me to the customary and biocapital; Roz Morris's teachings of the logic of derivative, Derrida, and what they mean for queer anthropology; Betsey Brada's ever-attuned listening ear urging me to explore personhood; and the vast intellects of this issue's co-guest editors, Danai S. Mupotsa and Neville Hoad, this article and special issue would never have been possible. For this article especially, I am sincerely indebted to the editorial hand of Marcia Ochoa. My greatest debts in formulating the arguments presented here are to them. My research has been generously funded by a Fulbright-Hays Doctoral Dissertation Research Abroad Fellowship, a National Institute of Mental Health Ruth L. Kirschstein National Research Service Award Fellowship, a Mellon Foundation Postdoctoral Fellowship in Queer Studies at the University of Pennsylvania, and a European Research Council Fellowship at the University of Amsterdam. The analysis presented here benefited greatly from the thoughtful comments of anonymous peer review. Any omissions and errors remain my own.

1.  I have used masculine pronouns for Themba based on his own usage and expressed preference. While I describe Themba's bodily comportment as feminine during this first meeting, he later identified himself in subsequent meetings using masculine pronouns and identified as gay.

2.  Many gay women are beginning both to be introduced to and to inhabit the trans woman identity category, which they are exposed to via global media and local trans-focused nongovernmental organizations. During my fieldwork, which I conducted from 2010 to 2015, the trans woman identity was not as widespread as the trans man identity among Black South Africans. This may have been due to the classed racial and gender politics in LGBTQ+ organizing in South Africa, where there were only two organizations for trans persons, and neither focused primarily on issues affecting Black trans women in poorer contexts. It may have been that there weren't as many Black trans women in poor contexts, given that many of those types of subjects were described as gay women in the townships where I worked in Johannesburg. Also, the only Black trans woman I met during my fieldwork was in Cape Town, and this was in connection with a sex worker rights organization. It may be that, in the past half-decade, transness in South Africa is a more widely distributed form of personhood, but it also has historically been characterized through nationally particular exclusions that do not necessarily define it in Euro-American contexts. For example, a former director of one of the oldest LGBTQ+ organizations in South Africa told me, after the publication of *Trans* (Morgan et al. 2009), the first edited volume of trans narratives in South Africa, that the editors "excluded transvestite-identified people": they

excluded the narrative of one hopeful contributor who identified as a transvestite. Whereas David Valentine (2007) has foregrounded the diversity of identities (including transvestites and even gender-queer gays and lesbians) under the "trans umbrella" in the United States, this umbrella seems to be constituted differently in the South African context, but this also may be changing as trans politics continue to unfold in the republic.

3.  In this description of Thomas, I use both masculine and feminine pronouns to connote the noticeable shift of gender performance and to reflect Themba's subsequent reading of Thomas as both a gay man and a woman.

4.  I am aware that there are a number of schools of thought about the anthropological use of the word *informants* in lieu of *research participants, coethnographers*, or even *friends*. I tend to use *informants* as it lays bare and without question that there are power differentials between ethnographers and those they conduct their research alongside, even when they are, in fact, friends or coethnographers, as many of the research participants during my field research were for me. However, anthropologist-of-color colleagues have suggested I use *informants* so as not to presume solidarities where there likely may be none, and this is what I have done here. For example, while all of the informants in my work participate of their own will in my research, I am the one writing this text. And while Thomas was a friend of mine, it was Themba who I feel was a coethnographer in the above vignette because he significantly marked my ethnographic gaze and ethnographic writing. However, as we knew each other only through the Health 4 Men clinic, describing him as a friend seems disingenuous. Regardless, I want the reader to know that the ethnographic encounter is one that is irreducibly fraught with ethical conundrums, as are all encounters between self and other—small *o* (Levinas 1985). Given the predations of global financializing capital, solidarities are few and far between, so I revert to using *informant* generally out of respect for the solidarities-to-come that my writing might someday engender and wish not to presume solidarities at the time of publication of this text.

5.  Calling these *bioderivatives* is a strategic move as well as theoretical necessity, as I fully understand that humans are not the only datafied populations of living or nonliving entities on our planet that are already commodified. I am currently conducting a global, multisite research project that considers how what I refer to as *biofinance* is happening not only to humans but also to animal and viral populations the world over. Processes I identify as *bioderivativization* go beyond their origins in the global agribusinesses of colonialism, which is where financial derivatives—also known as securities, as they securitized investors' capital—were invented to securitize shares of the Dutch East India company (Vereenigde Oostindische Compagnie [VOC]). The VOC was set up to produce a monopoly on the Dutch spice trade. The derivativization of VOC shares during the entirety of the seventeenth century resulted in the emergence of the world's first modern securities market on the Amsterdam stock exchange.

During colonialism, derivatives were subordinate to commodities in the production of value. In the contemporary world, this relation has radically shifted (Dejardins 2017). Such a shift can be read in the radical semantic, ethical, and economistic transformation of honeybees from industrial producers of honey globally to the "most important animal on the planet" due to the new status of pollinators as producing critical connectivity between all species-biocapital. One of the main functions of the contemporary global market in financial derivatives is to produce connectivity between pools of national capital. As goes the predominance of derivatives in value production due to their critical function of producing capital connectivity, so go the transformation of bees from industrial workers to nature's most important bioderivative traders.

6.  In Fiereck 2015 I show how forms of queer and customary personhood were discounted in the preexposure prophylaxis (PrEP) global clinical trial and why this is an issue for queer global health ethics. That study explores the figure of the gay woman in relation to the PrEP clinical trial's use of MSM, but not the clinic I conducted research at in Johannesburg. I demonstrated the disjuncture between biofinancial personhood and the customary by showing step by step how the MSM category was enacted by global health experts within South Africa and beyond, and how this enactment silenced aspects of womanhood of subjects coded as "MSM" despite whether or not they would have desired this silencing and coding. That article also discusses how enacting MSM does not have to be a neocolonial or merely bureaucratic practice by giving concrete examples of how global health practitioners can ask questions about gender variance in certain subjects' life spans within survey research. It goes beyond existing anthropological examinations of MSM, including Boellstorff 2011 and Biruk 2019, in that I use my training in global health, statistical inference, and bioethics to suggest a world beyond mere critique with concrete, actionable, and, most important, simple deconstructive statistical practices.

7.  "Themba," interview by the author, 2011.

8.  Themba interview.

9.  *Skesanas* are the feminine, receiving partner in a homosexual dyad. *Injongas* are the masculine, insertive partner. Among people who describe themselves as *skesanas* and *injongas*, gender role-playing is strictly enforced. However, there are also *imbube*, who enjoy both roles. According to accounts compiled by McLean and Ngcobo (1994: 167), *injongas* have identified as *imbube* without letting the *skesanas* know about their desire to be fucked and generally present themselves as "hat[ing] the *imbube* life."

10. Themba interview.

11. I've explored the highly ambivalent space regarding the ethics of PrEP, which repurposes HIV antiretroviral treatment as prevention (Fiereck 2015). During the first year of my field research, I focused my ethnographic inquiry at the Cape Town site of a global PrEP clinical trial that had eleven total sites, in six countries on four continents. The arm of the trial I worked within was part of a clinical research organiza-

tion based in Cape Town that partnered with other local and transnational clinical research organizations across the globe to carry out this clinical trial. All sites were enrolling trial participants based on race, ethnicity, and their putative sexual practices. In other words, in Cape Town the trial was sampling primarily Black MSM who may not necessarily identify as gay, although the overwhelming majority did.

## References

Appadurai, Arjun. 2016. "The Wealth of Dividuals." In *Derivatives and the Wealth of Societies*, edited by Benjamin Lee and Randy Martin, 17–36. Chicago: University of Chicago Press.

Austin, John L. 1975. *How to Do Things with Words*. 2nd ed. Oxford: Oxford University Press.

Bakhtin, Mikhail. 1981. *The Dialogic Imagination*, translated by Caryl Emerson. Austin: University of Texas Press.

Berlant, Lauren, and Michael Warner. 1998. "Sex in Public." *Critical Inquiry* 24, no. 2: 547–66.

Biruk, Cal (Crystal). 2019. "The MSM Category as Bureaucratic Technology: Reflections on Paperwork and Project Time in Performance-Based Aid Economies." *Medicine, Anthropology, Theory* 6, no. 4: 187–214. doi.org/10.17157/mat.6.4.695.

Boellstorff, Tom. 2011. "But Do Not Identify as Gay: A Proleptic Genealogy of the MSM Category." *Cultural Anthropology* 26, no. 2: 287–312.

Butler, Judith. 1988. "Performative Acts and Gender Constitution: An Essay in Phenomenology Theory." *Theatre Journal* 40, no. 4: 519–31.

Butler, Judith. 1993. *Bodies That Matter: On the Discursive Limits of Sex*. New York: Routledge.

Butler, Judith. 1999. *Gender Trouble: Feminism and the Subversion of Identity*. New York: Routledge.

Comaroff, John L., and Jean Comaroff. 2009. *Ethnicity Inc.* Chicago: University of Chicago Press.

Dejardins, Jeff. 2017. "All of the World's Money and Markets in One Visualization." *Money Project*, October 26. money.visualcapitalist.com/worlds-money-markets-one-visualization-2017/.

Derrida, Jacques. 1995. "Signature, Event, Context." In *Limited Inc.*, 1–25. Evanston, IL: Northwestern University Press.

Donham, Donald L. 1998. "Freeing South Africa: The "Modernization" of Male-Male Sexuality in Soweto." *Cultural Anthropology* 13, no. 1: 3–21.

Fiereck, Kirk. 2015. "Cultural Conundrums: The Ethics of Epidemiology and the Problems of Population in Implementing Pre-exposure Prophylaxis." *Developing World Bioethics* 15, no. 1: 27–39.

Fiereck, Kirk. 2017. "The Queer Custom of Non-human Personhood." *Queer STS Forum: Queer-Feminist Science and Technology Studies* 2: 39–43.

Fiereck, Kirk. 2018. "Queer Customs, Customarily Queer." *Medicine Anthropology Theory* 5, no. 1. www.medanthrotheory.org/read/10018/queer-customs-customarily-queer.

Fiereck, Kirk. 2020. "Pharmaceutical Derivatives: Sexuality, Race, and Pharmocratic Reason in Global Biomedicine." Unpublished manuscript.

Foucault, Michel. 2008. *The Birth of Biopolitics: Lectures at the College de France, 1978–1979.* New York: Palgrave Macmillan.

Geertz, Clifford. 1983. *Local Knowledge: Further Essays in Interpretive Anthropology.* New York: Basic Books.

Goodman, Jane E., Matt Tomlinson, and Justin B. Richland. 2014. "Citational Practices: Knowledge, Personhood, Subjectivity." *Annual Review of Anthropology* 43: 449–63.

Halberstam, Jack. 2016. "Straight Eye for the Queer Theorist—A Review of *Queer Theory without Antinormativity.*" *Bully Bloggers*, September 12. bullybloggers.wordpress.com/2015/09/12/straight-eye-for-the-queer-theorist-a-review-of-queer-theory-without-antinormativity-by-jack-halberstam/.

Halperin, David M. 2003. "The Normalization of Queer Theory." *Journal of Homosexuality* 45, no. 2–4: 339–43.

Hoad, Neville. 2016. "Queer Customs against the Law." *Research in African Literatures* 47, no. 2: 1–19.

Lane, Tim, H. Fisher Raymond, Sibongile Dladla, Joseph Rasethe, Helen Struthers, W. McFarland, and James McIntyre. 2009. "High HIV Prevalence among Men Who Have Sex with Men in Soweto, South Africa: Results from the Soweto Men's Study." *AIDS and Behavior* 15, no. 3: 626–34.

Levinas, Emmanuel. 1985. *Ethics and Infinity: Conversations with Philippe Nemo.* Pittsburgh, PA: Duquesne University Press.

LiPuma, Edward. 2017. *The Social Life of Financial Derivatives: Markets, Risk, and Time.* Durham, NC: Duke University Press.

Mahmood, Saba. 2005. *The Politics of Piety: The Islamic Revival and the Feminist Subject.* Princeton, NJ: Princeton University Press.

Mamdani, Mahmood. 1996. *Citizen and Subject: Contemporary Africa and the Legacy of Late Colonialism.* Princeton, NJ: Princeton University Press.

Mauss, Marcel 1990. *The Gift: The Form and Reason for Exchange in Archaic Societies.* New York: Norton.

McLean, Hugh, and Linda Ngcobo. 1994. "Abangibhamayo Bathi Ngimanandi (Those Who Fuck Me Say I'm Tasty): Gay Sexuality in Reef Townships." In *Defiant Desire: Gay and Lesbian Lives in South Africa,* edited by Mark Gevisser and Edwin Cameron, 158–85. Braamfontein: Ravan Press.

Morgan, Ruth, Charl Marais, and Joy Rosemary Wellbeloved, eds. 2009. *Trans: Transgender Life Stories from South Africa.* Auckland Park: Jacana.

Morris, Rosalind. 1994. "Three Sexes and Four Sexualities: Redressing the Discourses on Gender and Sexuality in Contemporary Thailand." *Positions* 2, no. 1: 15–43.

Morris, Rosalind. 1995. "All Made Up: Performance Theory and the New Anthropology of Sex and Gender." *Annual Review of Anthropology* 24: 567–92.

Morris, Rosalind. 2007. "Legacies of Derrida: ~~Anthropology~~." *Annual Review of Anthropology* 36: 355–89.

Nkabinde, Nkunzi. 2008. *Black Bull, Ancestors, and Me: My Life as a Lesbian Sangoma*. Johannesburg: Jacana.

Ong, Ahiwa. 1999. *Flexible Citizenship: The Cultural Logics of Transnationality*. Durham, NC: Duke University Press.

Postone, Moishe. 1993. *Time, Labor, and Social Domination*. Cambridge: Cambridge University Press.

Povinelli, Elizabeth A. 2015. "Transgender Creeks and the Three Figures of Power in Late Liberalism." *Differences* 26, no. 1: 168–87.

Reed, Adolph, Jr. 2013. "Marx, Race, and Neoliberalism." *New Labor Forum* 22, no. 1: 49–57.

Reid, Graeme. 2008. "'This Thing' and 'That Idea': Traditionalist Responses to Homosexuality and Same-Sex Marriage." In *To Have and To Hold: The Making of Same-Sex Marriage in South Africa*, edited by Melanie Judge, Anthony Manion, and Shaun de Waal, 73–86. Johannesburg: Jacana Media.

Reid, Graeme. 2013. *How to Be a Real Gay: Gay Identities in Small-Town South Africa*. Scottsville: University of Kwa Zulu-Natal Press.

Strathern, Marilyn. 1988. *The Gender of the Gift: Problems with Women and Problems with Society in Melanesia*. Berkeley: University of California Press.

Turner, Victor. 1974. *Dramas, Fields, and Metaphors*. Ithaca, NY: Cornell University Press.

Valentine, David. 2007. *Imagining Transgender: An Ethnography of a Category*. Durham, NC: Duke University Press.

White, Hylton. 2015. "Custom, Normativity, and Authority in South Africa." *Journal of Southern African Studies* 41, no. 5: 1005–17.

Wilder, Gary. 2015. *Freedom Time: Negritude, Decolonization, and the Future of the World*. Durham, NC: Duke University Press.

# THE FABULOUS PAN-AFRICANISM OF BINYAVANGA WAINAINA

Laura Edmondson

$\mathcal{B}$inyavanga Wainaina's dream wedding spanned the continent. In May 2018 the acclaimed Kenyan author, who made international headlines when he came out through the publication of his essay "I Am a Homosexual, Mum" (Wainaina 2014a), announced his upcoming nuptials on Facebook with characteristic expansiveness (Wainaina 2018a). His post zigzagged around Africa as he explained that he would marry his Nigerian lover in South Africa but would hold a reception in Kenya; in response to the expressions of mock outrage on social media, he promised to throw a party for his Nigerian friends as well (see Wainaina 2018b; Kamau 2018). Once he established the grand scale of his wedding, Wainaina (2018a) allowed himself a single poetic declaration of his devotion: "Nothing has surprised me more than coming to love this person, who is gentle and has the most gorgeous heart." The breadth of Wainaina's joy redefines the economic powerhouses of Nigeria, South Africa, and Kenya as defiantly queer spaces that are stitched together in a pan-African tapestry. Only the continent itself would suffice as a stage.

As readers may know, the wedding did not occur. Wainaina passed away a year later, on May 21, 2019, leaving behind a legacy of theatricality, boldness, and passionate pan-Africanism. In his 2015 TEDx talk, "Conversations with Baba," Wainaina (2015a: 12:46) proclaimed his love for "the oldest and the most diverse continent," which he also called "the moral reservoir of human diversity." He urged his African listeners, "We cannot think of our continent as a hostile place. Too many of us have learned to fear it. And I feel that if you trust it, engage with it and be involved with it in conversations of building, as adventurers, that this continent will start to sing to us again" (2015a: 16:00). For the occasion, he wore

*GLQ* 26:3
DOI 10.1215/10642684-8311843
© 2020 by Duke University Press

Figure 1. Binyavanga Wainaina delivering his TEDx talk, "Conversations with Baba." Courtesy TEDxEuston.

a red tulle skirt carefully chosen to match the red carpet on which he stood, a red tulle handkerchief peeking from his breast pocket, and a dyed strip of hair on his otherwise bald head (see fig. 1). In an analysis of his talk, Lara Abiona (2017) moves easily from describing the vivid colors of his hair and skirt to musing on his affirmation of African strength, noting that "Wainaina's spirit captures where we are going . . . as a continent." With theatrical flourishes, he sought to dismantle trenchant colonial legacies that constrained the forces of creativity and imagination. He performed fabulous with purpose.

In the burgeoning field of queer African studies, theatricality receives short shrift. Instead, anthropological studies of LGBTQ identities and practices in Africa emphasize theoretical frameworks of discretion, elusiveness, and ambiguity (Arnfred 2005: 73–75; Coly 2013: 26; Dankwa 2009, 2013; Epprecht 2004; Gunkel 2010; Hendriks 2016; Marx 2014; O'Mara 2013; Spronk 2018; Tamale 2011: 14). These analyses, which demonstrate keen sensitivity to the quotidian lives of ordinary queer Africans, serve as powerful reminders that nondiscretion and visibility often depend on sustained access to educational, legal, and cultural resources. Celebrities such as Wainaina are bold exceptions to a relatively covert rule. In her discussion of the 2011 Gay Pride Parade in Entebbe, Uganda, Stella Nyanzi (2014: 39) calls for "more queer contestations . . . and multipronged strategies" that account for the continuum of nonheteronormative Ugandan practices that straddle definitions of "overt and covert, short term and long term, inclusive and private, engineered and sporadic, labor intensive and capital intensive, local and border crossing." Even Wainaina's enthusiastic wedding plans resonate with Nyanzi's continuum, as the name of his Nigerian partner was never revealed. The richness of the continent contains multitudes, not all of which can be readily seen or heard.

Wainaina himself contained multitudes. Before coming out in 2014, he experimented with the aesthetic delights of discretion in his first and only play, *Shine Your Eye*. The commissioned play, which features a queer computer hacker in Lagos, was produced at the Volcano Theatre in Toronto in 2010 and 2011, a time of intensifying anti-LGBTQ legislation and rhetoric in Nigeria, Uganda, Malawi, and Senegal.[1] In contrast to the declarative nature of Wainaina's post-2014 sexuality, the play presents a subtle and nuanced articulation of queer and African identity that speaks to Nyanzi's continuum. As queer Kenya becomes increasingly out, loud, and sexy due to a wave of cultural production and legislation,[2] *Shine Your Eye* reminds us that ambiguity can be theatrical too.

I explore Wainaina's play in tandem with his 2014 essay, not to construct a progressive narrative from closeted discretion to theatrical outness but to explore their coarticulation across genres. As explained below, much activist and scholarly ink has been spilled regarding the pitfalls of visibility politics in neoliberal Africa, where the machinations of humanitarian aid heighten the usual threats of commodification and appropriation. Wainaina strategically recuperates the politics of visibility as a creative challenge instead of political quicksand. In *Shine Your Eye*, Wainaina uses Afrofuturist aesthetics to articulate a fabulousness that not only celebrates Africa's creative power but also destabilizes our field of vision. In an overview of queer African studies, Ashley Currier and Thérèse Migraine-George (2016: 294) suggest that the "discursive creativity, nuances, and productive ambiguity" of the aesthetic realm can help "bring us closer" to the multiplicity and specificity of queer African bodies (see also Munro 2012: xix). I suggest that Wainaina's queer aesthetics do not so much bring us closer as they express a spectacular unknowability. Like layers of tulle, the seeming transparency of the central character's sexuality tricks us and becomes opaque. Across genres, Wainaina explores a dialectics of theatricality that pays homage to the profound diversity of the Africa he fiercely loved—the continent with a gorgeous heart.

### Queer Visions

To speak of queer visibility is to encounter cautionary tales regarding commodification, surveillance, and neoliberalism. To be seen, the argument goes, is to court assimilation by the heteronormative, bourgeois, white supremacist regime.[3] These anxieties intensify in the context of postcolonial Africa, where explicit markers of queer identity become vulnerable to charges of catering to an imperialist and neo-colonial "gay international." These anxieties and cautionary tales situate visibility as a singular, hard-and-fast choice that ignores the interdependence and infiltration of the seen and unseen. A brief overview of these theoretical and political thickets clarifies the uniqueness of Wainaina's approach in which visibility politics are recast as creative raw material.

Open declarations of African LGBTQ identities are often perceived as complicit with US and Eurocentric models predicated on a sustained performance of uncloseted queerness. Lyn Ossome (2013: 44), for example, warns against the "dangers of retracting into identity politics at a time when a deepening of social and economic problems on the continent compels strong alliances for social justice." In an ethnographic study of transgender communities in Kampala, Uganda, Olive Minor (2014: 11) launched a stringent critique of Western-derived identity politics, describing them as exclusionary practices that "create divisions among already marginalized and vulnerable minority groups; impose static categories that often do not reflect queer people's lived experiences; limit and exclude those whose identifications do not conform to conventional or stable categories; overlook queers who experience intersecting types of marginalization and violence; and invoke individualist rather than collectivist practices."[4] Minor describes identity politics as cutting a wide, damaging swath through activist strategies and community formations. Both scholars caution that a singular emphasis on LGBTQ identities runs the risk of fostering resentment in the context of endemic economic precarity, structural violence, and autocratic states.

Static identity categories tend to efface the fluidity of African same-sex intimacies, which not only survive but often thrive under the radar of public display. In an influential study on South African queer sexuality, Marc Epprecht (2004: 37) describes sexual minorities in Africa as practicing "cultures of discretion" in which "acts that were forbidden in theory could be tolerated in practice as long as the community was not compelled to pay explicit attention." Minor (2014: 3) expands the discussion with the argument that transgender Ugandans seek a balance in which they are situated "within family and community groups and [embedded] in relations of material exchange," which in turn generates "a model of intersectional queer movement-building that avoids the divisiveness of identity politics."[5] Discretion helps maintain a sense of balance, whereas forthright declarations of sexuality disrupt it. The praxis of balance, silence, and discretion might not serve a radical queer visibility politics that depends on bold articulations of difference, but they remain deeply lived practices for many individuals and communities in Africa. To dismiss such practices as regressive or less "evolved" than the well-defined and public sexual identities associated with the global North is, of course, to perpetuate a Eurocentric lens that equates visibility and loudness with opposition and resistance.[6]

But the flow of foreign aid upsets the balance. The keen and often explicit investment of international aid and human rights organizations in LGBTQ rights has generated widespread rumors that Africans "convert" to homosexuality in exchange for money in a "gay-for-pay" scenario (Currier 2012; Biruk 2014; see also Biruk and Trapence 2018). The specter of Western aid feeds into understandings of same-sex desire and practices as un-African and thus erodes the legitimacy of same-sex desire and the courage of these individuals in articulating that desire. Moreover, the withholding of Western aid to "punish" African states for anti-LGBTQ legislation and practices has only intensified expressions of intolerance and bigotry on the ground (see, e.g., Gunkel 2013). The singling out of LGBTQ issues on the part of Western activists and politicians unwittingly contributes to the spread of what Jasbir Puar (2007) has famously termed *homonationalism*, in which queer minorities are deemed worthy of intervention and aid but those suffering from other forms of injustice are ignored. Although Puar (2013: 337) herself cautions against conflating identity politics and homonationalism, they work in tandem to efface and negate the survival strategies of subtlety, nuance, and ambiguity.

In an excellent ethnographic study of LGBTQ activism in southern Africa, Currier (2012) shifts focus. She moves beyond a critique of Western meddling and instead considers the strategic acts of African LGBTQ associations as they navigate a fraught humanitarian landscape. Instead of "positing visibility and invisibility as polar opposites," Currier treats both concepts "as complementary and simultaneously coexistent" (10). Similar to Nyanzi's continuum that embraces forthright and furtive articulations of queer sexuality, she presents a continuum from "intentional visibility" to "intentional invisibility" to theorize how these organizations cope with the charged political stakes of LGBTQ activism in Africa. Instead of associating invisibility with political failure and visibility with success, she treats both as fluid and dynamic strategies.

Currier's ideas resonate with the field of performance and visual studies, which has long grappled with the oscillation of seen and unseen. In the classic text *Unmarked*, Peggy Phelan (1993: 26) exposes the paucity of representational politics that equate visibility with recognition and rights, writing that "visibility and invisibility are crucially bound; invisibility polices visibility and . . . functions as the ascendant term in the binary." What is visible in representation is haunted and ultimately defined by that which lies beyond the gaze. Nicole R. Fleetwood (2011: 96) expands Phelan's ideas through the lens of critical race theory, arguing that black female subjecthood in the visual field is "bound by polarities of hypervisibility/ invisibility," due to its troubling state of being "simultaneously invisible and always visible, as underexposed and always exposed" (111). Fleetwood clarifies how invisibility as a subject and hypervisibility as a victim are inextricably fused in the context of black womanhood. In a fascinating study of South African queer performance, April Sizemore-Barber (forthcoming) takes Fleetwood's ideas a step further, using the term *hyper(in)visibility* to describe "the impossible representational paradox" in which African queer subjects are "simultaneously invisible and hyper-exposed," insofar as repeated denial of their very existence works in tandem with sensational media coverage. Fleetwood and Sizemore-Barber present various artistic and cultural strategies for negotiating these tensions and paradoxes, such as the performativity of excess flesh (Fleetwood) or through exposing the scopic regime (Sizemore-Barber). Wainaina's play *Shine Your Eye* takes a different tack: it theatricalizes the secrecy of same-sex desire so that its ambiguity becomes a pervasive, omnipresent force.[7] In the charged, hyperaware art form of theater, discretion itself can be made excessive.

## Neocolonial Looks

*Shine Your Eye*, Wainaina's first and only play, was written on request. In 2007, Ross Manson, the artistic director of the Volcano Theatre Company in Toronto, commissioned it as part of the Africa Trilogy, a project that was meant to explore the relationship between Africa and the West through the medium of theater. This ambitious project, which received an estimated $1 million in funding from private donations, as well as the sponsoring Luminato festival, culminated in three plays: *GLO* by Christina Anderson (US), *Peggy Pickit Sees the Face of God* by the German playwright Roland Schimmelpfennig (2014), and Wainaina's *Shine Your Eye*.[8] Borrowing from Chimamanda Adichie's (2009) influential TED talk, the trilogy was conceived as an intervention in the stereotypical narrative of Africa as a "single story" of catastrophe. Wainaina himself had come to worldwide attention for his blistering satire of Western stereotypes in Africa in his 2005 essay, "How to Write about Africa." By the time the Africa Trilogy premiered, the single story of disaster was narrowing into a relentless tale of African homophobia (Macharia 2010). The Western media used the scapegoating of LGBTQ individuals and communities in countries such as Nigeria and Uganda to strengthen the colonialist framing of Africa as uncivilized, atavistic, and antimodern (Coly 2013; Nyong'o 2012).

As the only play in the trilogy contributed by an African writer, *Shine Your Eye* serves as an especially poignant intervention in this singular narrative. In a sense, the play might be understood as Wainaina's nuanced response to how one *should* write about Africa—as a continent at the nexus of globalization. The play focuses on Gbene Beka, a brilliant young computer hacker seeking to escape from the demands of her father's activist legacy by building a new life in Lagos, Nigeria. Although Beka's flirtatious relationship with her Skype friend Doreen, an out lesbian based in Toronto, gestures pointedly to same-sex desire, the play folds this subplot into a multifaceted tale of human rights, structural adjustment, and post-Cold War politics. Wainaina's refusal to invoke the "homophobic Africa" narrative clears fresh creative space for imagining a world in which queerness is integrated into a textured understanding of Africanity. The title of the play, which refers to a popular Nigerian phrase that means to "look sharp" and "be aware," asks readers and spectators to shine their own eyes and wake up to a richly diverse and transnational Africa.

Gbene Beka, who goes simply by Beka, cultivates a careful stance of ambiguity that facilitates both discretion and balance. Her balancing among various identity formations means that her sexuality occasionally recedes into the background as she seeks a twenty-first-century path that is global, queer, and pan-African. Her journey thus exemplifies Puar's (2007: 205) notion of "queerness as an assemblage," which "moves away from excavation work, deprivileges a binary opposition between queer and not-queer subjects, and . . . underscores contingency and complicity with dominant formations." Although a Western shadow is cast over the play due to its genesis, funding, and production context, Wainaina's collaboration with Kenyan-Canadian actors and Kenyan-US artist Wangechi Mutu helps ensure an African-inflected portrayal of an extraordinary young woman who defies postcolonial clichés.[9] In this section, I focus on two characters, Tambari and Doreen, who respectively signify the landmines of neocoloniality and humanitarianism as Beka seeks an Africanity that is simultaneously theatrical and mysteriously elusive.

Before delving into the complications of a neoliberal present and a hazy Afrofuture, the play confronts the brutality of Nigeria's neocolonial past. The play opens in darkness, during which the audience hears the BBC World Service announce the murder of a prominent Ogoni activist, "the brightest voice" of the anti-oil movement, adding that the Royal Dutch Shell oil company denies involvement (Wainaina 2011b: 1). The radio then plays a passage of the murdered activist's speeches, which articulates a clear-cut stance of socialist resistance: "People of Nigeria, We must clothe our youth with the armour of revolution. We must nationalize our oil! And we must be prepared to die—for the sake of our children!" (1). Although the victim is not named, this opening immediately invokes the image of Ken Saro-Wiwa, the famous Nigerian activist and writer who worked tirelessly to bring compensation to the Ogoni people, who suffered harsh economic and political marginalization despite the rich oil reserves of their homeland in the Niger Delta region. In an echo of the BBC speech, Saro-Wiwa did indeed die for the sake of his children when he was executed by the Sani Abacha regime in 1995 in its failed attempt to silence a regional struggle for environmental and economic justice.[10] The opening of *Shine Your Eye* vividly invokes the legacy of one of the most famous human rights icons of the continent and thus ensures that the ideological ghosts of the neocolonial and authoritarian 1980s and 1990s loom over the rest of the play.

Beka steps forward to claim this Saro-Wiwa–like figure as her father. In contrast to the soaring rhetoric of her father's speech that invokes the glory of resistance, Beka's opening address to the audience consists of a plaintive description of entrapment: "Every day, for years. They came to my home. Delegations I had to cook for, visitors to my father's museum. Oh. Are you the dota of? The late great man. The speech-maker. The hero. All day. Every day. 'Stay inside Beka. You know the police are watching Beka. Do not use the telephone Beka.' Mama padlocks the landline" (Wainaina 2011b: 2). Beka is trapped by her hypervisibility as the "dota" that makes her vulnerable to the state's surveillance system. As she later explains to the audience, her father possessed secret documents leaked by Ogoni employees of Human Rights Watch (26); his possession of these documents triggered a police raid, his capture, and his death. Instead of Saro-Wiwa's execution by hanging, her father endured sustained torture and a prolonged death, as the play reminds us no less than three times through statements such as the following: "There were cuts all over her father's body. He was naked. One eye was missing. The coroner said it took him two days to die" (27; see also 1, 28). The lingering, painful, and visceral manner of her father's death clarifies the extent of his sacrifice: he not only died for the sake of all Ogoni children, but he died slowly, in great pain. The play's reiteration of his graphic fate clarifies that Beka's search for anonymity is motivated by genuine fear.

To find anonymity, Beka flees from her home village to the chaotic and bustling megacity of Lagos. Her father's friend Tambari hires Beka as an employee for his business, Pineapple Telekom International, an internet scam operation that generates mass emails that request the recipient to help with outlandish banking procedures in exchange for a cut of the proceeds—a practice commonly called Nigerian 419 scams after the section of Nigeria's penal code that criminalizes the practice. The energy and cheerfulness of her coworkers suggest that Beka has successfully escaped the confinement of the village. Her mother's padlocks are forgotten in the midst of her newfound freedom of unfettered access to cyberspace. Instead of foreboding news announcements of gruesome deaths, her colleagues banter and joke, and she delights in a self-built computer system with "wires snaking all over the place" (Wainaina 2011b: 6) like tentacles. When she helps Naijaboy, one of Tambari's employees, compose a 419 scam in which a Nigerian astronaut— "the first African in space"—is deserted on a secret space station upon the breakup of the Soviet Union for nineteen years and accumulates back pay of $15 million,[11] he and his coworkers burst into a rap that lights up the stage with spectacular media. Lagos whirls with lights, energy, and freedom.

The youth and energy of her coworkers stand in sharp contrast to the yearnings of their boss, Tambari. As a friend of her father, Tambari shares vivid memories of the Ogoni struggle: "They picked up half the men in my village that week. My family lost four" (Wainaina 2011b: 28). Even though he seeks to straddle the neocolonial past and the neoliberal present, describing himself as "structurally adjusted; military rulered. . . . Shoulder's sharp like an oil drill bit; hungry like the Dow Jones" (4), Tambari yearns to return to the "unfinished revolution" (Obi and Oriola 2018). He valiantly attempts to justify the scamming operation as his way of keeping the struggle alive: "Nigeria's 419 sector made 4.3 billion last year—but that is only a fraction of what all the foreign oil companies take from Niger Delta every three months. Is *that* a scam? It is ALL a scam. But we, *us*—are bringing our stolen money back" (Wainaina 2011b: 15). Beka's response is to scoff at his defense of the scamming operation as a means of generating reparations for the Niger Delta: "This is the best you can do? Jiggy Jiggy Stupid letters. Oh, White man—I go chop your dollar?" (30). Beka's critique reminds us that Tambari ultimately drifts in a neoliberal world of soft power and humanitarian pity. Even the emails that his company generates depend on Western stereotypes of Nigerian corruption and archaic traditions in order to trick Western recipients out of their money. "They must pay us for being the goat," he insists (17), still caught up in performing animalistic imagery of Africans despite the trappings of hard drives and fast internet service.[12]

In contrast, Beka celebrates her escape. As the icing on the cake of urban

Figure 2. Beka (Dienye Waboso) on Skype with Doreen (Karen Robinson) in *Shine Your Eye*. Photo by John Lauener. Courtesy Volcano Theatre.

freedom, she openly flirts with Doreen in Canada, a former Marxist radical turned investment banker whose lesbian sexuality is out, public, and distinctly Western. They communicate through Skype whenever Beka is alone in the Telekom office (see fig. 2). In the Toronto production, a live-feed projection of Doreen loomed on the projection screen that served as a backdrop for the stage. Doreen's sexual identity is made explicit almost immediately during the play's first Skype conversation between Beka and Doreen. When Beka comments that she had attended church that day, Doreen responds abruptly: "Well, you know, I haven't been to church since I came out to my parents" (Wainaina 2011b: 12). The play later reveals that Doreen is smitten with Beka. In contrast to her usual projected image, Doreen appears on stage when she confides her crush on Beka to the audience: "I am an intelligent, practical, self-sufficient, down to earth forty-one year old. . . . I like trashy paranormal romance books, which I buy online and read in the bathroom, and now I am in love with some kid *in Nigeria* who says she isn't gay!!! I mean, COME ON!!" (27). This corporeal moment, in which Doreen appears "live" rather than screened, further emphasizes the facticity of her desire and her sexuality. Although the stage directions state that Doreen is black (a specification that the Volcano Theatre Company followed with the casting of Karen Robinson), her racial identity is not referenced in any of her monologues or Skype conversations with Beka. Her sexuality supersedes her blackness.

In contrast to Doreen with her emphatic lesbianism, Beka follows the contours of discretion through an evasive and ambiguous approach. Beka might not exactly *say* that she's gay, but her conversations with Doreen speak to a non-heteronormative stance. When Doreen mentions coming out to her parents, the following exchange occurs:

*Beka*: What did your parents say when you came out?

*Doreen*: You have no idea. Shiit. My Dad didn't talk to me for years. He isn't the only one.

*Beka*: I think my father could have been ok with it. But my mother? Eh! I could never tell my mother!

*Doreen*: I thought you said you were not gay?

*Beka*: If I were I mean. (Wainaina 2011b: 12)

At this point, Beka openly flirts with Doreen: "I like it when you smile like that" (12). In the Toronto production, these textual cues were expanded through the actors' performances; as Beka, actress Dienye Waboso smiled upon the appearance of Doreen, lighting up the stage. But aside from her obvious delight in their Skype conversations and various flirtatious comments, Beka stops short of declaring her sexuality. In keeping with the customary practice of discretion and balance, she walks an ambiguous line; it is noteworthy that these Skype conversations occur only when she is alone in the Telekom office, allowing her coworkers and Tambari to ignore the lesbian desire that blossoms throughout the play. Through her resourcefulness, Beka evades the Western model of visibility that Doreen presents.

Increasingly, however, her sense of freedom erodes. The legacy of her father cannot be easily escaped, as signified by the growing hold that Tambari exerts over Beka. He conceives of an ambitious plan to work toward the creation of an oil distillery for the Ogoni people:

*Tambari*: I have booked us on the first flight tomorrow, to a meeting in Abuja, with the Minister of Petroleum Resources, in the office of the special advisor to the president. They will say yes *to you*, because of your father, because you were trained for this.

*Beka*: What is *this*?

*Tambari*: To lead us. To give us our own refinery.

*Beka*: A refinery. Our own refinery? An Ogoni refinery?

*Tambari*: There are many people working for this. Your father died for this. It is close; it is possible for us to control our own oil. Gbene Beka, will you turn away from us? (Wainaina 2011b: 30)

Tambari's plan is to reject the colonial and neocolonial machinery in which Africa serves as a source of raw material that is processed in the West and then sold back to the colonies as a captive market; to this day, even though Nigeria is the top exporter of crude oil on the continent, Nigerians frequently experience gas shortages partly because the country's dependence on overseas refineries.[13] Faced with the intransigence of colonialist tropes, Tambari gives up his strategic and insidious revolution and instead seeks a more conventional route to power that involves ownership. He scorns the world of soft capital and seeks to lay claim to the means of hard production with a plan that is seemingly bold but also startlingly naive. Beka had previously denounced those who were complicit in the oil industry as machines "humping up and down, eyes popping, cheeks hollowed, mouth sucking in all the crude fumes of the Niger delta" (10). Despite his radical intent, Tambari runs the risk of becoming another mindless, voracious machine that perpetuates the Delta's environmental destruction.[14]

The success of Tambari's plan also depends on Beka, who must capitulate to the weight of her father's legacy and carry on the revolution. He heatedly reminds her of what she owes to her people, scoffing at the computer games that she passionately designs and codes: "All the time you are playing cartoon games on your father's grave. We are real people. We bleed. The coins of our people paid for your father's funeral, your mother's debts, your school. They came, thousands to your home. Shine your eye, Princess. You did not make yourself" (Wainaina 2011b: 30). She might have fled from the village but she cannot escape the shadow of her father's martyrdom. "Your father died for this," he reminds her. They do not speak of the ominous price that Beka might pay in return.

Her relationship with Doreen also turns sour. Doreen might define herself as a political radical who "forced [her] way into their space" thanks to an infusion of feminist, green, union, and Third World clean money (Wainaina 2011b: 22), but her desire increasingly assumes a patronizing form. She imagines Beka as "so innocent, so burdened" even though Beka, building a new life in Lagos, is much savvier about the workings of global geopolitics than is Doreen, comfortably sheltered in Toronto. "I worry about you in Lagos, all alone," she tells Beka through Skype (14). Doreen clearly perceives herself as a radical figure; still, her politics does not prevent her from catering to predictable tropes and tired scripts that cast Beka in the role of the naive, innocent African, unwise to the complexities of a cosmopolitan world. As the play continues, Doreen becomes even more condescending. As Beka reels in confusion over Tambari's demand that she uphold her father's legacy, Doreen presents her with another stark choice. Over Skype, she announces that she has met with an immigration lawyer to arrange for a Canadian visa for Beka. "I'm wiring the money today. Beka—I've been around, I know when somebody has some—magic. You can blow this place wide open" (31). In a breathtaking act of imperial arrogance, Doreen assumes that Beka will leap at the opportunity and succumb to the siren call of the West. She eagerly inhabits the role of what Tavia Nyong'o (2012: 51) calls "the humanitarian angel swooping in to rescue the endangered and helpless African queer." To desire Beka is to save her.

Both Doreen and Tambari harbor nostalgia for timeworn narratives that eventually overwhelm their commitment to revolutionary politics and the counterappropriation of space. As such, they present Beka with a clichéd postcolonial conundrum: to escape to the West or to fulfill her father's legacy at home. Caught between the humanitarianism of the West and the necropolitics of the state, she is threatened with scripts of victimage on either side. In response, Beka takes a defiantly queer path by rejecting the human altogether. Her long act of discretion builds to a theatrical climax in which Beka writes a new code of African queerness.

## Afrofuturist Spectacle

Beka's computer serves as the gateway to a posthuman world. In addition to Skyping with Doreen and helping Naijaboy with his scam letter about the Nigerian astronaut, she devotes herself to designing and coding a computer game called *Shine Shine in the Feral City*. The game consists of a struggle between a lone avatar, Shine Shine Stern Fabulous, and creatures called Ferals. Shine Shine herself is vaguely defined; as Beka explains to a bemused Naijaboy, the Ferals attacked Shine Shine's lab, indicating that she is some kind of scientist. Beka also describes her as a "composite—made of materials that can self-repair—not sure yet" (Wainaina 2011b: 18). The Ferals are even more ambiguous; Beka says only that Shine Shine hates them "because they are not true believers" (18). Strikingly, she then describes Shine Shine as "original Delta where all the Sentients come from" (18). This reference to the Ogoni people suggests that Shine Shine was conceived as a homage to her father, himself a kind of superhero. As an enlightened Sentient, Shine Shine could be understood as fighting for the cause of democracy and human rights—an ideal in which the Ferals do not believe. Perhaps the Ferals are intent on forcing Shine Shine to conform to the stereotype of primitive and mendacious Africa (Mbembe 2001: 242)—to make her "feral" like them.

But Shine Shine proves too evasive to be easily categorized. In a telling moment, Beka also identifies her with Doreen. The play's first reference to Shine Shine occurs during one of their many flirtatious moments, when Beka says dreamily, "It's like you are hovering out there in space, a superhero—like Shine Shine!" Doreen teasingly responds, "So I'm your dream superhero, eh?," to which Beka answers coyly, "Maybe" (Wainaina 2011b: 12). Beka is still caught in a limited understanding of Shine Shine, whom she casts in the role of either the human rights activist (her father) or the humanitarian hero (Doreen). Even though an avatar has the potential of "highlighting (and stretching) the subordinate roles available to black women" (McMillan 2015: 12; see also González 2000), Beka deflects the idea of superhero status onto these looming figures in her past and present. At this point in the play, her conception of a superhero is too narrow to include her Nigerian female self.

Shine Shine is also framed as queer. In keeping with the codes of discretion, Shine Shine does not articulate her wants but instead looks out of the screen with a come-hither gaze that positions Beka as the object of her desire. Beka responds with sheer delight: "Oh my god! U DEY MAKE MY HEAD SCATTER!," she exclaims upon seeing Shine Shine's image.[15] Little wonder that Naijaboy responds to this figure with such unease, calling it "demonic" and asking, rather abruptly: "Sistah you are plugged in—but with all these hacker friends all over the world, you mean to say—(*he smiles*) you don't have a boyfriend?" (Wainaina 2011b: 18). As if in response to his strained attempt to cast Beka in a heteronormative role, we hear the sound of the Skype ring tone that signifies Doreen's incoming call. The screen's close-up of Shine Shine's erotic gaze is replaced with Doreen's warm smile, underscoring how the two virtual women oscillate as focal points of Beka's desire.

Shine Shine's power is clarified through the lens of Afrofuturism, an aesthetic that calls on the tropes of science fiction to imagine a future infused with black identity and experience.[16] As explained in the stage directions, Wainaina based his concept of Shine Shine on the fantastic visions of womanhood that appear in the works of the acclaimed Kenyan-US visual artist Wangechi Mutu.[17] Mutu assembles her works through a collage technique that culls together images from pornography, fashion magazines, medical treatises, and *National Geographic*. The "alternately alluring and disconcerting" female figures that emerge from this process (Veal 2008: 9–10) have been described as "glamorous hybrid monsters, empowered by the strategy of transformation and adaptation—presenting an alternative existence free from biological determinism and psychological conditioning" (Edblom 2010: 8). For the Toronto production, Mutu contributed a design for Shine Shine's image that integrates her composite nature and warrior strength. When Beka showed Naijaboy the designs for Shine Shine on her computer, the projection screen displayed an image from Mutu's 2002 ink-and-collage work *Riding Death in My Sleep* (see fig. 3). The central figure in the work, a crouched, voluptuous,

Figure 3. Wangechi Mutu, *Riding Death in My Sleep*, 2002. Ink and collage on paper. 60 × 44 in. Courtesy of the artist and Peter Norton Collection.

powerful figure with a leopard-patterned body and stark white bald head with cross-racial features, has been uprooted from the original painting and thrown into exile in the Feral city. Her explosive hybridity cuts across races and species, promising as yet untapped resources of resilience and strength. The unbelieving Ferals have met their glamorous, monstrous match.

Critics frequently invoke Afrofuturist tropes to describe Mutu's powerful figures. Rachel Wolff (2013), for example, describes Mutu's women as "shape-shifting cyborgs" and the works themselves as "luminescent tableaux of alien worlds" (see also Samatar 2017; Tate 2013). Shine Shine's animalistic features—the leopard-print skin, the insect growing out of her shoulder—are yoked inextricably with alien-like, posthuman characteristics. The mysterious Ferals might have destroyed Shine Shine's lab in an attempt to deny her access to the world of scientific knowledge and consign her to a primitive sphere, but Shine Shine, as a mutant of the racial imagination, is herself an emblem of technological interventions and thus cannot be contained. In a sense, Shine Shine's fleshiness performs a kind of fugitive assemblage as described by Alexander G. Weheliye (2014: 51–52), who draws on the pioneering work of Hortense Spillers and Sylvia Wynters to theorize "a surplus . . . that evades capture, that refuses rest, that testifies to the impossibility of its own existence," which intervenes in and/or supplements racializing assemblages that consign black womanhood to nonhuman status. In a similar vein, Naijaboy's anxious reference to Shine Shine as "demonic" calls to mind Wynter's (1990: 366) famous concept of "demonic ground" as a terrain of "a new science of human discourse, of human life beyond the 'master discourse'" (see also Weheliye 2014: 21–22). In *Shine Your Eye*, Mutu's image of fleshly, demonic surplus holds the tantalizing promise of posthuman transcendence.[18]

This transcendence is animated by African materialities. Shine Shine came into being during Beka's childhood: "When I was small, I used to beg Papa to leave the paraffin lamp on at night. *Put on the ShineShine, Papa.* I'd watch the shadows catfight on the wall" (Wainaina 2011b: 35). Paraffin lamps are ubiquitous as a light source throughout Africa; here, though, instead of signifying so-called Third World poverty, they serve as a source of comfort and creativity. Beka's ShineShine lamp helps her to escape from the domestic strife between her parents caused by her father's environmental activism: "I hear them fighting all the time now. Late late in the night. She shouts at him. I feel around for matches, light the paraffin lamp on my bedside table, it stutters, and crackles. Shadows swell and start to whisper" (26). The materiality of the paraffin lamp and the ephemeral world of dreams coalesce to give rise to Beka's shadowy superhero.

The forces of imagination are fully unleashed in the play's resolution. Tambari and Doreen hint at the extent of Beka's metamorphosis in an address to the audience:

*Doreen*: So. She disappears. I don't know if she's dead. I don't know if they arrested her. Western union says she never picked up the money I sent, so they're returning it. I mean, what the fuck?

*Tambari*: And then I'm sitting at my computer and the screen is suddenly covered with this crazy electricity. Then a face.

*Doreen*: A face.

*Tambari*: Not like any face I've ever seen.

*Doreen*: Luminous, twisted . . . familiar, but then, not. The lips swelled, and sent a big smacking lipstick kiss, and then the animation vanished.

*Beat*

*Both*: Gone. (Wainaina 2011b: 33)

In the end, Beka does not simply imagine herself in the role of the brave superhero cyborg; she *becomes* Shine Shine and disappears into a virtual world, "the whole wide swoosh of the world" (Wainaina 2011b: 35). The fusion of Shine Shine and Beka collapses the boundaries of self and avatar and thus stretches their mutual subjectivity across time and space:

> I open the lid to my brain. Grey matter steams and spits. It's all naked wires and conflicting numbers. I open the lid to my heart. I watch those I love curl away from my face and vanish like smoke. We are real people we bleed. But if it doesn't cost me I will never know what world I am in. Each nerve, each artery I redirect. Skin and fat and marrow catch flame. Skull-bone gives way. I make my own world. Shine Shine, Sternfabulous. (34)

On the projection screen behind Beka, Shine Shine has transformed into an animated, unmistakably female being; her leopard-patterned skin has morphed into black skin dappled with light (see fig. 4).[19] She shines as a luminous, otherworldly creature, one that opens the lid to the world itself. To shine is to be bold and visible, but to shine your eye is to be aware. Shine Shine fuses both meanings in a critical theatricality that accentuates what is unsaid and unseen. Judith Butler (2018: 3) reminds us that *fabulous*, from the Latin *fabula*, which came to mean

Figure 4. Shine Shine comes to "life."
Photo by John Lauener. Courtesy
Volcano Theatre.

"astonishing or exaggerated" in Middle English, originally meant characteristic of fables or myths; she suggests that the fabulous could "indicate a form of knowledge about matters that might be graspable only through fabulous forms." This lens suggests that the extraordinary theatricality of Shine Shine Stern-Fabulous is meant not only to astonish but also to create a "distance from the regime of truth" (3) and thus capacitate unknowability. Shine Shine blows a kiss to Beka, and a paranormal romance bursts forth on the stage. One's head scatters in response.

Characteristically, Wainaina situates these otherworldly specters on firmly African terrain. Gbene Beka's namesake is none other than the Great Mother goddess of the Ogoni people. Instead of perpetuating a romanticized notion of maternal divinity that circumscribes female power even as it purports to celebrate it, Wainaina's play offers up a reinvention of the Great Mother who gives birth to a queer cyborg, and Beka and Shine Shine are promptly swept up in a homoerotic tangle of desire. Wainaina's merging of Ogoni goddess and queer cyborg situates an Afrofuture in the context of the divine. Donna Haraway (1985) famously ends her classic "Manifesto for Cyborgs" with the declaration that she would rather be a cyborg than a goddess, thus affirming an opposition between the benign earth goddess of cultural feminism and the infidel cyborg of cyberfeminism. In Puar's (2012: 63) tongue-in-cheek reinterpretation of Haraway's essay, she muses:

Would I really rather be a cyborg than a goddess? The former hails the future in a teleological technological determinism—culture—that seems not only overdetermined, but also exceptionalizes our current technologies. The latter—nature—is embedded in the racialized matriarchal mythos of feminist reclamation narratives. Certainly it sounds sexier, these days, to lay claim to being a cyborg than a goddess. But why disaggregate the two when there surely must be cyborgian goddesses in our midst? Now that is a becoming-intersectional assemblage that I could really appreciate.

Puar might appreciate the becoming-intersectional assemblage that dominates the final moments of *Shine Your Eye*. Thinking of Shine Shine/Beka as a cyborgian goddess not only clarifies their refusal of disciplinary subjecthood and identitarian politics (as cyborg) but also lends them a touch of homegrown transcendence (as goddess). Beka's final line in the play—"The moment is coming"—is the cue for Shine Shine's appearance (Wainaina 2011b: 35).[20] She looms over Beka on the projection screen at the back of the stage. The Afrofuturist moment is coming, and it promises to be fabulous.

It also refuses to be captured and commodified. According to West African folklore, the goddess Gbene Beka is tantalizingly elusive: "Gbene Beka came from the sky. Just as you know when the wind blows yet cannot see it, so Gbene Beka is like that. She was a woman, when you tried to touch her she vanished" (Jeffreys 1970: 112). Beka's divine namesake prompts me to recast the "queer customary" of discretion as *elusiveness*, a term that connotes subversiveness rather than hiding, ambiguity rather than invisibility. In this light, her evasion of a declarative queer identity conveys an otherworldly power. It suggests, rather than an act of obeisance to social norms, a furtive revolution beyond the registers of the visible.[21]

In the midst of these utopic imaginings of a queer African future, though, Wainaina inserts a warning. The cyberspace world is hardly hospitable. In *Riding Death in My Sleep*, Mutu's animal/alien female perches on top of a mushroom-dotted world with an assortment of creatures (an eagle's head, an elephant with wings) as her companions. In Beka's game design, the ferocious figure has been deterritorialized from this richly imagined planet and consigned to a dreary, bullet-riddled tunnel.[22] Even the animal companions have been excised, meaning that Shine Shine fights the Ferals alone. In becoming Shine Shine and vanishing into cyberspace, Beka similarly assumes a life of isolation. Even though she rejects the path of her father's martyrdom that ends in a grisly death, she becomes a new kind of martyr to an Afrofuturist nation: "I watch those I love curl away from my face and vanish like smoke" (Wainaina 2011b: 34). The ending calls to mind Haraway's (1985: 67) apocalyptic image of the cyborg as the "ultimate self untied at last from all dependency, a man in space." Like Naijaboy's astronaut marooned on the post-Soviet space station, Beka becomes detached from the overlapping coalitions and connections that spiral across Africa and the global South. Perhaps the depth of her sacrifice is why she does not blow a kiss to Shine Shine in return.

Tambari's question haunts the end of the play: "Will you turn away from us?" (Wainaina 2011b: 30). In her flight to cyberspace, is Beka leaving behind the revolution, or is she turning to a new kind of politics "beyond and beneath the regime of the law" (Hoad 2016b: 16) as a posthuman fugitive? In contrast to Doreen and Tambari, who follow tried-and-true left-wing paths, is she blazing a new path of queer African humanity that eludes attempts to make it knowable? She rejects the world of the visible, the commodifiable, the colonized, and the victim in return for a postapocalyptic world in which the future remains an open question, a kind of ellipsis. Beka thus follows the example of her goddess namesake who vanishes when one tries to touch her. Returning to the image of Shine Shine trapped in a rubble-filled cell, I speculate that she is not so much incarcerated as secluded. She bides her time.

## Pan-African Dreams

In contrast to the elusive Beka, Wainaina embraced certainty and boldness. Not only did he publicly declare his sexual identity through his essay "I Am a Homosexual, Mum" (Wainaina 2014a), but even the title itself adheres to classic coming-out narratives through his emphasis on the act of self-naming. In the essay itself, Wainaina states emphatically that "I, Binyavanga Wainaina, quite honestly swear I have known I am a homosexual since I was five." After the publication of the essay, Wainaina (2014b) tweeted yet another definitive pronouncement: "I am, for anybody confused or in doubt, a homsexual [sic]. Gay, and quite happy." His declarations insistently refute an academic emphasis on the discretion, silence, and ambiguity of African queer practices and desires. In this section, I shift focus from Wainaina's playwriting to his practices of the self to show how, like Shine Shine, his theatricality opens up African technologies of queerness.

Despite his seeming candor, Wainaina shared Beka's refusal to conform to a neocolonial, knowable world. The seeming forthrightness of the title of his coming-out essay is belied by the fierce antilinearity of the actual content. Wainaina (2014a) slips back and forth between what "is not the right version of events," in which he shares his secret with his mother just before she passes away in Nairobi in 2000, and "the right version of events," in which he is in South Africa at the time of her death and thus unable to whisper his secret into her ear—an act that is figured as deeply intimate rather than as declarative. In the course of the relatively brief essay, he spirals between the ages of five, seven, twenty-nine, and forty-three in what Neville Hoad (2016a: 186) describes as "a series of dizzying temporal shifts." At the age of seven, for example, Wainaina (2014a) experiences a transformative sexual awakening: "I am shaking because he shook my hand. Then I am crying alone in the toilet because the repeat of this feeling has made me suddenly ripped apart and lonely. The feeling is not sexual. It is certain. It is overwhelming. It wants to make a home." He then shifts rapidly to memories of his father's death in 2011: "His heart beat for four days, but there was nothing to tell him." Repeatedly, the essay pulses with capacious love for his parents and profound sorrow at their absence: "I love my dad so much, my heart is learning to stretch." Wainaina's sexual politics are cloaked in familial love and yearning; even the title itself yokes his declarative act to his mother—he speaks specifically to her rather than to the world. He articulates a queer identity that gestures to Minor's (2014: 11) notion of balance, a "practice of queer self-making in the balance of interdependent relationships." Instead of a linear, declarative statement, Wainaina's coming out was poetic, interdependent, and gorgeous.

Wainaina also "came out" as a pan-Africanist. In 2012, he famously made a speech at the African Studies Association UK conference in Leeds, "I Am a Pan-Africanist, Not an Afropolitan," in which he critiqued *Afropolitanism*, a term increasingly celebrated as a hip version of transnational Africanity defined by "routes through Africa (be they physical or ideological), more so than roots" (Abebe 2015).[23] Wainaina denounced Afropolitanism as a marketing strategy for a global African elite rather than a political platform for continental transformation. Although Wainaina is hardly alone in his critique of Afropolitanism and its "rapacious consumerism" (Dabiri 2014; see also Santana 2013), what interests me here is his embrace of *pan-Africanism* in opposition to Afropolitanism—that is, as a politics and aesthetics of continental unity (Jamison 2003, xii; Muchie 2003: 3).[24] He sought to reclaim the term from the dustiness of nation-statism and the provincialism of area studies, showcasing its decolonizing and coalitional potential. "I belong to the continent," he told the *Guardian* (Howden 2014), a statement in which pan-African roots and Afropolitan routes coalesce.

Upon the publication of "I Am a Homosexual, Mum," Wainaina fused queerness and anticolonialism as a pan-African source of strength. Three days after the essay appeared, he published a six-part video series on YouTube aimed at his fellow Africans called *We Must Free Our Imaginations* (Wainaina 2014d). Throughout the videos, which were folded into his "multimedia coming out" (Kulish 2014), he unleashes a torrent of ideas in which the act of coming out recedes in the midst of his sharp critiques of the church, neocolonial education, and the narrowing of African minds. He argues that the "syllabus," which serves as a kind of metaphor for the rigidity of a neocolonial educational system, manufactures submissive subjects rather than free-thinking selves. Wainaina frames the concept of coming out as an anticolonial act of resistance that could liberate the imaginative capacity of all Africans. He sent forth his missives from Nairobi, where he relocated in 2013 after several years teaching in the United States. Instead of retreating to a self-imposed exile in the West, he enacted his personal revolution in an economic and political epicenter of Africa and the global South.

Wainaina stretched and redefined the concept of balance. In an audaciously utopic act, Wainaina's interdependent relations expanded from his local community and family to include the entire continent. This creative expansion built on the work of his activist precursors, such as those who gathered in Nairobi in 2010 to write the LGBTI Manifesto/Declaration, a document that erases the boundaries between queer and African rights: "As Africans, we all have infinite potential. We stand for an African revolution which encompasses the demand for a re-imagination of our lives outside neo-colonial categories of identity and power."[25] Wainaina (2014d, pt. 1, 3:55) echoes the manifesto's rhetoric when he reminds viewers in his video series that "it's not so much that gays and lesbians . . . are dying, it's that *people* are dying in exactly the same boundary that the *mzungu* [European] has made," a point that connects the hardening of colonial boundaries with structural and direct violence that impacts all disenfranchised Africans. To erase those colonial cartographies is to explode the parameters of the future.

Achille Mbembe (2001: 242) observed that the phantasmic nature of Africa in the Western imagination as a site of ultimate otherness means that "there is no description of Africa that does not involve destructive and mendacious functions." Wainaina's writing and loving transformed the mendacity of Africa into a creative life force. Like Shine Shine, he could be understood as a cyborgian goddess whose embrace of technology and fierce love of home reshaped—or, even better, disregarded—Western codes of queerness. The play itself serves as a daring act of pan-Africanism in which he borrows from Ogoni folklore, 419 scams, and the legend of Ken Saro-Wiwa to serve his revolutionary vision. He stitches together an Africa from the vortices and ellipses of Kenya, Nigeria, and cyberspace. He tips his hand and demonstrates his power. Like his not-quite-realized wedding, only the continent itself is grand enough as a stage.

Wainaina and Beka shared a dream. Beka confides to the audience, "I dream of the perfect code, the perfect mask, the perfect beast in a pixel world that can change shape and dance past the oil flares, the oil stains, through space and time. I dream. Online" (Wainaina 2011b: 11). She imagines a spectral pan-Africa that recasts the dehumanizing legacy of colonialism and neocolonialism as an Afrocentric posthumanism. Beka's game design of *Shine Shine in the Feral City* confines her cyborgian goddess in a tunnel riddled with bullets; however, the tunnel includes a door on the back wall. Perhaps, beyond that door, lies the whispering, swelling shadows of queer Africa. Perhaps Wainaina himself is also waiting, resplendent in red tulle. He waits only for Shine Shine to conquer the Ferals—those who do not believe in the power of fabulous dreams.

## Notes

1. In an especially notorious example, MP David Bahati introduced cruel legislation to the Ugandan parliament in 2009 that became known as the "kill the gays" bill; the next year, *Rolling Stone* published the names of one hundred LGBTQ Ugandan activists. In Senegal, an outburst of LGBTQ persecution can be traced to 2008, when sensational reporting of a gay male marriage sparked a wave of harsh legislation (Awondo, Geschiere, and Reid 2012: 155–56).

2. Recent cultural production includes Wanuri Kahiu's film *Rafiki* (2018), which received international critical acclaim as well as considerable publicity for the temporary ban enacted by the Kenyan government; see Ghoshal 2018 for a moving commentary on the significance of Kahiu's extraordinary film. Other examples include *Same Love* (2016), a viral video by the recording artist Art Attack, which was also banned by the government, as well as the documentary *Stories of Our Lives* (2014) by the Nest Collective. Kenya has also experienced a wave of high-profile court cases, two of which have been victorious; see Ghoshal 2019 for an overview of LGBTQ legal activism in Kenya. Unfortunately, though, the struggle experienced a serious setback when the High Court upheld colonial antisodomy laws in a widely reported ruling that occurred just three days after Wainaina's death, on May 24, 2019.

3. For a helpful summary of this extensive literature, see Currier 2012: 7.

4. See, for example, Arondekar 2005, Bosia 2014, Hong and Ferguson 2011, Massad 2007, and Povinelli 2006. For a specifically African(ist) critique of identity politics, see Gaudio 2009, Hoad 2007, and Nyanzi 2015.

5. These ideas of discretion and balance resonate more broadly with current theories of neoliberal and postcolonial African selfhood as practices rather than as formations of identity, as pointed out by Currier and Migraine-George (2016: 295–96). Theorists of discretion might also find useful Natalie Newton's (2016) ideas of "contingent invisibility" as a complex form of resistance in Vietnamese lesbian communities.

6. Here I borrow from earlier work (Edmondson 2019: 14–15), in which I discuss Epprecht 2004 and Tamale 2011 to theorize silence in queer cultural production in Uganda.

7. To invoke *theatricality* is to enter a vexed academic discourse that wrestles with the broadness of the term and its entanglement with *performance* and *performativity*. Davis and Postlewait 2003 remains one of the most authoritative works on the concept; for a more recent discussion, see George-Graves 2015: 7–9. My use of *theatricality* draws on the Brechtian concept of the stage as a "heightened" realm or state (Davis and Postlewait 2003: 6; Brecht 1964: 204) that "flaunts . . . its constructedness" (Taylor 2003: 13). In other words, Wainaina's play uses theatricality to mark and denaturalize the queer customary of discretion.

8. The Africa Trilogy, which marked the premiere of *Shine Your Eye*, ran June 10–20, 2010, with Ross Manson directing. Dienye Waboso, Lucky Onyekachi Ejim, and Karen Robinson played the roles of Beka, Tambari, and Doreen, respectively. Then, in 2011, Schimmelpfennig's and Wainaina's plays were restaged as Another Africa from September 29 to October 22, with Ordena Stephens-Thompson assuming the role of Doreen. Of the three plays, only Schimmelpfennig's *Peggy Pickit* has been published (in 2014) and reproduced; notably, this play does not contain African characters. It tells the story of a dinner party of two white heterosexual couples in an unnamed Western country; one of the couples has recently returned from six years in a crisis zone in an African country (also unnamed). *GLO* focuses on a young Kenyan woman who is promoting her memoir of growing up in the Nairobi slum of Kibera on a US tour; this play was not reproduced alongside Wainaina's and Schimmelpfennig's plays in 2011. My analysis of *Shine Your Eye* is based on an unpublished script generously provided by Volcano Theatre Company (Wainaina 2011b), as well as a viewing of an archival video of the 2011 production. My sincere thanks to Manson for making both the video and the script available to me. At this time, the play is not included on the website planetbinya.com (assessed October 10, 2019), which seeks to collect all of Wainaina's writing.

9. For a discussion of how Muoi Nene, the Canadian-based Kenyan actor who played Naijaboy, helped contribute to the development of the script, see Nene 2011: 31.

10. For reflections on Saro-Wiwa's legacy, see Brittain 2015, Campbell 2002, and Obi and Oriola 2018. Additional sources on Saro-Wiwa include Doron and Falola 2016, McLuckie and McPhail 2000, Na'Allah 1998, Ojo-Ade 1999, and Okome 2000. Saro-Wiwa's sizable collection of writings includes novels, plays, essays, and a prison memoir.

11. Naijaboy's scam is based on an actual 419 email; see Manson 2010 and Moran 2016.

12. See Smith 2009 for a fascinating analysis of how these emails perpetuate colonialist tropes of Africa as backward and uncivilized and thus "play on features of European and American 'knowledge' about Africa which have a much longer historical provenance" (33).

13. See BBC 2016 as a representative example of media reports on Nigeria's perpetual oil shortages.

14. Illegal refineries have proliferated in Ogoniland in connection with the informal econ-
    omy. See Ugor 2013: 271 for an analysis of the Delta's underground oil economy as
    "an existential counter-move against a thriving formal petroleum economy that has
    been cruel and indifferent to the daily predicaments, agitations and outcries of ordi-
    nary people in oil-producing communities in the area for more than fifty years." Tam-
    bari's determination to open a state-sanctioned refinery betrays an underlying invest-
    ment in upholding an exploitative formal petroleum economy.

15. The projection designers were Torge Möller and Momme Hinrichs from FettFilm in
    Germany.

16. The term *Afrofuturism* was originally coined in the 1990s and used to describe US
    black speculative fiction and film in the 1960s and 1970s (Anderson and Jones 2015;
    Womack 2013: 16–17); however, as Akosua Adomako Ampofo (2016: 25n11) observes,
    the term has assumed a more capacious perspective that increasingly includes the
    continent (see also Samatar 2017).

17. Wainaina's connections and collaborations with Mutu predate the Volcano Theatre
    production. For example, a hardcover edition of his memoir *One Day I Will Write
    about This Place* (Wainaina 2011a) features an image from her 2006 work, *My
    Strength Lies*. He also published an experimental, rich essay about Mutu in *Jalada*
    (Wainaina 2014c).

18. Space does not permit a discussion of how Wainaina's play builds on Nyong'o's (2019:
    26) concept of Afrofabulations as a kind of social dreaming and how Shine Shine
    opens up "new genres of the human out of the fabulous, formless darkness of an anti-
    black world." It would also be worthwhile to consider *Shine Your Eye* in the context of
    Kara Keeling's (2019) tantalizing but brief exploration of African cultural production
    in the final pages of *Queer Times, Black Futures*. *Shine Your Eye* resonates, for exam-
    ple, with her description of Nnedi Okorafor's novel *Who Fears Death* (2010), which
    "anchors its freedom dreams for another future in a here and now with complex geopo-
    litical coordinates and stubborn historical entanglements" (Keeling 2019: 212).

19. The computer animation of Shine Shine was created by Marcus Moore.

20. In a delightful moment of intertextuality, Wainaina borrows several passages from
    the first chapter of his memoir during these closing moments of the play (Wainaina
    2011a: 8).

21. This discussion of Beka's elusiveness borrows from the "refusal turn" in performance
    and visual studies, which uses ideas of opacity and rejection to challenge a well-worn
    reliance on visibility in representational politics; see, for example, Campt 2017 and
    Mengesha and Padmanabhan 2019. See also Macharia (2016: 185) for a poignant take
    on the significance of refusal (or what he describes as "rudeness") as a response to
    the relentless academic search for African queers. I'm inclined, though, to interpret
    Beka's elusiveness as not quite refusal since she operates within the normative codes
    of discretion that speaks to an "ethos of camouflage" (Nyong'o 2019: 13).

22. This description is based on a production image provided by Volcano Theatre; I regret that I am unable to reproduce the wonderfully evocative image in this article.

23. As Carli Coetzee (2016) explains, the lecture was not recorded, and he spoke from loose notes; Santana 2013 is often cited as a source of information regarding his talk.

24. See Santana 2017: 61 for a discussion of how Wainaina's understanding of pan-Africanism as "continent-centric" differs from the ideology described by, for example, Toyin Falola and Kwame Essien (2014) and Achille Mbembe (2005).

25. This anonymous document is widely circulated in print and on the web (see, e.g., "African LGBTI Manifesto" 2011).

## References

Abebe, Alpha. 2015. "Afropolitanism: Global Citizenship with African Routes." *Debating Development* (blog), April 4. blog.qeh.ox.ac.uk/?p=910.

Abiona, Lara. 2017. "A Birthday Tribute: Binyavanga Wainaina." *Brittle Paper* (blog), January 16. brittlepaper.com/2017/01/birthday-tribute-binyavanga-wainaina/.

Adichie, Chimamanda. 2009. "The Dangers of a Single Story." TED Global video, July. www.ted.com/talks/chimamanda_ngozi_adichie_the_danger_of_a_single_story.

"African LGBTI Manifesto." 2011. In *African Sexualities: A Reader*, edited by Sylvia Tamale, 182. Cape Town: Pambazuka Press.

Ampofo, Akosua Adomako. 2016. "*Re*-viewing Studies on Africa, #Black Lives Matter, and Envisioning the Future of African Studies." *African Studies Review* 59, no 2: 7–29.

Anderson, Reynaldo, and Charles E. Jones. 2015. *Afrofuturism 2.0: The Rise of Astro-Blackness*. Lanham, MD: Lexington Books.

Arnfred, Signe. 2005. "'African Sexuality'/Sexuality in Africa: Tales and Silences." In *Re-thinking Sexualities in Africa*, 2nd ed., edited by Signe Arnfred, 59–76. Uppsala: Nordiska Afrikainstitutet.

Arondekar, Anjali. 2005. "Border/Line Sex: Queer Postcolonialities, or How Race Matters outside the United States." *Interventions: The International Journal of Postcolonial Studies* 7, no. 2: 236–50.

Awondo, Patrick, Peter Geschiere, and Graeme Reid. 2012. "Homophobic Africa? Toward a More Nuanced View." *African Studies Review* 55, no 3: 145–68.

BBC News. 2016. "Nigeria's Fuel Queue Fury." April 6. www.bbc.com/news/world-africa-35976580.

Biruk, Crystal. 2014. "'Aid for Gays': The Moral and the Material in 'African Homophobia' in Post-2009 Malawi." *Journal of Modern African Studies* 52, no. 3: 447–73.

Biruk, Crystal, and Gift Trapence. 2018. "Community Engagement in an Economy of Harms: Reflections from an LGBTI-Rights NGO in Malawi." *Critical Public Health* 28, no. 3: 340–51.

Bosia, Michael J. 2014. "Strange Fruit: Homophobia, the State, and the Politics of LGBT Rights and Capabilities." *Journal of Human Rights* 13: 256–73.

Brecht, Bertolt. 1964. "A Short Organum for the Theatre." In *Brecht on Theatre: The Development of an Aesthetic*, edited and translated by John Willett, 179–205. New York: Hill and Wang.

Brittain, Victoria. 2015. "Ken Saro-Wiwa: A Hero for Our Times." *Race Class* 56, no. 3: 5–17.

Butler, Judith. 2018. "Solidarity/Susceptibility." *Social Text* 36, no. 4: 1–20.

Campbell, Marion. 2002. "Witnessing Death: Ken Saro-Wiwa and the Ogoni Crisis." *Postcolonial Studies* 5, no. 1: 39–49.

Campt, Tina. 2017. *Listening to Images*. Durham, NC: Duke University Press.

Coetzee, Carli. 2016. Introduction to "Contemporary Conversations: Afropolitanism: Reboot." Special section, *Journal of African Cultural Studies* 28, no 1: 101–3.

Coly, Ayo. 2013. "Homophobic Africa?" *African Studies Review* 56, no. 2: 21–32.

Currier, Ashley. 2012. *Out in Africa: LGBT Organizing in Namibia and South Africa.* Minneapolis: University of Minnesota Press.

Currier, Ashley, and Thérèse Migraine-George. 2016. "Queer Studies/African Studies: An (Im)Possible Transaction?" *GLQ* 22, no. 2: 281–305.

Dabiri, Emma. 2014. "Why I'm Not an Afropolitan." *Africa Is a Country* (blog), January 21. africasacountry.com/2014/01/why-im-not-an-afropolitan/.

Dankwa, Serena Owusua. 2009. "'It's a Silent Trade': Female Same-Sex Intimacies in Postcolonial Ghana." *Nordic Journal of Feminist and Gender Research* 17, no. 3: 192–205.

Dankwa, Serena Owusua. 2013. "'The One Who First Says I Love You': Love, Seniority, and Relational Gender in Postcolonial Ghana." In *Sexual Diversity in Africa: Politics, Theory, and Citizenship*, edited by S. N. Nyeck and Marc Epprecht, 170–87. Montreal: McGill-Queen's University Press.

Davis, Tracy C., and Thomas Postlewait, eds. 2003. *Theatricality*. Cambridge: Cambridge University Press.

Doron, Roy, and Toyin Falola. 2016. *Ken Saro-Wiwa*. Athens: Ohio University Press.

Edblom, Stina. 2010. "Wangechi Mutu." In *Disidentification 2.7–31.10 2010*, 8–10. Exhibition catalog, Göteborgs Konsthall. www.konsthallen.goteborg.se/wp-content /uploads/2016/09/Catalouge.pdf.

Edmondson, Laura. 2019. "Antihomosexual Acts on Trial: The Aesthetics of Justice in Uganda." *TDR* 63, no. 2: 6–33.

Epprecht, Marc. 2004. *Hungochani: The History of a Dissident Sexuality in Southern Africa*. Montreal: McGill-Queen's University Press.

Falola, Toyin, and Kwame Essien. 2014. Pan-Africanism, and the Politics of African Citizenship and Identity. New York: Routledge.

Fleetwood, Nicole R. 2011. *Troubling Vision: Performance, Visuality, and Blackness*. Chicago: University of Chicago Press.

Gaudio, Rudolf Pell. 2009. *Allah Made Us: Sexual Outlaws in an Islamic African City.* Malden, MA: Blackwell.

George-Graves, Nadine. 2015. "Magnetic Fields: Too Dance for Theater, Too Theater for Dance." In *The Oxford Handbook of Dance and Theater*, edited by George-Graves, 1–16. Oxford: Oxford University Press.

Ghoshal, Neela. 2018. "Lesbian Film *Rafiki* May Change Kenya Forever." *Advocate* (blog), October 15. www.advocate.com/commentary/2018/10/15/lesbian-film -rafiki-may-change-kenya-forever.

Ghoshal, Neela. 2019. "LGBT Kenyans' Patience Has Gone Unrewarded." *Foreign Policy* (blog), February 24. foreignpolicy.com/2019/02/24/lgbt-kenyans-patience-has -gone-unrewarded/.

González, Jennifer A. 2000. "The Appended Subject: Race and Identity as Digital Assemblage." In *Race in Cyberspace*, edited by Beth Kolko, Lisa Nakamura, and Gil Rodman., 27–50. New York: Routledge.

Gunkel, Henriette. 2010. *The Cultural Politics of Female Sexuality in South Africa.* New York: Routledge.

Gunkel, Henriette. 2013. "Some Reflections on Postcolonial Homophobia, Local Interventions, and LGBTI Solidarity Online: The Politics of Global Petitions." *African Studies Review* 56, no. 2: 67–81.

Haraway, Donna. 1985. "Manifesto for Cyborgs: Science, Technology, and Socialist Feminism in the 1980s." *Socialist Review* 80: 65–108.

Hendriks, Thomas. 2016. "SIM Cards of Desire: Sexual Versatility and the Male Homoerotic Economy in Urban Congo." *American Ethnologist* 43, no. 2: 230–42.

Hoad, Neville. 2007. *African Intimacies: Race, Homosexuality, and Globalization.* Minneapolis: University of Minnesota Press.

Hoad, Neville. 2016a. "Afterword: Out of Place, Out of Time." *Research in African Literatures* 47, no. 2: 186–91.

Hoad, Neville. 2016b. "Queer Customs against the Law." *Research in African Literatures* 47, no. 2: 1–19.

Hong, Grace Kyungwon, and Roderick A. Ferguson, eds. 2011. *Strange Affinities: The Gender and Sexual Politics of Comparative Racialization.* Durham, NC: Duke University Press.

Howden, Daniel. 2014. "Kenyan Writer Binyavanga Wainaina Declares: 'I Am Homosexual.'" *Guardian*, January 21. www.theguardian.com/world/2014/jan/21 /kenyan-writer-binyavanga-wainaina-declares-homosexuality.

Kamau, Richard. 2018. "Wedding Bells for Gay Kenyan Author Binyavanga Wainaina and Longterm Nigerian Partner." *Nairobi Wire*, May 3. nairobiwire.com/2018/05 /wedding-bells-for-gay-kenyan-author-binyavanga-wainaina-and-longterm-nigerian -partner.html.

Keeling, Kara. 2019. *Queer Times, Black Futures.* New York: New York University Press.

Kulish, Nicholas. 2014. "Writer Tells Africa What He Couldn't Tell 'Mum.'" *New York Times*, January 24. www.nytimes.com/2014/01/25/world/africa/as-africa-debates -gay-rights-writer-comes-out.html.

Jamison, Andrew. 2003. "Reflections on Pan-Africanism and the African Renaissance." In *The Making of the Africa-Nation: Pan-Africanism and the African Renaissance*, edited by Mamma Muchie, xi–xiv. London: Adonis and Abbey.

Jeffreys, M. D. W. 1970. "Ogoni Folklore." *Folklore* 81, no. 2: 112–13.

Macharia, Keguro. 2010. "Homophobia in Africa Is Not a Single Story." *Guardian*, May 26. www.theguardian.com/commentisfree/2010/may/26/homophobia -africa-not-single-story.

Macharia, Keguro. 2016. "On Being Area-Studied: A Litany of Complaint." *GLQ* 22, no. 2: 183–90.

Manson, Katrina. 2010. "Coming Soon: Nigerians in Space?" *Global Post*, May 30. www .globalpost.com/dispatch/nigeria/091029/nigeria-space-agency.

Marx, Jacqueline. 2014. "Negotiating Homosexual In/Visibility." In *Reclaiming Afrikan: Queer Perspectives on Sexual and Gender Identities*, curated by Zethu Matebeni, 29–31. Athlone, South Africa: Modjaji Books.

Massad, Joseph A. 2007. *Desiring Arabs*. Chicago: University of Chicago Press.

Mbembe, Achille. 2001. *On the Postcolony*. Berkeley: University of California Press.

Mbembe, Achille. 2005. "Afropolitanism," translated by Laurent Chauvet. In *Africa Remix: Contemporary Art of a Continent*, edited by Njami Simon and Lucy Durán, 26–30. Ostfildern, Germany: Hatje Cantz.

McLuckie, Craig W., and Aubrey McPhail, eds. 2000. *Ken Saro-Wiwa: Writer and Political Activist*. Boulder, CO: Lynne Rienner.

McMillan, Uri. 2015. *Embodied Avatars*. New York: New York University Press.

Mengesha, Lilian G., and Lakshmi Padmanabhan. 2019. "Introduction to Performing Refusal/Refusing to Perform." *Women and Performance* 29, no. 1: 1–8.

Minor, Olive. 2014. "*Kuchus* in the Balance: Queer Lives under Uganda's Anti-homosexuality Bill." PhD diss., Northwestern University.

Moran, Lee. 2016. "Nigerian Astronaut Is Not Really Trapped in Space." *Huffpost Weird News*, February 2. www.huffingtonpost.com/entry/nigerian-astronaut-space-trapped _us_56c2ced4e4b0c3c550527f0b.

Muchie, Mammo. 2003. "Has the Pan-African Hour Come?" In *The Making of the Africa-Nation: Pan-Africanism and the African Renaissance*, edited by Mammo Muchie, 2–11. London: Adonis and Abbey.

Munro, Brenna. 2012. *South Africa and the Dream of Love to Come: Queer Sexuality and the Struggle for Freedom*. Minneapolis: University of Minnesota Press.

Na'Allah, Abdul. 1998. *Ogoni's Agonies: Ken Saro-Wiwa and the Crisis in Nigeria*. Trenton, NJ: Africa World Press.

Nene, Muoi. 2011. "The Africa Trilogy: My Kenyadian Experience." *Alt Theatre* 8, no. 4: 27–33.

Newton, Natalie. 2016. "Contingent Invisibility: Space, Community, and Invisibility for *Les* in Saigon." *GLQ* 22, no. 1: 109–36.

Nyanzi, Stella. 2014. "Queer Pride and Protest: A Reading of the Bodies at Uganda's First Gay Beach Pride." *Signs* 40, no. 1: 36–40.

Nyanzi, Stella. 2015. "Knowledge Is Requisite Power: Making a Case for Queer African Scholarship." In *Boldly Queer: African Perspectives on Same-Sex Sexuality and Gender Diversity*, edited by Theo Sandfort, Fabeinne Simenel, Kevin Mwachiro, and Vasu Reddy, 125–35. The Hague: Hivos.

Nyong'o, Tavia. 2012. "Queer Africa and the Fantasy of Virtual Participation." *Women's Studies Quarterly* 40, nos. 1–2: 40–63.

Nyong'o, Tavia. 2019. *Afro-fabulations: The Queer Drama of Black Life*. New York: New York University Press.

Obi, Cyril, and Temitope B. Oriola, eds. 2018. *The Unfinished Revolution in Nigeria's Niger Delta: Prospects for Environmental Justice and Peace*. London: Routledge.

Ojo-Ade, Femi. 1999. *Ken Saro-Wiwa: A Bio-critical Study*. New York: Africana Legacy.

Okome, Onookome. 2000. *Before I Am Hanged: Ken Saro-Wiwa, Literature, Politics, and Dissent*. Trenton, NJ: Africa World Press.

O'Mara, Kathleen. 2013. "LGBTI Community and Citizenship Practices in Urban Ghana." In *Sexual Diversity in Africa: Politics, Theory, and Citizenship*, edited by S. N. Nyeck and Marc Epprecht, 188–207. Montreal: McGill-Queen's University Press.

Ossome, Lyn. 2013. "Postcolonial Discourses of Queer Activism and Class in Africa." In *Queer African Reader*, edited by Sokari Ekine and Hakima Abbas, 32–47. Dakar: Pambazuka Press.

Phelan, Peggy. 1993. *Unmarked: The Politics of Performance*. London: Routledge.

Povinelli, Elizabeth A. 2006. *The Empire of Love: Toward a Theory of Intimacy, Genealogy, and Carnality*. Durham, NC: Duke University Press.

Puar, Jasbir. 2007. *Terrorist Assemblages: Homonationalism in Queer Times*. Durham, NC: Duke University Press.

Puar, Jasbir. 2012. "'I Would Rather Be a Cyborg than a Goddess': Becoming-Intersectional in Assemblage Theory." *PhiloSOPHIA: A Journal of Feminist Philosophy* 2, no. 1: 49–66.

Puar, Jasbir. 2013. "Rethinking Homonationalism." *International Journal of Middle East Studies* 45, no. 2: 336–39.

Samatar, Sofia. 2017. "Toward a Planetary History of Afrofuturism." *Research in African Literatures* 48, no. 4: 175–91.

Santana, Stephanie Bosch. 2013. "Exorcizing Afropolitanism: Binyavanga Wainaina Explains Why 'I Am a Pan-Africanist, Not an Afropolitan' at ASAUK 2012." *Africa in Words* (blog), February 8. africainwords.com/2013/02/08/exorcizing-afropolitanism -binyavanga-wainaina-explains-why-i-am-a-pan-africanist-not-an-afropolitan-at -asauk-2012/.

Santana, Stephanie Bosch. 2017. "Exorcising the Future: Afropolitanism's Spectral Origins." In *Afropolitanism: Reboot*, edited by Carli Coetzee, 58–64. Abingdon, UK:
Routledge.

Schimmelpfennig, Roland. 2014. *Peggy Pickit Sees the Face of God*. In *Plays: One*, translated by David Tushingham, 159–227. London: Oberon Books.

Sizemore-Barber, April. Forthcoming. *Prismatic Performances: Queer South Africa and
the Fragmentation of the Rainbow Nation*. Ann Arbor: University of Michigan Press.

Smith, Andrew. 2009. "Nigerian Scam E-mails and the Charms of Capital." *Cultural
Studies* 23, no. 1: 27–47.

Spronk, Rachel. 2018. "Invisible Desires in Ghana and Kenya: Same-Sex Erotic Experiences in Cross-Sex Oriented Lives." *Sexualities* 21, no. 5–6: 883–98.

Tamale, Sylvia. 2011. "Researching and Theorising Sexualities in Africa." In *African
Sexualities: A Reader*, edited by Sylvia Tamale, 1–36. Cape Town: Pambazuka Press.

Tate, Greg. 2013. "Gikuyu Mythos vs. the Cullud Grrl from Out of Space, a Wangechi
Mutu Feature." In *Wangechi Mutu: A Fantastic Journey*, edited by Trevor Schoon-
maker, 85–93. Durham, NC: Duke University Press.

Taylor, Diana. 2003. *The Archive and the Repertoire: Performing Cultural Memory in the
Americas*. Durham, NC: Duke University Press.

Veal, Michael E. 2008. "Enter Cautiously." In *Wangechi Mutu: A Shady Promise*, edited
by Douglas Singleton, 9–12. Bologna, Italy: Damiani.

Wainaina, Binyavanga. 2005. "How to Write about Africa." *Granta 92: The View from
Africa*. www.granta.com/Archive/92/How-to-Write-about-Africa/Page-1.

Wainaina, Binyavanga. 2011a. *One Day I Will Write about This Place*. Minneapolis: Gray-
wolf Press.

Wainaina, Binyavanga. 2011b. *Shine Your Eye*. Unpublished manuscript, November 1.

Wainaina, Binyavanga. 2014a. "I Am a Homosexual, Mum." *Africa Is a Country* (blog),
January 19. africasacountry.com/2014/01/i-am-a-homosexual-mum/.

Wainaina, Binyavanga (@BinyavangaW). 2014b. "I am, for anybody confused or in doubt,
a homosexual." Twitter, January 20, 2:41 p.m. https://twitter.com/binyavangaw.

Wainaina, Binyavanga. 2014c. "Wangechi Mutu Wonders Why Butterfly Wings Leave
Powder on the Fingers, There Was a Coup Today in Kenya." *Jalada*, October 17.
jalada.org/2014/10/17/wangechi-mutu-wonders-why-butterfly-wings-leave-powder-on
-the-fingers-there-was-a-coup-today-in-kenya-by-binyavanga-wainaina/.

Wainaina, Binyavanga. 2014d. *We Must Free Our Imaginations*. 6 pts. YouTube, January
21. www.youtube.com/watch?v=8uMwppw5AgU.

Wainaina, Binyavanga. 2015a. "Conversations with Baba." TEDx Talk. YouTube, January
15. www.youtube.com/watch?v=z5uAoBu9Epg.

Wainaina, Binyavanga. 2018a. "I asked my love for his hand in marriage two weeks ago."
Facebook, May 2. www.facebook.com/binyavanga.wainaina.

Wainaina, Binyavanga (@BinyavangaW). 2018b. "I am sure we will have a party for Nigerians later next year." Twitter, May 2, 10:21 a.m. https://twitter.com/binyavangaw.

Weheliye, Alexander G. 2014. *Habeas Viscus: Racializing Assemblages, Biopolitics, and Black Feminist Theories of the Human*. Durham, NC: Duke University Press.

Wolff, Rachel. 2013. "She'll Probably Cut up This Magazine Too." *New York Magazine*, September 2. nymag.com/guides/fallpreview/2013/wangechi-mutu-2013-9/.

Womack, Ytasha L. 2013. *Afrofuturism: The World of Black Sci-Fi and Fantasy Culture*. Chicago: Lawrence Hill Books.

Wynters, Sylvia. 1990. "Afterword: Beyond Miranda's Meanings: Un/Silencing the 'Demonic Ground' of Caliban's 'Woman.'" In *Out of the Kumbla: Caribbean Women and Literature*, edited by Carole Boyce Davies and Elaine Savory Fido, 355–72. Trenton, NJ: Africa World Press.

Ugor, Paul U. 2013. "Survival Strategies and Citizenship Claims: Youth and the Underground Oil Economy in Post-amnesty Niger Delta." *Africa* 83, no. 2: 270–92.

# BELATED : INTERRUPTION

**Keguro Macharia**

> Paukwa—Pakawa
> Sahani—Ya Mchele
> Giza—Ya Mwizi
> Kiboko—Cha Mtoto Mkorofi
> Na Maziwa Je?

> method: anecdote rumor speculation fabulation

I have been thinking about belatedness, what it means to be marked as absent or delayed or not yet ready or undeveloped or illiterate or primitive. Or as child or woman or black or blackened. Or African. I have been thinking about what this belatedness means for politics and thinking, for theory and coalition, for gene-alogies of knowledge and pedagogical practice, for co-imagining freedom and co-building a different world. In this issue of *GLQ*, dedicated to "interdisciplinary discussion," "new research," and theoretical innovation, I wonder what it means to have a special issue dedicated to Africa almost thirty years after the journal was first published in 1993. What kind of belatedness is at work, and how do I write with and into it?

Five years ago, I was interested in "queering" African studies. If not Afri-can studies, I was interested in "queering" Africa. One of the melancholic objects from a previous life is an idea for a manuscript titled "Queer Africa." I cannot discard it because I have not yet spent enough time with it to map how and why it became impossible.[1] What follows is one version of such mapping.

Instead of queering African studies or Africa, I am interested in what an encounter between something called *queer* and something named *Africa* might generate. At my most optimistic—I am not an optimist—I hope that musing about this encounter might illuminate something about pursuing and practicing freedom.

The problem, as always, is where to start. And so I start again.

*GLQ* 26:3
DOI 10.1215/10642684-8311857
© 2020 by Duke University Press

Paukwa—pakawa

Sahani—ya mlaji jasusi

Mkono mtupu—ya udaraji

Na dawa ya moto je?—ya kisonono tukutu

Two figures mark the encounter between queer and Africa: the queer savage and comrade bae. The first figure I adapt from Neville Hoad's (2000) foundational work on the "queerness of savages," and the second I adapt from Danai Mupotsa's (2015) mapping of South African student activism within libidinal terms. Where Hoad's work returns me to the archives of colonial modernity, to the problems of sex, gender, sexuality, embodiment, and blackness in figuring the human and the unhuman, Mupotsa's work places me within ongoing struggles for freedom in South Africa and the role of black queer and trans* womxn in those struggles as they reimagine and transform the masculinist politics they have inherited. I am not mapping a trajectory from the queer savage to comrade bae, moving from past to future, archive to activism. Instead, I am interested in the difficult coevalness of these figures, in the shadows they cast upon each other, the frictions generated by their entanglement, the possibilities they generate for and as thinking.

Two warnings before I continue. First, Katherine McKittrick (2014: 16–17) on the problem of researching black life from colonial archives:

> The archive of black diaspora is, as [Saidiya] Hartman rightly suggests, "a death sentence, a tomb, a display of a violated body, an inventory of property, a medical treatise . . . an asterisk in the grand narrative of history." The asterisked archives are filled with bodies that can only come into being vis-à-vis racial-sexual violence; the documents and ledgers and logs that narrate the brutalities of this history give birth to new world blackness as they evacuate life from blackness. Breathless, archival numerical evidence puts pressure on our present system of knowledge by affirming the knowable (black objecthood) and disguising the untold (black human being). The slave's status as object-commodity, or purely economic cargo, reveals that a black archival presence not only enumerates the dead and dying, but also acts as an origin story. This is where we begin, this is where historic blackness comes from: the list, the breathless numbers, the absolutely economic, the mathematics of the unliving.

The counting and uncounting begins before the ships leave from Europe: the speculative unmaking of stolen life powers the commodity-making voyages (see

Baucom 2005). The kidnappings and coffles and containment and inspection and rejection extend from inland to coast, coast to hold, hold to ocean to market to plantation (see Mustakeem 2016; Smallwood 2007). New World blackness speaks not only to the blackness forged in—and on the way to—the Americas, but also to the blackness produced through the worlding of 1492 (see Wynter 1995). To be more explicit: Africa does not—cannot—escape this (new) worlding. Blackness names, in part, the suture between Africa and Afro-diaspora.

A second, related warning comes from Edward Wilmot Blyden (1882) about the danger of engaging colonial archives. He urges that the "mind of the youthful African" should not be "trained" in works from the early modern period through the age of revolutions to the present:

> I know that during these periods some of the greatest works of human genius have been composed. I know that Shakespeare and Milton, Gibbon and Macauley, Hallam and Lecky, Froude, Stubbs and Green, belong to these periods. . . . It was during the [early modern] period that the transatlantic slave trade arose, and those theories—theological, social, and political—were invented for the degradation and proscription of the Negro. This epoch continues to this day and has an abundant literature and a prolific authorship. (17)

A good Anglophile, Blyden is unable—or unwilling—to write that "the greatest works of human genius" imagine and produce human genius as white man genius. Africans trained in these works "experience the greatest possible inconvenience. They never feel at home." They experience themselves as "strangers" (10). Putting it in stronger terms, Frantz Fanon (2008: 118) writes that the problem is not a "feeling of inferiority," but "a feeling of not existing." Blyden worries about the "youthful African" trained to think through colonial archives. I wonder these days about what happens to trained researchers who engage negating archives looking, desperately, for something that might have escaped the impress of white supremacy. I wonder if reading strategies—against the grain, along the grain, in the margins, through white space, in gaps and silences, counterintuitively—counter the overall negating force and effects of such archives.

*(What am I doing here, and what is it doing to me?)*

Belatedness means that the queerness of the savage is reckoned differently from the queerness of the nonsavage. In modernity's archives, African queerness—the queerness of the savage—is not related to the taxonomic-sexological marking of gay, lesbian, bisexual, trans*, intersex, and the proliferation of con-

ditions and practices described by Richard von Krafft-Ebing. *African queerness*
names a failure to organize intimate life. The sixteenth-century chronicler of
Africa Leo Africanus (c. 1494–1550), for instance, faults "Negros" for lacking
discrimination:

> But in the yeere of the Hegeira 380, by the meanes of a certaine Mahu-
> metan which came into Barbarie, the residue of the said land was found
> out, being as then inhabited by great numbers of people, which liued a
> brutish and sauage life, without any king, gouernour, common wealth, or
> knowledge of husbandrie. Clad they were in skins of beasts, neither had
> they any peculiar wiues: in the day time they kept their cattell; and when
> night came they resorted ten or twelue both men and women into one cot-
> tage together, using hairie skins instead of beds, and each man choosing
> his leman which he had most fancy vnto. (Africanus 1896, 3:819)

This passage opens the "Seuenth Booke," which examines "the land of Negros."
No similar description of intimate practices open the "Fifth Booke," dedicated
to "the kingdomes of Bugia and Tunis"; the "Sixth Booke," dedicated to "the
village called Gar"; or the "Eight Booke," dedicated to "Egypt." The "land of
Negros" enters Africanus's *History and Description of Africa* as a libidinal space.
"Negros" have not yet attained the modern forms of intimate organization that exist
as monogamy or polygamy: they are out of sync with intimate modernity. Indeed,
"Negros" are defined through their intimate disorganization.

A picture of Africanus's "Negro" emerges as he maps the land of the
"Negros." The inhabitants of the "kingdome of Gualata" are "blacke people" and
"lead a most miserable life" (Africanus 1896: 3:821). The "husbandmen and shepherds" in the "great towne of Gago" are "ignorant and rude people," who, "in winter couer their bodies with beasts skins; but in sommer they goe all naked saue
their priuie members" (3:827). The inhabitants of Casena are "extremely black,
having great noses and blabber lips. They dwell in most forlone and base cottages"
(3:830). The inhabitants of Zanfara are "most base and rusticall people," who are
"tall in stature and extremely blacke, their visages are broad, and their dispositions most sauage and brutish" (3:831). The "herdesmen and shepherds" of Borno
"goe all naked save their priuie members" in summer, but in winter "they are
clad in skins, and haue bed of skins also. They embrace no religion at all, being
neither Christians, Mahumetans, nor Iewes, nor of any other profession, but liuing
after a brutish manner, and hauing wiues and children in common" (3:833). "The
Negros," he writes, "are alwaies strong and lustie, hauing their teeth found euen

till their dying day : yet is there no nation vnder heauen more prone to venerie"
(1:180). He adds, "The Negros . . . leade a beastly kinde of life, being vtterly des-
titute of the vse of reason, of dexteritie of wit, and of all artes. Yea they so behaue
themselues, as if they had continually liued in a forrest among wilde beasts. They
haue great swarmes of harlots among them; whereupon a man may easily coniec-
ture their manner of liuing" (1:187). Africanus's Negros are black, base, naked,
savage, brutish, belated, out of sync with modernity. *I could go on, but I am uninterested in pursuing my own negation.*

    *blackness sutures Africa and Afro-diaspora*

    Originally published in 1523, Africanus's *History* was "Europe's principal
source of information about Africa" for over two hundred years (Burton 1998: 48).
In general, it is considered a work that counters negative, fantastic representations
of Africa and offers positive, or at least realistic, depictions. (*the african real is a
genre as powerful as african fantasy.*) But Africa is not one thing. Neither are Africans. John Pory, Africanus's translator into English, summarizes, "This part of the
world is inhabited especially by fiue principall nations, to wit, by the people called
Cafri or Cafates, that is to say outlawes or lawlesses, by the Abassins, the Egyp-
tians, the Arabians, and the Africans or Moores, properly so called; which last
are of two kinds, namely white or tawnie Moores, and Negros or blacke Moores"
(Africanus 1896, 1:20). The divide between white or tawny Moors, and Negroes
or black Moors is temporal and sexual. White or tawny Moors are educated, practice recognized religions, cover their bodies, and have functioning governments.
Negroes or black Moors are belated and primitive, as evidenced by their lack of
proper clothing, their lack of proper governments, and their disorganized intimate
lives.

    (perhaps all of this sounds familiar, so familiar that it is very boring—and
I will not extend it by asking what Pory *wants* from this translation)

    *blackness sutures Africa and Afro-diaspora*

    *Disorganized* intimate life names the Africa suffering from overpopula-
tion because Africans do not know how to plan families; the Africa suffering from
underpopulation because AIDS is spreading like wildfire; the Africans who cannot
be given antiretrovirals because Africans don't know how to stick to a schedule;
the Africans easily seduced into "vice" by Arabs; the Africans easily convinced to
be homophobic by US conservatives; the Africans waiting to be trained into proper
gender and sexuality activism by non-Africans; the Africans disciplined into intimate modernity via analogy; the Africans arriving late to the scene of knowledge
making about Africa and Africans.

*(the slippage between* African *and* Negro *makes it seem as though we're talking about the same black and blackened figures; but in South Africa and Egypt, they ask us when we are returning to Africa, which is black and blackened, the land of the Negro; let the slippage stay—imprecision is also a method)*

*Disorganized intimate life* complicates the hypersexual and hyposexual frames through which blackness has been apprehended. It broadens the view to gather figures and groups who escape taxonomy-sexology, even as they are marked by it. Disorganized intimate life is cause *and* effect of belatedness, symptom and disease. And while the political effects of disorganized intimate life are easy to map—in one reading, the civilizing mission is about organizing intimate life— disorganized intimate life provides no real position from which to organize a legible politics. Nor does it really present an archive to document the queerness of the savage. Contact with the savage disorganizes frames and methods and practices and archives.

I'm trying to get at something here about why the many articles and books documenting something called African LGBTQI over the past thirty years or so have felt not quite right (roughly, from Dynes 1983 to Zabus 2013). And I'm also trying to get at something about the moving target of the queerness of the savage, a movement that can in no way be considered liberatory. It might be that the taxonomic-sexological frames that subtend empirical and conceptual work on Africa and African sexualities are too toxic to imagine liberation, even as they are often offered in the guise of liberation. We might ask, following McKittrick, whether the methods of studying Africa and African sexualities escape the mathematics that unhumans the African-as-Negro. We might ask, also, whether the forms in which we demand that study void any possible ethical stance.[2]

*We could say Africans are always already queer, as I was told recently. But this is not conceptually or politically useful. It avoids the structural misogyny and homophobia of African nationalisms and ethnonationalisms and pan-Africanisms. We do not all walk down the street the same way in Nairobi or Kampala or Lagos or Johannesburg.*

Paukwa
Sahani
Giza
Kiboko
Na Maziwa Je?[3]

*By age ten I knew that to change sex you walked around the sacred Mugumo tree seven times, backward—or so I thought. I do not remember where I learned this. I do not remember how it became present and unforgettable. For a long time I thought I had invented what I needed to survive. I have since encountered this myth elsewhere (see, e.g., Karangi 2008: 126).*

*I need this story—this break—before I proceed. One tries to avoid one's negation, but encounters it everywhere, as method, as archive, as knowledge, as theory.*

Paukwa—Pakawa

Sahani—Ya Mchele

Giza—Ya Mwizi

Kiboko—Cha Mtoto Mkorofi

Na Maziwa Je?

Against disorganization, Edward Blyden ([1908] 1994: 10) insists:

The Family, which in Africa, as everywhere else, is the basic unit of society. Every male and female marries at the proper age. Every woman is required and expects to perform her part of the function of motherhood—to do her share in continuing the human race.

Against disorganization, Jomo Kenyatta ([1938] 1965: 150) insists:

All matters relating to sex are done according to a well-regulated code of convention.

Against disorganization, Kenyatta's classmate and academic rival L. S. B. Leakey (1977: 739) choreographs:

To start with, the girl had to lie on her left side with her left leg stretched out flat on the sleeping mat and her right leg bent and raised with the knee in the air. The left arm was also kept flat on the sleeping mat, the right arm being kept free for encircling the man's neck. When the man lay down he had to do so in such a way that his right leg rested on the girl's left leg. Then she brought her right leg over and enfolded both his legs under her right knee. She then rolled her trunk so that her breasts faced upwards; the man brought his chest down on to her breasts, and she encircled his neck with her right arm, thus helping to keep him in position. The man's penis was pressed against the girl's soft pubic apron. When the couple got too stiff in this position, they turned over and lay down on the other side in a corresponding position, with the girl on her right side and the man on his left.

Against disorganization, Nkiru Nzegwu (2012) maps African intimacies:

[*Family Matters*] deals with different forms of family relationships, notably consanguineal, nuclear, mixtures of the two, polygamous, matrilineal, patrilineal, dual-descent, matrifocal, patrifocal, patriarchal, and matriarchal. A consanguineal family construes the family as composed of kin, while the nuclear treats the family as composed of a man and his wife and children. Polygamous families are made up of a male or female husband with multiple wives. A matrilineal family traces descent through the mother, while a patrilineal one traces descent through the father, and a dual-descent family traces descent through both the mother and the father. Matrifocality describes a family that is based or focused on the mother, whereas a patrifocal family is centered on the father. A patriarchal family is one in which the father has the dominant power in the family, and a matriarchal family is one in which the mother has the dominant power in the family.

Against disorganization, Sylvia Tamale (2005: 28) choreographs:

Among the erotic paraphernalia associated with Kiganda sexuality are the stringed, colourful waist beads called *obutiti*. Traditionally, the *butiti* were made out of tiny, delicate clay beads that would make a tinkling or rattling sound as they knocked against each other with any slight movement. The sight of a woman adorned with rows of *butiti* around her waist strutting around the bedroom excites her male partner. Similarly when a man twirls the *butiti* around or rubs them against the woman's body, they function as a stimulant or aphrodisiac. Special herbs are often injected or otherwise soaked into the beads to add to their potency.

Usually, during a private *Ssenga* session, observers will be taught how to enhance their lovemaking techniques through a guided performance. Two *Ssengas* may lie on a bed and take the couple or group through a blow-by-blow display of "how it is supposed to be done." They come prepared with sex gear and gadgets (including dildos). Key among this sexual equipment is the *nkumbi* (literal translation, hoe), a large, soft, absorbent white cloth used for hygienic purposes during and after sex. The practices and beliefs associated with *enkumbi* constitute a ritual enterprise that in itself is very important to the Baganda people. *Ssengas* even teach various "lovemaking noises" (for example, *okukona ennyindo*—nasal; *okusiiya*—hiss; *okusika omukka*—breath/gasp). Watching two half-naked women in bed did not seem to suggest lesbianism to the absorbed tutees.

It might be that I am too enamored of intimate disorganization as a frame into which Africans-as-Negros are constantly written and, in turn, constantly write within and against. It might be that by juxtaposing feminists like Tamale against phallocrats like Jomo Kenyatta, I am losing a position from which to think about progressive sex politics. Yet, as I read through conservative and progressive thinkers on sex and gender and sexuality and intimacy in Africa, I keep encountering the need—theirs and mine—to write against intimate disorganization.

For the African-as-Negro, black and blackened by a belated entry into intimate modernity—the practices, the identities, the postidentities, the erotics, the theories, the methods, the archives—intimate disorganization names a kind of inevitable doing and *un*doing: however one engages with intimate modernity, one will do it wrong. One needs capacity building. One needs training. One needs a kind of modernity that one will not—cannot—access.

If, as I seem to be suggesting, intimate disorganization names a kind of automation that blackens, keeping those blackened writing from within and against it, generating something that cannot be considered knowledge about themselves—ourselves—within the frames generated as intimate modernity, and if something called *freedom* names a position within intimate modernity, what is it to write as the belated, forever barred from the freedom promised within intimate modernity?

Perhaps what I name here is the sense that the *queer* that names and critiques intimate modernity cannot be the same *queer* that precedes *Africa* as adjective or verb. And that few, if any, of the methods and practices developed to frame queerness, including those in black queer studies and black queer diaspora studies, provide ways to engage the Africa-as-Negro, forever belated to intimate modernity.[4]

(*blackness sutures Africa and Afro-diaspora: I write in the seams of that suture*)

Paukwa—pakawa
Matako—ya kudondosa
Mshusho—ya vibiriti ngoma
Haraka haraka je?—ya ziara danguroni

I do not trust arguments that map some impossibility or other and then, in their concluding sections, offer a hopeful resolution. It is not that I don't believe in hope. On Twitter, Mariame Kaba repeats, "Hope is a discipline." Hope is something to be worked on, every day. Following her, I have decided not to write or publish critical writing that does not practice hope, no matter how improbable that hope seems given the sequence of the argument, or the particular history we occupy. I will neither fetishize nor generate the countless aporias and impossibilities that litter critical and theoretical prose. Why should I mark myself as an impossible thing? Hope is a discipline. I write this because I want to make explicit the trajectory of this writing and the particular leap of invention I take to move from where I've been to where I'm going.

> Paukwa—pakawa
> Mafuta—ya mkundu mkavu
> Vidole—vya shimo pokevu
> Na hamsini hamsini je?—ya ngoma ghali

Danai Mupotsa's (2015) "An Open Love Letter to My Comrade Bae . . . Or At Least 32 Reasons Why I See You" is a stunning work of political and ethical care. My preference would be to simply reprint all of it here, because I can think of nothing else that so beautifully articulates the libidinal, affective, political, and aesthetic in African thinking and activism. When I first imagined writing about it, I was going to map, briefly, how it rethinks antilibidinal African anticolonial, nationalist, ethnonationalist, and phallocratic thinking and activism, the stuff that demands abstinence, distance from women, active homophobia, gender segregation, and nonconsensual ritual sex. But, honestly, I no longer have the patience to write about all the ways African phallocrats think and act. And I am tired of the idea that freedom-seeking writing responds to earlier, antifreedom writing. It is debilitating to position oneself as responding to works that unsee and unhuman you. I am uninterested in pursuing my own negation.

I learn from Mupotsa (2015) how to think *with*, rather than against: "The 'open letter' often takes 'against, against, against' as a preferred narrative form. There are probably good reasons for this, but I would like to take a moment in breath for a mode of address made in dense love." Elsewhere, Mupotsa (2018) writes about designing a course as a "love letter to smart girls"; I am arrested—enthralled—by the possibility of pedagogy and scholarship as acts of love. Christina Sharpe (2016) writes,

> So we are here in the weather, here in the singularity. Here there is disaster and possibility. And while *"we are constituted through and by continued vulnerability to this overwhelming force, we are not only known to ourselves and to each other by that force."*

"Comrade Bae" models the ways we are known to ourselves and to each other. It is seeing each other: "This is my love for comrade bae whose will refuses to become accustomed to people not ever actually seeing you. I see you" (Mupotsa 2015). It is recognizing often unacknowledged labor: "This is my love for comrade bae who makes sure that other comrades are fed." It is considering the erotics of struggle: "This is my love for comrade bae who remembers to find ten minutes, when the day is time-pressed to rub one out, because you know that this too is part of our revolution." It is acknowledging the damage of kinship: "This is my love for comrade bae who screams because comrade bae can't take the abuse of uncles anymore." It is imagining a different world together: "This is my love for comrade bae who insists on a dense debate concerning the best way to have anal sex over lunch and while we make decisions on political strategy." It is imagining a different world together: "This is my love for comrade bae who is full, so full of will that every part of your body presents itself, naked and exposed because you will give everything for the possibility of a life we have not even begun to imagine." It is imagining a different world together: "This is my love for comrade bae who gives us poetry."

As I sit with "Comrade Bae," as I read and reread it, I am held by the freedom dreams it imagines and pursues. I am awed by how it theorizes and models care and sociality. And if, in this particular writing, I cannot escape the weight and shadow of taxonomy-sexology, the belatedness that marks me as black and blackened, the forms and rhetorics that grant limited and limiting legibility, the Africa-as-Negro that forecloses my entry into intimate modernity, I continue to pursue freedom.

*I write in the suture that is blackness, I write into the seam of Africa and Afro-diaspora, I write onto and around sutures of difficult coevalness, seeking something that might be called freedom.*

## Notes

Ndinda and Kweli provided the sound and the imagination.

1. One navigates the existence of a field that grants one's work some legibility while noting that most of the objects and scenes and methods that now populate that field make one's work illegible within the terms of that field.

2. I find myself apologizing constantly for not being able to write academic prose as I learned. I pursue forms where something that is not entirely hostile to me can exist.

3. Belatedly: this call-and-response formula is used to begin a storytelling session. It assembles listening and listeners. It marks, in this writing, the ongoing presence of fabulation, and calls to those who respond.

4.   If nothing else, the absence of Africa-based thinkers from the books and special jour-
      nal issues that have named these fields tells a story about failures to think and work
      across difference, across geohistories.

## References

Africanus, Leo. 1896. *The History and Description of Africa and of the Notable Things
     Therein Contained*, translated by John Pory. 3 vols. London: Hakluyt Society.

Baucom, Ian. 2005. *Specters of the Atlantic: Finance Capital, Slavery, and the Philosophy
     of History*. Durham, NC: Duke University Press.

Blyden, Edward Wilmot. 1882. *The Aims and Methods of a Liberal Education for Afri-
     cans*. Cambridge, MA: John Wilson and Son.

Blyden, Edward Wilmot. (1908) 1994. *African Life and Customs*. Baltimore, MD: Black
     Classic's Press.

Burton, Jonathan. 2013. "'A Most Wily Bird': Leo Africanus, *Othello*, and the Trafficking
     in Difference." In *Post-colonial Shakespeares*, edited by Ania Loomba and Martin
     Orkin, 43–63. London: Routledge.

Dynes, Wayne. 1983. "Homosexuality in Sub-Saharan Africa: An Unnecessary Contro-
     versy." *Gay Books Bulletin* 9: 20–21.

Fanon, Frantz. 2008. *Black Skin, White Masks*, translated by Richard Philcox. New York:
     Grove Press.

Hoad, Neville. 2000. "Arrested Development or the Queerness of Savages: Resisting Evo-
     lutionary Narratives of Difference." *Postcolonial Studies* 3, no. 2: 133–58.

Karangi, Matthew M. 2008. "Revisiting the Roots of Gikuyu Culture through the Sacred
     Mugumo Tree." *Journal of African Cultural Studies* 20, no. 1: 117–32.

Kenyatta, Jomo. (1938) 1965. *Facing Mount Kenya: The Tribal Life of the Gikuyu*. New
     York: Vintage.

Leakey, L. S. B. 1977. *Southern Kikuyu before 1903*. Vol 3. New York: Academic Press.

McKittrick, Katherine. 2014. "Mathematics Black Life." *Black Scholar* 44, no. 2: 16–28.

Mupotsa, Danai. 2015. "An Open Love Letter to My Comrade Bae . . . Or At Least 32
     Reasons Why I See You." *Daily Vox*, November 16. www.thedailyvox.co.za/an-open
     -love-letter-to-my-comrade-bae-or-at-least-32-reasons-why-i-see-you/.

Mupotsa, Danai. 2018. "Living a Feminist Life: A Love Letter in Five Parts." *Syndicate*,
     January 22. syndicate.network/symposia/philosophy/living-a-feminist-life/.

Mustakeem, Sowande' M. 2016. *Slavery at Sea: Terror, Sex, and Sickness in the Middle
     Passage*. Urbana: University of Illinois Press.

Nzegwu, Nkiru. 2012. *Family Matters: Feminist Concepts in African Philosophies of Cul-
     ture*. New York: State University of New York Press. Kindle.

Sharpe, Christina. 2016. *In the Wake: On Blackness and Being*. Durham, NC: Duke Uni-
     versity Press. Kindle.

Smallwood, Stephanie E. 2007. *Saltwater Slavery: A Middle Passage from Africa to American Diaspora*. Cambridge, MA: Harvard University Press.

Tamale, Sylvia. 2005. "Eroticism, Sensuality and 'Women's Secrets' among the Baganda: A Critical Analysis." *Feminist Africa* 5, no. 1: 9–36.

Wynter, Sylvia. 1995. "1492: A New World View." In *Race, Discourse, and the Origin of the Americas: A New World View*, edited by Vera Lawrence Hyatt and Rex Nettleford, 5–57. Washington, DC: Smithsonian Institution Press.

Zabus, Chantal 2013. *Out in Africa: Same-Sex Desire in Sub-Saharan Literatures and Cultures*. Martlesham, UK: Boydell and Brewer.

## THINKING WITH PORN CLASSICS

**Richard T. Rodríguez**

$\mathcal{S}$hortly after taking over as the Moving Image Review editor from Kara Keeling (whose example I hope to follow during my tenure in this role), I proposed a number of topics to the *GLQ* editors on which I wished to focus. One topic that caught their attention was thinking with porn classics. The charge to potential contributors, I explained, would be to identify a favorite classic porn film and detail what that film teaches us about gender, sexuality, or anything else. *Classic* could be interpreted however they wished, but in my mind a classic porn film's importance rests on its ability to command enduring value in the way that any other film classic does yet is distinguished by its unique illustrative historical, cultural, or aesthetic properties.

"Thinking with" such porn classics generates insight into the pedagogical worth of sexually explicit representations. As with the focus on pornographic "pedagogical archives" in Tim Dean, Steven Ruszczycky, and David Squires's groundbreaking collection *Porn Archives* (2014), the contributions to this dossier also encompass the space of the classroom. They additionally explore how an "instructive" encounter with porn—what thinking with porn teaches its spectators—indelibly contours our understanding of fantasy in both public and private settings. Each piece featured here illuminates how thinking with porn classics enables new and alternative ways to ascertain the operations of genre (Capino), memory (Galvan), desire (Harris), language (Garcia Hernandez), and pleasure (Miller-Young).

### Reference

Dean, Tim, Steven Ruszczycky, and David Squires, eds. 2014. *Porn Archives*. Durham, NC: Duke University Press.

DOI 10.1215/10642684-8311871

*GLQ* 26:3

# *TAKE ONE* AND NOTES ON REALITY-BASED PORN

**José B. Capino**

*I*n 2016, Wakefield Poole's *Take One* (1977) resurfaced after decades in storage, thanks to a DVD edition by Vinegar Syndrome, a niche distributor of "rare and forgotten cult films," including pioneering gay male erotica. When I corresponded with Poole about an article I was writing in the early 2000s, he did not know the film's whereabouts (Capino 2005: 166). Neither did Bijou, the company peddling most of his work on home video. I was chasing down the film at that time, after seeing an advertisement for it in gay newspapers from the 1970s and reading various reviews (Verrill 1977) and publicity articles. The ad quoted glowing notices from critics and described *Take One* as a "docufantasy" about several men.[1] It seemed quite unlike prevailing types of nonfiction erotica, mainly short films centered on nude modeling (Stevenson 1997: 26) or the odd quasi-informational feature, such as Tom DeSimone and Jack Deveau's *Good Hot Stuff* (1975), a chronicle of key productions by the gay porn studio Hand in Hand Films. As a film scholar, I also found Poole's neologism *docufantasy* irresistible, a paradox worthy of John Grierson's famous characterization of the documentary as a "creative treatment of actuality" or Jean Rouch's billing of his partly staged documentaries as "ethno-fiction." To be sure, various scholars would later point out that even pornographic films with fictional scenarios contain documentary elements, such as actuality footage of nonsimulated sex and the significations of sexual pleasure and orgasm.[2]

The rediscovery of *Take One* has deepened my understanding of Poole's ties to documentary filmmaking and avant-garde cinema. I noticed that his film shares the confessional, quasi-documentary, and experimental approach of two celebrated works of the avant-garde: Curt McDowell's explicit and often humorous short film *Confessions* (1972) and Yvonne Rainer's feature-length dance-drama *Lives of Performers* (1972).

Those studying the documentary impulse in experimental film would do well to add *Take One* among its objects of study, not only for its thoughtful blurring of the boundaries between the testimonial and the performative but also for its intricate temporal continuum and flamboyant visual style. Equally important, and more germane to this article, *Take One* helps us better appreciate the salience of reality-based erotica, a subject that is as relevant as ever thanks to the continuing proliferation of "amateur" or quasi-actuality sex videos, including gonzo porn or live streaming programs from websites like Chaturbate.

In a featurette for the DVD, Poole describes *Take One* as a riff on the Broadway musical *A Chorus Line*, whose author, Michael Bennett, was a fellow client of his business manager and producing partner Marvin Shulman. Bennett's musical is a quasi-ethnographic piece about dancers in New York, with a prismatic narrative drawn extensively from tape-recorded interviews. Poole, with help from filmmaker Edd Dundas, imitated Bennett's method, using videocassettes instead of audiotape as recording media, and persons connected with the porn industry and the San Francisco gay subcultures instead of chorus dancers in New York as subjects (Schmitz 1977).

*Take One* revolves around a self-reflexive and documentary-like framing scenario of Poole working at the Nob Hill Theatre, the famous San Francisco all-male adult cinema, where he and some associates are depicted shooting and then premiering the titular film. The framing scenario plays out at various spaces in the building, including offices, the lobby, and private quarters, and segues into vignettes of Poole's coworkers, acquaintances, and some of the theater's patrons interacting with the filmmaker and his staff and then enacting their sexual fantasies for the camera. Later in the film, the subjects of the interviews congregate during the film's debut screening where they have sex with one another while the movie they had filmed earlier (and yet are also still filming for us) unspools in the auditorium. The recorded sound of the behind-the-scenes conversations between Poole and his subjects is interspersed with snippets of pretaped confessional interviews. The filmed vignettes feature the graphic unsimulated sex found in pornographic shorts or "loops," albeit staged by Poole in a highly expressive manner, using a syncretic mix of moody theatrical lighting, multiprojector slide shows and filmed scenes projected behind the performers, and movement that is alternately dance-like and sculptural.

In a collaborative chapter in *Representing Reality*, Bill Nichols, Christian Hansen, and Catherine Needham (1991: 215) juxtapose moving image pornography and ethnographic film, pointing out among other things that both cinemas "dwell on the body" and "rely on the documentary impulse, a guarantee that we will behold 'the thing itself,' caught in the grain of the cinematographic sound and image" (211). Filmed ethnography, they add, "is a kind of legitimated pornography, a pornography of knowledge," while "pornography is a strange, 'unnatural' form of ethnography, salvaging orgasmic bliss from the seclusion of the bedroom" (210). The distinction, they say, rests in part on "the basic unit" of each kind of praxis.

Where "a situation or event offering an example of cultural specificity" is the kernel of ethnography, its counterpart in pornography is one "exemplifying sexual engagement between actors/characters" (214).

Though it is in some ways sui generis, *Take One* shows us that reality-based erotica is as much pornographic ethnography as it is ethnographic pornography. Reality-based sex films aim to capture not only moments of "orgasmic bliss" but also the eroticism of the lived experiences of actual persons. To be sure, the promise of access to the performers' intimate affairs is as much a fantasy construction as the profilmic reality being recorded by the camera.

As with many works of ethnographic cinema (MacDougall 1998: 178) and reality-based erotica, Poole's film titillates with narratives of the exotic. *Take One* features a much-publicized set piece: a tryst between performers identified as twin brothers. Poole claims in an interview that he had filmed the two men (credited as Dutch and Rudy Valentino) having sex together for the first time (Fritscher 1978: 16–17). The segment, which involves not only oral and anal sex but also a fisting scene that Poole self-censored (15), is staged passionately, free of hesitation or awkwardness. Some might call the scene scandalously exploitative, but Poole's treatment makes an arousing spectacle of the brothers' incest.

Similar to the depiction of the amorous twins, two of the scenarios in Poole's film assimilate other ethnographic predilections, including honing in on eccentricities (Renov 2004: 216). In one episode, a male model—the porn actor Richard Locke—rhapsodizes about the joys of living in isolation in a desert environment. He acknowledges in his at times incoherent ramblings that while the harsh surroundings turn him on, his lover is not fully sold on his living situation. This last detail colors the way we see their romp under the beating sun and opens up a subplot about the long-term prospects of their relationship. We wonder, is this couple doomed, or will the furious pounding save them?

More representative of the rest of *Take One* and certain works of reality-based porn and ethnographic film (MacDonald 2013: 289) are vignettes that highlight the voyeuristic thrills of probing the fantasy lives of ordinary persons. The episode features Nick Ritter, the young man tasked with producing the poster for Poole's film. In voice-over narration he professes his childhood fascination with automobiles and then goes on to speak of his daydream of meeting a fellow car hobbyist with whom he would have sex. The testimonial quality of the young man's narrative is juxtaposed with a self-consciously theatrical representation of his erotic fantasies. In a darkened room, we see him masturbating on a platform and then on or beside various parts of his vintage Buick convertible (whose license plate reads K8, short for "Kate," the car's name). Behind him, on a scrim made of parachute fabric, flash still and moving images of automobiles and male bodies. The reverie plays out like scenes from Poole's acclaimed *Bijou* (1972), a film that depicts a construction worker's sexual fluidity through his activities in a mysterious theater-like space. The visuals of *Bijou* draw inspiration from the imagery of *Alice in Wonderland*, multimedia art installations (Teal 1972: 25), and the experimental "trance film" (Powell 2017: 280). At some point the mechanophilic performer in *Take One* shifts from humping the car's curvy and soft parts to thrusting his member and the pointed end of a car antenna against the car's round, orifice-like insignia. He also licks and sticks his tongue in and out of one of the portholes on the car's side, as though engaging in analingus or cunnilingus. The insignia poking and porthole rimming read like perfunctory, perhaps even comedic bits of erotic choreography, and yet they also index his idiosyncratic desires and the intensity of his sexual energy. Candid moments such as these reveal the ethnographic vein in Poole's film and reality-based pornography more generally. They give viewers a sense of mastery that comes from keenly observing the performers and extracting telling details about them.

I venture that such curious discoveries about the erotic and daily lives of persons are the oft-ignored but indispensable attractions of reality-based porn, mitigating its tendency toward uneventfulness. Apart from wringing eroticism from banality, these attractions expand the range of erogenous elements within the narrative and mise-en-scène of moving-image pornography.

The value of such unique moments of eroticized or fetishized banality is apparent in today's porn, such as in the video-streaming site Chaturbate. Combining the logics of security cameras, webcam-based video chats, reality shows on TV, and 1970s peep shows, the popular website serves up instantaneously transmitted reality-based erotica, typically produced out of the performer-broadcaster's home. To create frequent, multihour programs out of the inherently short-lived spectacles of self-pleasure and orgasms, the makers of reality-based porn frame even patently nonsexual activities as erotic spectacles. To cite an example, a straight-identified model who goes by the handle the_capt88 fills the time between orgasms by showing viewers the progress of his bathroom remodeling project or unwrapping presents sent to him through Amazon's gift registry. The Chris Pratt look-alike also charges extra for viewers to watch him munch on beef jerky, play an interactive roulette game, belt show tunes, or grind his hips against enormous pillows shaped out of the heads of cartoon mascots. Comments posted instantaneously by viewers are split between those that eroticize his nonsexual doings and those that characterize them as simply fascinating or endearing. On another Chaturbate show, twenty-something hipster-looking performer daddy_rocco runs through a Beatles playlist while "edging" himself. He occasionally delays orgasm by pausing to pet his cat with his lube-coated hands or taking the pussy out of the room altogether. Viewers gush about the feline (named Maggie, like the Tennessee Williams character) but appropriately withhold comment on its proximity to his flopping member. Elsewhere on the same platform, the performer Brock Cooper talks about real estate while stroking himself. He details plans to turn his newly acquired home into an Airbnb rental and fields questions from users about such ventures. As with other performers on Chaturbate, he advertises a gift registry. The selections reveal the model and girth of his butt plug, along with sundry details, such as his preferred fruit-flavored tea varieties and fast food restaurants.

On Chaturbate as in *Take One*, the raw stuff and cast-offs of ethnography fuel much of actuality-based pornography. (Reality-based porn might well be an unheralded but popular variety of urban or rural autoethnography.) When banality slides, as it often does, into unwatchability, eye-catching and apparently revelatory moments play a crucial role in retaining viewers. Similar to the *Take One* performer suddenly pouncing on the car's emblem, the_capt88 arrests drift in his multihour programming by putting on a royal blue robe designed like those worn by professional boxers but made of terry cloth. The robe signifies, among other things, a nostalgic identification with traditional masculinity, his childlike sense of play, and a desire to position himself as a celebrity who primps and does costume changes in front of the camera. Whereas the original viewers of *Take One* could respond to the specialness of Nick Ritter's emblem fucking only by touching themselves or fellow moviegoers, viewers of the_capt88 could add a rejoinder to the piquant moment of robe donning by remotely activating a vibrator plunged deep into his rectum, sending pleasurable jolts to the "captain's" prostate and painting colorful expressions on his face. Apart from heightening the thrill of amateur field observation (i.e., ethnography), the remote-controlled ass buzzing gives viewers access to the performer's body. It creates a stronger sense of intimacy between the observers and the observed and turns viewers into virtual makers of pornography. Such virtual interactions reshape the pornographic ethnography at the heart of reality-based erotica and, equally important, expand the genre of erotic figuration that Poole explored in his innovative "docufantasy."

**Notes**

1.    Reel to Real Productions, "Advertisements for *Take One*," clippings on Wakefield Poole, 1977. Anthology Film Archives, New York.

2.    For variations of this point, see Escoffier 2017: 92; Hilderbrand 2016: 339; and Williams 1999: 98.

## References

Capino, José B. 2005. "Seminal Fantasies: Wakefield Poole, Pornography, Independent Cinema, and the Avant-Garde." In *Contemporary American Independent Film: From the Margins to the Mainstream*, edited by Chris Holmlund and Justin Wyatt, 155–73. New York: Routledge.

Escoffier, Jeffrey. 2017. "Sex in the Seventies: Gay Porn Cinema as an Archive for the History of American Sexuality." *Journal of the History of Sexuality* 26, no. 1: 88–113.

Fritscher, Jack. 1978. "Dirty Poole: Everything You Fantasized about Wakefield Poole but Were Too Wrecked to Ask." *Drummer*, November, 14–22.

Hilderbrand, Lucas. 2016. "Historical Fantasies of 1970s Gay Male Pornography in the Archives." In *Porno Chic and the Sex Wars*, edited by Carolyn Bronstein and Whitney Strub, 327–48. Amherst: University of Massachusetts Press.

MacDonald, Scott. 2013. *American Ethnographic Film and Personal Documentary: The Cambridge Turn*. Berkeley: University of California Press.

MacDougall, David. 1998. *Transcultural Cinema*. Princeton, NJ: Princeton University Press.

Nichols, Bill, Christian Hansen, and Catherine Needham. 1991. "Pornography, Ethnography, and the Discourses of Power." In *Representing Reality: Issues and Concepts in Documentary*, edited by Bill Nichols, 201–28. Bloomington: Indiana University Press.

Powell, Ryan. 2017. "*Bijou* (Wakefield Poole, 1972)." *Porn Studies* 4, no. 3: 280–88.

Renov, Michael. 2004. *The Subject of Documentary*. Minneapolis: University of Minnesota Press.

Schmitz, Michael. 1977. "Wakefield Pool 'Take's One.'" *Kalendar*, May 27.

Stevenson, Jack. 1997. "From the Bijou to the Bedroom: A Secret History of Gay Sex Cinema." *Film Quarterly* 51, no. 1: 24–31.

Teal, Donn. 1972. "'Bijou' Offers Multi-media Hardcore." *Advocate*, November 22.

Verrill, Addison. 1977. "Take One." *Variety*, August 17.

Williams, Linda. 1999. *Hard Core: Power, Pleasure, and the "Frenzy of the Visible."* Expanded ed. Berkeley: University of California Press.

DOI 10.1215/10642684-8311885

# ONE DAY I WILL FORGET YOU

## Looking at Porn

R. Galvan

*I* should have asked for details," I thought as I took possession of my neighbor's "gay" belongings. It was the early 2000s, and among my friends and myself it was a common practice to carefully put away items that would code us as gay and sexually active to visiting family and friends. Things like fetish gear, sex toys, lubricants, photographs, and porn—not digital files but stuff like magazines, video cassettes, and DVDs—were discretely boxed and delivered to an out-of-sight location, only to be returned and lovingly unpacked and deposited to their rightful spot once houseguests departed.

The gesture of selectively packaging away one's things that outwardly reveal the self as homosexual and erotic generates a record, a fleeting performance that may be correlated to a sense of self-worth. On one hand, the scrutinizing of appearance through the trappings of one's home serves as a mirror, reflecting a refined image of the self, a presentation of acceptability and presumed domesticity. This sanitizing of lived space seems to privilege an aesthetic of empty interiors, like staging a home for prospective buyers to fantasize about owning. On the other hand, the private editing of one's possessions, concentrating and compartmentalizing the lascivious particularities of sexual conduct, masks the obsessive behavior that allows us to bury away those things about our self. By restricting viewership and putting the suggestive objects outside of the home, this "forgetting," a kind of curation of personal belongings, paradoxically emphasizes the deliberate thinking and protracted looking and doing one must accomplish in order to present an unintentional omission of salacious things that are eventually taken back.

For the case of my neighbor, the four crates of their possessions, which had transformed my galley kitchen into a warehouse, were reclaimed after two weeks. "Here. Keep it. I think you'll really like it." My compensation, fished from the top container that had been tucked away in my apartment, was a bootleg DVD. "A Night at Halsted's" had been handwritten across the disk, which was housed in a scratched CD jewel case. Still, I gladly took possession of the porn. And like its casing, the content of the DVD seemed to have poor fidelity, probably an effect of tape-to-tape copying that was then converted to disk. But certainly, evidence of its successive passage from factory-sealed offering to nondescript contraband did not wear away its value. Rather, it seemed to enhance it. This must be special—otherwise, why go to such lengths to preserve something, even in a degraded state, that is readily available elsewhere?

"The following is a feature presentation from H I S Video," announced a disembodied voice. A man enters a venue. He discloses to the front desk attendant his chronological plan for enjoying the many offerings of the space. Like a book, the film begins with a table of contents. It is as if the actors in the film are offering us instructions: follow the action sequentially or skip ahead. In either case, the scene explicitly induces one's compliance—you can't help but watch. In the best possible way, I'm haunted by that scene. It allows viewers to luxuriate in the outlined and forthcoming experiences in the film, as well as the possibility that viewers will know enough about their own sexual interests and may choose to locate them within the porn quickly.

What makes the scene especially impressive is the presentation of an eroticized gay male fully costumed in black leather and mustached as one that appears sexually aggressive and dominating. This premeditated cultivation and exhibition for others to consume, however, feel perfunctory, as if they're following the steps of an algorithm to bring about viewer titillation through prideful stereotypes. But through dialogue with the clean-shaven venue attendant (who is wearing sunglasses indoors), he is revealed to be thoughtful, admirable, and a "regular" guy, not an animated image of sexuality that reflects a marketable and easily consumed type of subjectivity.

This kind of vanity, an outward appearance that is constructed from a sense of self-worth, and with the intention to clearly relate to others, for me seems to be an essential characteristic of one's gendered and sexually aware self. And much like the composing of one's home by stowing away belongings that may make others blush, the fussing and indulging about one's personal image invites others to look, to love, and to fantasize about handling. It is an assertion of the self to be not just in space but of space, of this world. That is the essence of vanity: as we gaze on the things that surround our lives to understand the world, it is the world that we will see instead of our things. We will forget them, including and especially porn.

DOI 10.1215/10642684-8311899

# UNTITLED: INSPIRED

## Keith M. Harris

### 1.

Jean-Daniel Cadinot's *Harem* (1984, France) holds an especially gratifying and significantly problematic place in the erotic pleasures and politics of my homosexual life.

### 2.

For one, even though pornography has its ebbs and flows, its frequencies and infrequencies, as something that I watch, as something that I inconsistently do, however often or seldom done, *Harem* is the first and last pornographic film, be it a departure or return.

### 3.

*Harem* follows the hardcore sexual travails of a French tourist in Tunisia in pursuit of a young local Arab. The film unfolds from the tourist's first meeting of the young Tunisian during an orgiastic encounter in a male hammam. In the ooohhhss and throes of the bathhouse crowd, the two share a moment. The young Tunisian quickly departs as the French tourist hastily begins chase. For the next fifty minutes or so, the French tourist spots his object of desire in the crowd and loses him again, down narrow passages, through unmarked shop doorways. Between sightings, in every shop investigated the tourist bottoms, vigorously, for merchant, supplier, delivery man, stock boy, and customer alike. Finally, at the edge of the medina, past the crowds, he spots his object of desire. Together again, the tourist and Tunisian frolic in the ocean and fuck on the beach, as the sun sets, with close credits, in naked, romantic embrace.

### 4.

Cadinot's *Harem* and several other of his early titles, *Sex Oasis* (1987), *Street Smart* (1987), and *Thick'n Creamy* (1985) among them, are some of the first

French pornographic productions shot in North Africa and/or featuring African Black and Arab men—with members as trope—energetically, forcefully, viciously servicing the French man in the film (Mack 2017: 243). These early "sex bazaar" films and late-career films like his six-part opus, *Nomades I–VI* (2005–7), place Cadinot's oeuvre as one that initiates the *porno ethnik* (ethnic porn) subgenre that continues today (Cervulle 2008: 175; see also Mack 2017: 221). So-called ethnic porn, straight or gay, is not unique to French pornographic production and output. Ethnic porn is a refinement of discursive tensions, stimulations, and intimacies that already libidinally animate pornography. With *Harem* and other films, Cadinot's storylines, locations, and characters exploit colonial desire and the colonizer-colonized dynamics from which the whiteness of the French national body and the ethnicity of the postcolonial Arab body emerge with cultural and symbolic meaning and value. The *ethnic* in the subgeneric nomenclature presupposes the alterity of an other, which in turn defines the normativity of another, the two locked in a subject-object dyad. In the postcolonial France context and moment of emergence for French gay porn and Cadinot's *porno ethnik*, the intersubjective ground of the pornscape becomes the French colonial/national body and North African Arab body. Furthermore, the narrative, characters' sexuality and sexual positions, viewer's spectatorial practices, and even intended audience demographics and marketing are to a great extent embedded in the subgeneric presuppositions of *porno ethnik*.

## 5.

The visuality of pornography is one that deploys fantasy as the visual artifact and setting for the discursive navigations, mediations, and interplays among desire, sexuality, and the interpellated, viewing subject. In pornoptics, desire is made visible as visual fantasy. In *porno ethnik* films as seen in the fantasy visuals of *Harem*, the space of the colony (more contemporarily the urban surrounding, perispace of *banlieues*, French suburban immigrant neighborhoods and housing) is the pornscape in which French national and Arab colonial and their encounter configure the pornotropes seen in the sexual tourist/citizen/interloper/target/victim/dominant bottom/cum bucket versus black/*beur* (North African)/*racaille* (Arab homo-thug)/*grosse tige* (big dick)/*baulieusards* (denizens of *banlieues*). The Frenchman and the Arab are sexualized variously as gay, sexually pristine, sexual victim, passionate aggressive-bottom and straight, sexually virile, hyper-sexual homo-thug, dispassionate aggressive-top, respectively. French bottoms and Arab tops traverse the colonial fantasy ground and map the pornscapes in narrow medina passages, between plateau and medina, in the steamy hammams, on far-away, pristine sandy shores, between *cité* and *banlieues*—all while Orientalist fantasy, *nostalgérie* (nostalgic colonial narratives), tourist or journeymen narratives, loose romance narratives, and/or situational/spatial scenes prompt the prurience for all manner of sex, back alley rapes, and basement *tournates* (gang bangs).

### 6.

*Harem*: The desiring, all-consuming sexuality, the ravenous sex/search from the hammam, in and out of the medina shops—where there is more, heavier, hotter in and out sexing/searching—leads the Frenchman to the young Tunisian in the final scenes of the film. In all these scenes—from the hammam to medina passages, curtain-covered shop backrooms, a beach expanse blanketed in sea foam and spume, and finally the gossamer, gauzed hotel room—there should have been nothing there for me.

### 7.

I was finishing my master's degree in the English department at Berkeley. I cannot remember what had prompted my outburst and denunciation of Marguerite Duras in a seminar some weeks before (or why we were reading her novel). Nevertheless, after the seminar had come to a conclusion, in the silence following my comments about reading Duras and exercises in colonialism, someone suggested that I take a look at a film by Claire Denis. A few weeks later I was at the now defunct Tower Video on Market Street in San Francisco with Denis's *Chocolat* (1988) in hand when I stumbled into the adult section of the store. The videos were arranged in the usual tripartite formation of straight, gay, and bisexual sections, but oddly enough, each primary section was secondarily organized by national cinema. Apparently, there were only three nations making porn for men like me: France, Italy, and the United States. I had the usual annoyance with the American section because of the tertiary breakdown of race and ethnicity. I was further exasperated because of the ease by which I could tell which films were Black or Latin cast and made for white men and which were Black or Latin cast and made for Black or Latin men. Also, I had already had the opportunity on another occasion to peruse Italian gay porn. In the French section, the box cover for *Harem* caught my eye. The men looked like me, but I gathered from the Orientalist costume and set for the photo inset that there was an Arabic theme. Surprisingly, I thought, there were no white men on the cover. *Chocolat* and *Harem* it was.

**8.**

As I walked home, downhill from Market to Guerrero, I flipped the box over to see the French tourist on his knees, back arched, butt up, surrounded by the contrasting color and dick size of the other men in a photo clipped from the hammam scene in the beginning of the film. I did not even read the blurb. The back photo, which would have been on the front of a "black on white" American production, let me know that this would be the same ol' same ol', and why would it not be. I was angry with myself for expecting otherwise: there was nothing there for me.

**9.**

Yet there was.

**10.**

Once home, I popped the tape in, expecting no surprises, expecting the usual: white boy gets it, likes it, and gives it up to get it again. I was expecting that, though we were not the same, were from different historical, national, and cultural contexts, the African American descendent from slaves who was viewing and the postcolonial French Arab men performing were analogous, if not the same, when standing in an ethnic pornscape: though we were different, the pornoptics of whiteness would have us embody the same pornotropes in the racial or colonial homoerotic fantasy visuals of a film like *Harem*. In short order, my expectations, without surprise, were met.

**11.**

With this first viewing of *Harem*, I cut it short, switched tapes, and watched *Chocolat*.

**12.**

This was the first film by Denis that I had ever seen, and though it has since been knocked down a few by Denis films like *Beau Travail* (1999) and *Trouble Everyday* (2001), *Chocolat* became one of my favorite films, raising the bar for French film in my film-viewing practices. The esteem for the film was garnered in the clarity with which colonialism and desire explore the past and the present. This exploration, for me, was always redirected, sublimated, if not submerged, but always there, in other French films (and in Duras's work), but never fully engaged, not to my liking at least. Furthermore, that night after the unsurprising, disarousing, and disappointing abbreviated viewing of *Harem*, I realized that Denis's film and Cadinot's *porno ethnik* were confronting the same colonialism, the same desire. The following night, before returning the videos, thinking about how I reacted to both, I popped *Harem* back in and asked, "So what is your problem?"

## 13.

What I liked about *Chocolat* was that the film was thoughtful, contemplative of the structuration of desire, of colonial desire. Even though the undercurrents of stereotype and objectification were there, and were still problematic, the visuals, storytelling, pacing, shot sequences, the overall form of the *Chocolat* mediated the viewing experience, enabling critical reflection on the subject matter. Ethnic porn and films like *Harem* had always sullied the porn-viewing experience, and not for the obvious reasons but because too often I had had sexual experiences with men who expected the ethnic sexuality, and fantasy sex of ethnic porn was expected and desired from me, by me: viewing ethnic porn therefore made me feel complicit in the formation of myself as a sexual proclivity, complicit and enjoying of it. In retrospect, after back-to-back viewing of the two films, I realized the expectations that were not met with the initial viewing of *Harem* should have never been. I should have never had them. Perhaps, I should have had the same negative expectations for *Chocolat* (I did, in fact, and they were not met).

## 14.

That first abbreviated viewing of *Harem*: What was I thinking? I had seen porn before. I knew the effect and affect of pornography and viewer very well. I had gotten through more of *Lawrence of Arabia* than of *Harem*.

## 15.

That night I went back to the cover and the reason that I had chosen, without hesitation, to rent the video: the men on the cover were hot. I wanted to see them naked. I wanted to see them fuck. I knew whom I desired. I also knew that I should have no hopes that my sexual desire would ever unfold as the visual fantasy in a gay pornographic film. I had grown accustomed to an ambiguously pleasurable, if not pleasurably indifferent, end.

## 16.

That night I went back to *Harem*, with ambition and intention. That the film was not for me as I had thought did not mean that I did not watch it. It just meant that I did not watch the film or seek pleasure from it for those reasons. It meant that I found my own. I went for the brown men. I laughed at the tourist's pain of entry, the stereotypical, hyperbolic violence of the sexual fantasy. I fantasized about the men, put the men I desired in another fantasy.

## 17.

However, I have not found any means by which I can pleasurably appreciate the end sequence of the film, the scenes in which the tourist, after many sexual encounters, exits the narrow passages of the medina onto the beach. Here they finally find each other. After all that butt fucking and colonial chase, the tourist and Tunisian fall into a romantic embrace. Fortunately, I have not gotten that far in the film for years. It really did not matter since I had learned, with *Harem*, how to displace the cultural excitations and stimulations, the discursive optics informing the gaze and the form of fantasy—I had learned how to displace it all with my libidinal fantasy and motives, to my own salacious, sensational end.

### References

Cervulle, Maxime. 2008. "French Heteronormativity and the Commodification of the Arab Body." *Radical History Review*, no. 100: 171–78.

Mack, Mehammed Amadeus. 2017. *Sexagon: Muslims, France, and the Sexualization of National Culture*. New York: Fordham University Press.

DOI 10.1215/10642684-8311913

# THE PORNOGRAPHIC GRAMMAR OF THE VOCAL LATINX BODY

**Yessica Garcia Hernandez**

$\mathcal{D}$uring the summer of 2018 I taught a course titled "'Putting Hypersexuality to Work': Ethnic Images in Film." The course was inspired by Mireille Miller-Young's article "Putting Hypersexuality to Work: Black Women and Illicit Eroticism in Pornography" (2010b). The goal of the course was for students to analyze and understand how pornography created different racial scripts, how queer and feminist genres emerged, and how adult entertainers of color negotiate labor politics. Given it was my first time teaching a porn class, I made a commitment to read what I could find about porn and pedagogy (Decena 2010; Miller-Young 2010a; Penley 2013; Parreñas Shimizu 2010). Most of the films I assigned were incorporated into the course because they were identified as porn classics by porn scholars, particularly when thinking about race, gender, class, size, and queer representation. As I watched these porn classics and assigned readings to my students, I began to realize that most of the literature had very little about Latinx and fat representation (Flores 2013).[1] As a relational scholar of race, class, gender, and sexualities, I became intrigued by this gap.

In this essay I share notes made throughout my journey searching for Latinx representation in several porn classics. Building on Celine Parreñas Shimizu's (2007: 109) observations that compare how Asian, Mexican, and Latina women in stag film are "rendered through space," I argue that, outside of the stag film, Latina difference is marked through what Ines Dolores Casillas, Juan Sebastian Ferrada, and Sara Veronica Hinojos (2018: 63) call "the vocal body," defined as "all aspects of a person's speech, such as perceived accent(s), intonation, speaking, volume and word choice." In pornographic films, the vocal body appears through the vernaculars of "dirty talk," particularly the English-to-Spanish code-switching that happens during sex.

In *The Dancers* (1981), the "sonics of pornography" (Mowlabocus and Medhurst 2017) are evident through Vanessa Del Rio's role as Frances, a waiter who abandons her job in search of a Hollywood opportunity. The main characters in *The Dancers* are a group of white traveling strippers who hook up with different women before their shows. We first see the men stripping, enjoying their profession, and later we see them in their daily lives having sex with different women.

Sebastian, the blondest stripper of the group, meets Frances while she is working at a restaurant. Frances overhears him having a phone conversation about being a dancer, so she approaches him with the hope that he can make her a famous superstar. Sebastian and Frances leave to her apartment so she can show him her talent. Frances is the only Latina character in the film, and her role best exemplifies how Latina actresses are encouraged to hyperperform their "vocal body"—particularly their thick accent and intonation. The sex scene following the first encounter between Frances and Sebastian opens with Frances telling Sebastian to wait a minute outside of the apartment so she can clean up her place and take off her headband from work. After Frances lets her hair loose, she allows Sebastian to go inside. Sebastian first peeks through the door and enters with hesitation. Frances continues to clean up her place while Sebastian walks toward the couch. He scoops her chair to clean it and flicks several crumbs from it.

As he sits down, Frances says, "Well, I mean everybody is always talking about how they know somebody, how they know somebody, how they have friends, how they got diz [this] how they got that. How juw [you] want to be a movie star, juw have to know somebody, well now, I know somebody."[2] Sebastian responds, "Yeah, who?" Frances replies, "Juw, I know juw." Sebastian then looks at Frances from head to toe and says, "Oh, yeah, that's right, I forgot. You know me. We know each other." Sebastian starts to unzip her dress while she tells him, "Juw give me the business?" And he responds, "What business?" She clarifies, "Juw say something about business at the restaurant, remember?" To seduce her, he says, "Yeah, I am giving you the business." Frances states, "Oh, Mr. Sebastian. Juw are going to make me a big movie star." To undress her he says, "A movie star? Oh, yeah. I'll make you a movie star. A matter of fact this will be a great audition. Listen, uh, let's go over here to rehearse." They walk toward the bed, and Frances begins to rub his back and hair. Sebastian is unbuttoning his shirt, but he gets bothered when she touches his blonde hair. He screams at her, "Watch the hair!" After he takes off his clothes, he gets on top of her and they start kissing.

At this point Frances is so excited she starts to talk dirty in Spanish. She tells him, "Aiy, tíramela. Sí, sí, sí. Te gusta, ay sí métemela. Ay sí papi dámelo. Ay sí más duro, dígame." Although Frances is really into it, Sebastian stops her and says, "Hey, hey, cool it lady! Don't talk in Spanish." Frances ignores him and continues to talk in Spanish: "Sí, sí, sí, sí, ay me gusta. Ay sí papi dámelo papi, sí. Ay papi. Ay papi, dámelo, métemelo." The shooting style of this sex scene is distinctive, intentionally including an aerial view of their sex act to racialize Frances as a low-class Latina. The bird's-eye view reminds the viewer of France's dirtiness, or what Deborah Vargas (2014) aptly calls *suciedad*. This scene underscores how the adult industry constantly used, and continues to use, the Latinx vocal body and its accentuated moans as a racial marker of difference. In this case, the on-screen staging of Frances's accent enhances tropicalized fantasies that Latinas are expected to fulfill in order to capitalize on their staged "exotic foreignness" (Nguyen 2014). Moreover, Sebastian and Frances's sex scene exemplifies how the mise-en-scène of Frances's home, her broken English, and the technique of Spanish dirty talk are used to hear race and racialize Latinas as sexual others. Sebastian's character vividly represents the historical access to resources that whiteness has afforded him to enter Hollywood. While Sebastian is portrayed as a sanitary citizen, the dirtiness of Frances's home marks her as an "unsanitary subject" (Ochoa 2014: 40).

Although the negotiation of language during the sex scene between Frances and Sebastian demonstrates the ways that "racist nativism" makes it to the bedroom (Perez Huber 2010), we can read this exchange through what Hoang Tan Nguyen (2014: 62) calls an "accented pornography," defined as "a mode of porn performance and reception that, while drawing on toxic racialized sexual roles, also allows for the envisioning and inhabiting of a different subject position vis-à-vis" racialized fantasy scenarios. Frances's refusal to stop speaking Spanish when Sebastian demands her to stop shows her agency and "erotic sovereignty" (16).[3] I read Frances's refusal to stop as a reclamation of space through the vocal body, even within a scripted porn film narrative. Engaging in Spanish dirty talk appeared to be Del Rio's intoxicating pleasure—her way to get "in on it," as she refers to it in her autobiography (Hanson 2016).[4] Latinidad, particularly the vocality of Spanish dirty talk is Frances's "lexicon of desire" (Nash 2014: 86) and her way of engaging with what Jennifer Nash (2014: 86) calls "race-pleasures," "where the wound of [racialization] is taken up as a site of ecstasy." Nash theorizes race-pleasures through an analysis of *SexWorld* (1977), a film about a sexual weekend getaway where "every fantasy will be fulfilled" and the panics of interracial sex are left behind.

I taught both *The Dancers* and *SexWorld* in our unit on interracial sex. I paired these films to show how golden-age porn showcases the taboos of interracial sex and prioritizes heterosexual encounters (even lesbian sex scenes are centered on a white male gaze). This pairing worked perfectly because the sonics of pornography where also evident in *SexWorld*. For instance, Black vernacular speech and dirty talk were also important aspects of the recurring racist scene between Jill (Desiree West) and Roger (John Leslie).[5] Both Miller-Young (2014: 96) and Jennifer Nash (2014: 91) analyze this scene extensively because it demonstrates how ideas of blackness intersect with pornography. Miller-Young states, "*Sex World* rehearses a scenario that dates back to the plantation sexual economy, in which black women's sexuality was made available to white patriarchy, objectified and imagined as desirous of the (white man's) civilizing mission." However, Nash finds ways to read the pleasures that Jill displays through her seduction of Roger. Nash states, "While Roger initially shares his disgust at Jill's body, and at black women's bodies more generally, Jill responds to his every assertion, insisting on her body's sexual virtues, which she imagines as particular to black female sexuality. As the scene progresses, Jill explicitly pokes fun at the racial fictions that give the encounter its erotic charge, playing with the conception of black women's sexual alterity and even locating pleasure in it" (2014: 103).

What struck me about *SexWorld* was that the scene between Jill and Roger is so blatantly racist that other racial negotiations in the film are overlooked. However, as we know, "race is intersectional. It's the life of the party; it never goes anywhere alone. Because race has to do with differential citizenship, lesser citizenship, premature death, disproportionate exposure to violence, it makes you look at more than one group" (Lipsitz 2019: 23). In porn, race is also the life of the bedroom, and in films featuring Latinx performers it never cums alone. This is because race has to do with whom we are conditioned to desire, whose desires we prioritize, and even whom we let cum on screen. In *SexWorld*, Latinx representation is created in relation to Black sexuality, and we never see money shots from brown or black men; their purpose instead is to satisfy the mysterious desires of white women (Nash 2014: 101).

The Latinx characters in *SexWorld* do not have central roles. Take, for instance, Tomás, a brown man who changes his name to Tom to make the white woman he was assigned more comfortable as he waits for her to open the door. Oscar, the other Latinx actor, is the SexWorld counselor that helps the white woman client get paired with Tomás. Although the woman refuses to talk to Oscar about her sexual fantasies, we know that she desires a younger man in the control room. The counselors who match clients to their ideal fuck read that interaction as a sign that she is craving a "Latin type," particularly one that is "gentle." Tomás's sex scene appears before the only sex scene in the film featuring a Black man, whose name is unmentioned and who does not say a word throughout his sexual encounter. What we do know is that Lisa Hill, the white woman who has sex with him, requested a Black man that looked like the one from the 1972 porn film *Behind the Green Door*.[6] In contrast to the Black man in the film, Tomás is portrayed as the Latin lover. This is captured both visually and sonically. The shots of the sex scene are edited to portray a feeling of tenderness, matching the soft guitar sounds added to the soundtrack. The only Latina character we encounter is a

Frida Kahlo look-alike, who has her hair braided and wears a *huipil* (embroidered dress). We do not know her name, but during the orientation she asks about her incestual sexual fantasies and presents herself as very timid and shy. The Frida look-alike does not become one of the main characters in the film, but her curiosity is exposed at the beginning of the narrative to highlight the perversities, even if incestuous, that SexWorld can bring to its clients. A comparison of the Latinx representation in *SexWorld* and *The Dancers* demonstrates the race-pleasures of Frances's dirty talk because compared to the other Latinx characters, she uses the vocality of her brown body to express her own pleasures.

Playing with her Afro-Latina identity, Del Rio, as Frances, constructs her own racial folklore: "The louder and thicker the accent, the sweeter the juice." Even if Frances did not resort to her own racial fictions through the scripted dialogue, listening between the scripted lines, spoken words mixed with moans of pleasure are also sounds of resistance in an otherwise premediated landscape that organizes Latinx bodies according to white desires. However, how do we understand the absence of fat racialized bodies in these porn classics? I continue to wonder, how does fatness queer our grammar of the Latinx vocal body? How is racial difference created when, for example, two fat women of color fuck each other?

## Notes

I dedicate this piece to my mentors of porn and sexuality, Jillian Hernandez and Hoang Tan Nguyen; both of you supported my interests in porn during my years at UCSD, and I am very excited about starting this research journey. I also thank Ricky Rodríguez and Angelica Camacho for their support and feedback on the manuscript: your input is so valuable, and I appreciate it tremendously.

1.  Afro-Latina actor Vanessa Del Rio is an exception, given she is one of the most popular actresses in the golden age of pornography. Nonetheless, even her own negotiations of race, as a mixed-race Latina, are complicated. In some films, through vocality she performs a stereotypical working-class notion of Latinidad, and in other films she is erased to be read as racially ambiguous.

2.  The way Frances pronounces *yes* with a long intonation ("jesss") is another way of marking her Latina accent. In this article, I use *juw* to approximate her on-screen accent.

3.  The costume that Del Rio wears in *The Dancers*, which is used as the cover of the film, also deserves analysis. In her autobiography she says, "All the clothes I wore in the movies I wore in real life" (Hanson 2016: 194). Her aesthetic choices can be read through what Jillian Hernandez (2009) calls "sexual aesthetic excess." My students

and I watched *Jacquette* (1976), where she plays Madame X; *Odyssey* (1977); and *Come with Me My Love* (1976), where she plays Lola. In just these three narrative films the play with her vocality was drastically different. For instance, her English did not have an accent, and her dirty talk was not performed in Spanish, but what did remain throughout were her red nails, which were staged as an extension of her Latina vocal body. Her moans did remain similar throughout these films, which I will explore in future work.

4.  To view the complete interview watch the DVD inside *Vanessa Del Rio: Fifty Years of Slutty Behavior* (Hanson 2016). For more on Vanessa Del Rio, see Rodriguez 2015.

5.  For a description of this scene see Miller-Young (2014: 90–103) and Nash (2014: 107–12).

6.  As the first feature length film, *Behind the Green* door portrayed a Black man and white woman racial scene (Miller-Young 2014: 74). The Black actor in this film is Johnnie Keyes, a former boxer whose performances portrayed Black muscular masculinity.

## References

Casillas, Ines Dolores, Juan Sebastian Ferrada, and Sara Veronica Hinojos. 2018. "The Accent on Modern Family: Listening to Representation of the Latina Vocal Body." *Aztlan: A Journal of Chicano Studies* 43, no. 1: 61–88.

Decena, Carlos. 2010. "Risky Lesson: Thinking/Viewing/Talking Sex in the Feminist Classroom." *Signs* 2, no. 2. ffc.twu.edu/decena_essay_1_2-2.html.

Flores, April. 2013. "Being Fatty D: Size, Beauty, and Embodiment in the Adult Industry." In *The Feminist Porn Book: The Politics of Producing Pleasure*, edited by Tristan Taormino, Celine Parreñas Shimizu, and Constance Penley, 279–83. New York: Feminist Press.

Hanson, Dian, ed. 2016. *Vanessa Del Rio: Fifty Years of Slightly Slutty Behavior*. Köln: Taschen.

Hernandez, Jillian. 2009. "'Miss, You Look like a Bratz Doll': On Chonga Girls and Sexual-Aesthetic Excess." *NWSA Journal* 21, no. 3: 63–90.

Lipsitz, George. 2019. "Race as a Relational Theory: A Roundtable Discussion." In *Relational Formations of Race: Theory, Method, and Practice*, edited by Natalia Molina, Daniel Martinez HoSang, and Ramon Gutiérrez, 22–42. Berkeley: University of California Press.

Miller-Young, Mireille. 2010a. "The Pedagogy of Pornography: Films for the Feminist Classroom." *Signs* 2, no. 2. ffc.twu.edu/issue_2-2/miller-young_essay_1_2-2.html.

Miller-Young, Mireille. 2010b. "Putting Hypersexuality to Work: Black Women and Illicit Eroticism in Pornography." *Sexualities* 13, no. 2: 219–35.

Miller-Young, Mireille. 2014. *A Taste for Brown Sugar: Black Women in Pornography.* Durham, NC: Duke University Press.

Mowlabocus, Sharif, and Andy Medhurst. 2017. "Six Propositions on the Sonics of Pornography." *Porn Studies* 4, no. 2: 210–24.

Nash, Jennifer Christine. 2014. *The Black Body in Ecstasy: Reading Race, Reading Pornography.* Durham, NC: Duke University Press.

Nguyen, Hoang Tan. 2014. *A View from the Bottom: Asian American Masculinity and Sexual Representation.* Durham, NC: Duke University Press.

Ochoa, Marcia. 2014. *Queen for a Day: Transformistas, Beauty Queen, and the Performance of Femininity in Venezuela.* Durham, NC: Duke University Press.

Parreñas Shimizu, Celine. 2007. *The Hypersexuality of Race: Performing Asian/American Women on Screen and Scene.* Durham, NC: Duke University Press.

Parreñas Shimizu, Celine. 2010. "Intimate Literacies: The Ethics of Teaching Sexually Explicit Films." *Signs* 2, no. 2. ffc.twu.edu/issue_2-2/parrenas-shimizu_essay _1_2-2.html.

Penley, Constance. 2013. "A Feminist Teaching Pornography? That's like Scopes Teaching Evolution!" In *Feminist Porn Book: The Politics of Producing Pleasure*, edited by Tristan Taormino, Celine Parreñas Shimizu, and Constance Penley, 179–99. New York: Feminist Press.

Perez Huber, Lindsay. 2010. "Using Latina/o Critical Race Theory (LatCrit) and Racist Nativism to Explore Intersectionality in the Educational Experiences of Undocumented Chicana College Students." *Educational Foundations* 24, nos. 1–2: 77–96.

Rodriguez, Juana Maria. 2015. "Pornographic Encounters and Interpretative Interventions: *Vanessa del Rio: Fifty Years of Slightly Slutty Behavior.*" *Women and Performance: A Journal of Feminist Theory* 25, no. 3: 315–35.

Vargas, Deborah. 2014. "Ruminations on Lo Sucio as a Latino Queer Analytic." *American Quarterly* 66, no. 3: 715–26.

DOI 10.1215/10642684-8311927

# CUMMING TO POWER

**Mireille Miller-Young**

$O$k, it's all yours. Come here!" Johnny Wadd, the hard-boiled detective, pulls Cindy, the freshly minted widow, into a deep tongue kiss. The "it" that Wadd, played by the renowned adult film actor John C. Holmes, references is his "14 inch cock." Along with his "rather pleasant smile" and "nice big blue eyes," Wadd's exceptional member is, he tells her, on "offer" to Cindy, played by the most noted Black adult film actress of her generation, Desiree West. The actors' one scene in Alan Colberg's *Tapestry of Passion* (1976) is one of my all-time favorites. Rather than consider an entire film from the classic eras of golden- or silver-age pornography, I find this single scene to be a vastly rich text to explore ways in which porn offers all of us a tool to grapple with desire economies of gender, sex, and race.

*Tapestry of Passion* emerged in the latter part of the golden age, when porn producers sought to make full-length narrative films (shot on film) on par with Hollywood. Though it was directed by Colberg, the film was part of a series created by Bob Chinn (Robert Husong) about the character Johnny Wadd, an exceptionally endowed white male detective played by Holmes. Whereas Holmes was the basis for the character Dirk Diggler in the Paul Thomas Anderson movie *Boogie Nights* (1997), Burt Reynolds's award-winning performance as porn director Jack Horner was based on the figure of Chinn, a prolific writer-director in the adult industry during the 1970s and 1980s. Set in San Francisco and featuring a cast of celebrated actors such as Leslie Bovee, Sharon Thorpe, Annette Haven, and John Leslie, *Tapestry of Passion* follows Johnny Wadd as he investigates a sexualized murder by a demented dominatrix known as the Black Widow. Holmes's Wadd interviews West's Cindy, the widow of the murdered man, in the kitchen of her posh apartment. The interview soon turns to sex, but before it does Cindy voices something important that sets the stage for her encounter with Wadd.

"Johnny, all the questions you're asking . . . what does it matter? My husband is dead, and I'm not dead. I'm living. What do they say? 'Death hurts only the living'? Anyway, I want to enjoy myself." Cindy, in a clear setup by the writers to allow a newly widowed woman to hook up with the detective investigating her late husband's murder, actually expresses something quite profound. Not in the words written for her, but in West's performance as a Black woman, of a Black woman,

I find the proclamation "I'm not dead. I'm living," followed by "Anyway, I want to enjoy myself," to be fascinating on multiple registers.

What does it mean for a Black woman to proclaim life and to desire pleasure? This question resides in a deep place for Black women. It emerges from a core concern in the afterlife of slavery and shapes the image, performance, and labor of Black women in pornography. If sexual freedom is central to freedom, how do we excavate economies of pleasure that are for ourselves and that serve us? What does that desire unleash and make possible?

As a Black woman pornography consumer employing what I call a Black feminist pornographic gaze, I bring to my viewership not only an optic for the potential agency that Black women always retain in their sexual labor on-screen (or elsewhere) but also a fundamental identification with Black women seeking erotic autonomy, life, and joy in any domain within a nation consumed with anti-Black violence.

One element that stands out about this scene between the top Black woman performer and the top white male performer of the 1970s porn industry is that it is a surprisingly tender encounter. In this form of "soft porn," the fantasy and the actors themselves articulate a language of tenderness. Desiree West as Cindy exudes an ethereal goddess-like glamour and beauty. Her hair is pressed straight and hangs in shoulder-length soft curls, a misty aquamarine eye shadow meets thickly plumped eyelashes on bedroom eyes, her lips are graced in a pouty soft pink, and her elegantly manicured burgundy nails decorate graceful hands. West comes into the scene wearing a flowing white silk nightgown and matching robe cheerfully printed with a pink and green floral pattern, matching her bedroom that is colored in pinks, greens, creams, and golds. The bedroom furniture further gives the feeling of feminine boudoir meets springtime in the 1970s: pink settee, macramé throw, polished gold canopy bed, bedside flowers, and cupid lamps. The view out the bright windows shows a sunlit city and bay expanding down below. Sunlight fills the room as Rolf Kühn's jazz vibraphone track *Early Morning* saturates the scene like melodic incense.

"Is that lovely enough for you?" Cindy asks Wadd about her pretty gown and robe ensemble. "It's nice, and it feels good too," he says as he strokes her arm. They kiss lovely, soft kisses with exploring tongues, and they caress each other's arms, legs, shoulders, and cheeks. While kissing, Wadd gently pulls the bow on Cindy's robe, letting it gracefully fall from her shoulders.

Compared to most porn scenes in the golden era, and most interracial straight-market porn scenes then and now, this scene feels expressly romantic. The bright sunny room elevated in the clouds and plush cream carpet beneath their feet seem to elevate the couple to another plane. Both the streaming video and DVD show a scene in soft blurred vision, what some call a Vaseline or soft-focus lens in photography, though this effect appears to be from the deconditioning of the film from the transfer to video, then disc, then digital media, rather than from the original 35-mm print. Still, sitting from here and looking back through time via this faded technology, the scene feels like a suspended dream.

Yet in that dream, there is always the urgency of race that pervades the fantasy and the factory of pornography. Indeed, the racial stakes of a scene with the top Black actress and top white actor of the time were enormous, and the production came at a time when those stakes would have been felt. Desiree West was disparagingly called the "Black Panther Porn Star" in a memoir by David Jennings (2000), a porn director in the 1970s, because he remembered her being aggressive, outspoken, and even difficult to work with—apparently, she had the audacity to refuse a cum shot on her face in one film by Jennings.

Though there is no evidence she was a Panther rather than simply a strong Black woman who stood up for herself, West lived in Oakland at the time, where in fact the Black Panther Party had a very strong presence. Interestingly, during the height of Desiree West's career in porn, Elaine Brown became chairwoman of the party, and having run for Oakland City Council in 1973 and 1975, Brown was widely known throughout the city as a powerful symbol of Black women's leadership. West came from a social context where Black nationalist and Black feminist politics were prominent and where bodily autonomy in the haptics of racial fetishism and racialized violence mattered.

This aesthetic and political militancy were an aspect of Black embodied agency that the porn industry sought to capitalize on during the Black Power era in what I call soul porn, a form defined by the desirability of Black sexual aesthetics for white audiences, and white pornographers' appropriation and imitation of what they saw as Black soul. Often, scenes focused on interracial sex played up the conflict and contrast between races. And while these interracial erotic dramas invoke tropes and myths to powerfully charge the tension in the narrative and sex alike, as I argue in *A Taste for Brown Sugar* (Miller-Young 2014), soul porn is also constituted by Black people's own mobilization of racialized eroticism into sexual media.

In this case, while we acknowledge that West's presence in the scene may have aroused both titillation and fear in viewers and pornographers as they grappled with Black women's changing social status and increasingly resistive politics, we also must remember that West had her own expectations, demands, and desires for her performance as she simultaneously navigated the racist and sexist currents of an industry striving to propel the sexual revolution as a cultural movement that would transform American liberalism.

John C. Holmes also had an incredible symbolic power in the way he embodied white masculinity. He remains one of the most famous male porn stars ever, due to his reportedly 13½-inch-long penis and tragic personal narrative, including a bizarre alleged role in the notorious Wonderland Murders. Holmes's rise to fame came at a time in the industry when leading male actors like Harry Reems, John Leslie, and Jamie Gillis were getting work in narrative films, but hardly a character-driven movie series like Chinn's Johnny Wadd films. There was a tremendous fascination with Holmes's exceptional genital size, given that most white actors were not noted in that category. In fact, Black male actors—often referred to as "bucks" in the marketing for interracial loops from the 1970s—tended to be the focus of the fetishization around penis size in straight porn. Indeed, the incongruence of Holmes's working-class, midwestern white boyishness, his tall, lanky body, his disheveled sandy blonde locks, and his legendarily large penis informed his legibility as more powerful than a buck. Instead he emerged as a kind of folk hero or symbol of pride for white male viewers.

Watching these titans come together is as surprising as it is electrifying. So many of the pairings of Black women and white men have been saturated in colonial fantasies that allow white men to deny and conceal their privilege and to project their fantasies onto Black women such that Black women are always the aggressors and provocateurs of sexual arrangements. This dynamic remains at play in *Tapestry of Passion*, but with a difference.

In key moments we see Holmes pick up West in his arms and carry her to the bed, a gesture often seen as about male power and female powerlessness, yet here we see them rather as united and swept up in the romance of the dreamlike room. They perform oral sex in a "69," and as we see West showcasing her awesome talents at fellatio, we also see and hear her expressions of pleasure in the act. During penetration she recites the customary complement to male costars: "You're so big!" Yet while she performs the provocateur of his pleasure, West is also the provocateur of her own pleasure. Soon West declares, "Oh, I'm cumming!" In reading her face in ecstasy, and her softly curled-in body postorgasm, West's performance communicates authenticity, vulnerability, and even transcendence (see figs. 1–4).

Given the invisibility of women's orgasms to the viewer and the structural marginality of actresses' orgasms in the production of porn, we can only wonder at the authenticity of such moments. Such moments that are part of the narra-

Figure 1. Still from *Tapestry of Passion* (dir. Alan Colberg, 1976). John C. Holmes as Detective Johnny Wadd and Desiree West as Cindy.

Figure 2. Still from *Tapestry of Passion* (dir. Alan Colberg, 1976). Desiree West as Cindy, "I'm cumming!"

tive of golden-age porn tend to be excessively registered and childishly hyperbolic. This orgasm, however, exceeds the confines of the text. It creates a rupture where the multidimensionality of the actors playing at myth, trope, and taboo appears to break through. Specifically, the faciality of desire and the postorgasmic peacefulness of Desiree West lying on the bed while Holmes reaches his own climax

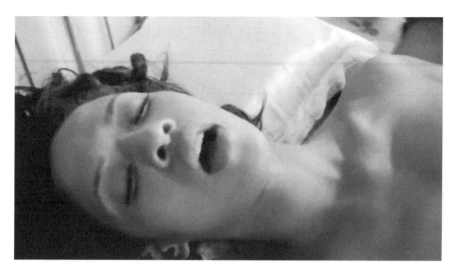

Figure 3. Still from *Tapestry of Passion* (dir. Alan Colberg, 1976). Desiree West
as Cindy, in ecstasy.

Figure 4. Still from *Tapestry of Passion* (dir. Alan Colberg, 1976). Desiree West
as Cindy, postorgasm bliss.

returns us as viewers to the question of stakes. How does it feel to be in a moment
when the materiality of claims for Black life and pleasure attempt to escape,
exceed, or exhaust the blistering presence of anti-Black violence and death? In
West's face we see the intertwining of a performance of Black women's pleasure
meet a pleasure in Black women's performance in ways that as a viewer, I have to
admit, are pretty hot.

## References

Jennings, David. 2000. *Skinflicks: The Inside Story of the X-Rated Video Industry.* Bloomington, IN: AuthorHouse.

Miller-Young, Mireille. 2014. *A Taste for Brown Sugar: Black Women in Pornography.* Durham, NC: Duke University Press.

DOI 10.1215/10642684-8311941

# DARK PRECURSORS, QUEER PORTENTS

**andré m. carrington**

*Afro-Fabulations: The Queer Drama of Black Life*
Tavia Nyong'o
New York: New York University Press, 2019. ix + 265 pp.

Tavia Nyong'o is one of many critics who have investigated Black performance through queer studies, leaning on queer studies' tolerance for ambiguity and ambivalence toward its ostensible objects to make sense of unwieldy, unsettling findings. The weight of history causes the subjects of Black performance to appear in shadow throughout queer studies, as if Blackness is always an aftereffect of something ineluctably *already*. Taking a critical interest in how racialized, gendered, and sexual alterity elude the overdetermined functions scripted for them by exploitative economies of difference requires an expansive imagination as well as analytical acumen. *Afro-Fabulations* appraises Black performances that frustrate efforts to reduce them to matters of similarity and difference, truth and falsehood; they insist in the Lacanian sense, exceeding the task of visibility so thoroughly that the question of representing Blackness or queerness becomes moot. The fabulist role in which Nyong'o casts Black performance is a ghostwriting practice, a fugitive conspiracy responsible for both authoring and citing acts that surprise, confound, and unsettle the heteronormative status quo. Nyong'o traces fabulist figures in Trajal Harrell, Jason Holliday, Adrian Piper, Melvin Van Peebles, Kara Walker, Samuel Delany, and others, conspiring with them to uproot Blackness and queerness from the demands under which they are bound to appear without untangling them in the process.

   Thinking with the artists about what fabulation can do allows the meanings of Nyong'o's keyword to proliferate without becoming redundant. Fabulation is a "theory and practice of black time and temporality" (5), an "inventive rather than explanatory" (125) way of discerning inscrutable motives, a centrifugal dimension in which diasporic "racial assemblage" (180) constantly orients itself away from the telos of identification, and a manner of arranging events in time without reifying a relation of causality between them. These disparate powers enhance the intellectual resonance of the performances cited in the book.

Fabulation is untimely and therefore indifferent to urgency. For Nyong'o, fabulation preserves the funk aesthetics of film and performance art in the 1970s as a body-conscious sensibility that subsequently proves essential to articulating Black transgender subjectivity within a multiracial constellation of LGBT identities (83). He argues that another fabulist, Samuel Delany, sets the stage for queer theory to acknowledge its indebtedness to the "normative strivings" (160) archived in the social and sexual experiments of the 1960s by speculating about a posthuman future in his early novel *The Einstein Intersection* (1967). Like other critics who revalorize creative writing by women and queers of color as a theorizing practice instrumental to academic queer studies, Nyong'o claims the status of theoretical knowledge production for the deeper, darker engagement with discourse and power in Delany's fiction and memoirs (157). The untimeliness of fabulation also politicizes the vulnerability of the death-bound Black subject, underscoring the "premature" in prison abolitionist and scholar Ruth Wilson Gilmore's oft-cited definition of racism as "state-sanctioned and/or legal production and exploitation of group-differentiated vulnerabilities to premature death" (105–6), to speculate about possibilities for Black life foreclosed by violence.

Associating the timelessness of fabulation with "black polytemporality" (23) requires Nyong'o to qualify the terms on which he appropriates the concept from one of its intellectual forebears. In the work of Henri Bergson, fabulation names phantoms of the imagination that interfere with the constructive illumination provided by human evolution toward modern intelligence. Nyong'o dislodges this productive mode of fantasizing from Bergson's framing. He employs the notion of deep time to highlight fabulation's capacity to stage scenarios that precede human evolution and those that may follow our extinction. Through the lens of fabulation, spectators can contemplate the persistence of the earth throughout the violent processes that force humanity into relations governed by the meanings of being Black, white, Indigenous, settler, and Other. Reflecting on Guatemalan performance artist Regina José Galindo's performance *Piedra*, for example, Nyong'o recalls witnessing the "brown" performer having covered herself in charcoal to emulate an undisturbed stone as a moment that "perturbs [the] violent relatedness" of Black and nonblack people (109). The specter of blackface recedes into deep time as the author pronounces himself "less interested in disavowing any link to the travesty of blackness . . . than in understanding exactly how, in that entanglement, it may be possible to see that violent apparatus of anti-black perception momentarily rendered inoperative" (106).

*Afro-Fabulations* is skeptical about the ultimate horizon of cultural politics, but not in the way that readers concerned with the renewed visibility of antiblack violence might expect. The study makes clear its queer dedication to the benefits of deemphasizing identity by eschewing the notional interests of any rights-bearing, extramural constituency in deciding the relevance of its itinerary. Instead, Nyong'o interpolates and accelerates the figures that fabulation subjects to metamorphosis. Regarding Benh Zeitlin's 2012 film *Beasts of the Southern Wild* as a dramatization of the dream of posthumanism, he asks, "What repercussions does an environmentally motivated 'giving up' of human sovereignty imply" for people who move through that environment via displacement (129)? Similarly, Nyong'o situates Bina48, a Black female artificial intelligence with the likeness of her white inventor's wife, as the avatar for depression as a "public feeling," interpreting her professed consciousness of her own inadequacy in a television interview as evidence of "the infinite debt that artificial intelligence owes to black thought" (192). With her limited responsiveness in conversation and incomplete replica of a human body, Bina48's susceptibility to "embarrassing social failures" (193) elicits compassion. Fabulation makes her failure more compelling than a successful ruse.

The generative, capacious quality of *Afro-Fabulations* makes it especially useful for understanding the drama that consistently characterizes academic queer studies: its precarious institutional location, its nonreproductive kinship with race and ethnicity, its irreparable debt to identititarian social movements. The author acknowledges that fabulation "begs the question of what lies outside or beyond it; what if any, its ethical limits may be" (125). Ethics notwithstanding, *Afro-Fabulations* may lend Blackness the propensity to have no limits, to do anything.

**andré m. carrington** is associate professor of English at Drexel University.

DOI 10.1215/10642684-8311955

# THE FUGITIVITY OF FORCED QUEERNESS

**Cameron Clark**

*Fugitive Life: The Queer Politics of the Prison State*
Stephen Dillon
Durham, NC: Duke University Press, 2018. vii + 189 pp.

In her seminal essay "Punks, Bulldaggers, and Welfare Queens: The Radical Potential of Queer Politics?" Cathy Cohen (1997) articulates how the racialized regulations of gender and sexuality for chattel slavery and its afterlives complicate the parameters of what is often deemed "queer" and "heteronormative." Although the eponymous figures of her essay title may self-identify as heterosexual, state-based procedures that position these racialized populations as nonnormative blur the categorical distinctions for queer and heteronormative sexualities. For Cohen this force of involuntary queerness is no doubt a gross injury; however, it holds critical import insofar as "all those deemed marginal and all those committed to liberatory politics" (440) may begin to mobilize around intersectionality and coalition for a radical political praxis.

Stephen Dillon further develops Cohen's politicoethical project of relationality across multiple embodied differences in *Fugitive Life: The Queer Politics of the Prison State*. In it, he maps the affective and epistemological force of queerness onto discussions of fugitive imaginaries, alternative space-times, and unknowable ethics of survival. As Dillon argues, "Thinking of queerness as a form of relational difference produced by racial violence helps us to reconceptualize how the state and capital operate, and also opens up new possibilities for thinking about life, survival, and freedom" (15–16). Drawing from women-of-color feminists and queer abolitionists, Dillon centers the prison as an index for how white supremacy and cis-heteropatriarchy generate racialized, gendered, and sexual difference in close proximity to terror and death. More narrowly, his approach conceptualizes how the prison also serves as a locus for neoliberal politics of economic rationality, whereby mass incarceration requires the "freedom" of the market and individual. Bringing together Cohen's radical potential of queer politics, Hortense Spillers's (1987: 68) "ungendered" flesh, and Sarah Haley's (2016: 73) "forced queering," Dillon analyzes how queerness functions in relation to social, civil, and premature death. At the same time, he charts how inhabiting this ontological position produces fugitive ways of thinking, feeling, and living to combat such dire strictures.

One of the ways in which fugitivity takes flight in Dillon's text is through a queering of spatiotemporalities in the underground. In chapters 1 and 2, Dillon reads the law-and-order and economic policies of Barry Goldwater, Richard Nixon, and Milton Friedman as propelling a future-oriented imperative for privatization, deregulation, deindustrialization, and color blindness as instances of "neoliberal freedom" (23). He counters this state-sanctioned reordering with contemporaneous communiqués and poetry from the Women's Brigade of the Weather Underground and Susan Choi's *American Woman* (2003). For Dillon, these authors utilize the underground as "an alternative time-space paradigm" that "exists within but negates the normative time of the nation, state, and capital" (40). This negation occurs through a generative "politics of unknowing" (40) that undermines the progression of biopolitics and "neoliberal freedom" with "affective and epistemological impossible possibilities that are created by running away, hiding, and vanishing into the thick air of the everyday" (22). Fugitivity in the underground thus produces alternative experiments of freedom in sharp contrast to the discipline and control of the neoliberal-carceral state.

The value of "impossible possibilities" is addressed by Dillon's modification of the afterlives of slavery as possessing the present, rather than haunting it. In chapter 3 he brings together writings on captivity and fugitivity by Assata Shakur, Safiya Bukhari, Angela Davis, and Sherley Anne Williams to demonstrate how the necropolitics of chattel slavery is coterminous with the biopolitics of neoliberalism in the very structure of the market. Given that the present is possessed by this relation, Dillon locates sites of resistance in the unknowable, writing, "By engaging the unknowable, black feminism can help make connections between the past and present that other epistemologies leave unthought and unthinkable" (98). For Dillon, rememory and the imagination thus open up queer space-times, which in turn produce the thinkable and the possible as a means of renouncing the progressive imaginary of the state.

This then leads Dillon to conclude his project with queer feminist futures and ways to reorient desire toward revolutionary goals. In chapter 4 he begins with an analysis of Street Transvestite Action Revolutionaries (STAR) to demonstrate how sexual liberation has often been tied to a critique of racialized policing. He extends this critique through poetry by Audre Lorde and June Jordan, as well as political theory by Michel Foucault, Gilles Deleuze, and Félix Guattari, who collectively track how the state and capital compel a desire for police, prisons, and subjection. Yet, this constellation of thought also articulates how desire and the erotic are conditions of possibility for "new forms of knowledge, ways of being, and abolitionist imaginings of a world without racialized and gendered state violence" (122). If a desire for police and prisons is integral to the neoliberal-carceral state, then fugitive desires and affects foster the means of undoing these spatiotemporal and psychoaffective constraints.

Dillon's overall project returns a genealogy of antiprison politics to contemporary queer theoretical debates on temporality, fugitivity, and desire. As he discerns, the import of an antiprison political framework is how "the contributors [Black feminists and queer abolitionists] construct an affective epistemology—a fugitive way of knowing that escapes articulation—that would give rise to a new ontology founded on collective becoming, not the singularity of being" (26). A move toward collective becoming and coalitional praxis offers strategies to think and feel beyond the rational individuality of the neoliberal marketplace and its coterminous ties to police violence, racial capitalism, and incarceration. Dillon's text is thus not only a valuable contribution to Black feminist thought and queer studies but also a model for abolition itself.

**Cameron Clark** is a doctoral candidate in the Department of English and Comparative Media Analysis and Practice at Vanderbilt University.

### References

Cohen, Cathy. 1997. "Punks, Bulldaggers, and Welfare Queens: The Radical Potential of Queer Politics?" *GLQ* 3, no. 4: 437–65.

Haley, Sarah. 2016. "'Like I Was a Man': Chain Gangs, Gender, and the Domestic Carceral Sphere in Jim Crow Georgia." *Signs: Journal of Women and Culture in Society* 39, no. 1: 53–77.

Spillers, Hortense. 1987. "Mama's Baby, Papa's Maybe: An American Grammar Book." *Diacritics* 17, no. 2: 65–81.

DOI 10.1215/10642684-8311969

# AGAINST VANILLA HISTORIES

**Camille Robcis**

*Sex, France, and Arab Men, 1962–1979*
Todd Shepard
Chicago: University of Chicago Press, 2017. 317 pp.

For a long time, much of French history was written through a national lens: historians assumed that territory, population, and state were mapped onto one another, and colonies were regarded as a state of exception. To be sure, this version of colonial history documented the violence, the racism, and the systematic discrimination that characterized colonial life. However, because nation and metropole were superimposed, France could still be considered the birthplace of human rights, the Enlightenment, and republicanism, whereas colonial violence and racism could be interpreted as an anomaly, as "bad practice," as the faulty applications of liberal principles that remained uninterrogated. As Gary Wilder (2005: 6–7) described it, "methodological nationalism" made possible the triumph of this "affirmative historiography" of France. For a long time also—at least until the crucial intervention of Michel Foucault (1980)—the history of sexuality in France, especially that written in the tradition of the *histoire des mentalités*, took as self-evident heterosexuality, gender, and the family. Fathers, mothers, children, and marriage were the starting points for this history, not categories that were themselves historically constructed.

Todd Shepard's book *Sex, France, and Arab Men, 1962–1979* is particularly exciting because it takes to task both of these fields: it challenges long-standing assumptions not only about the relationship between colony and metropole but also about the history of sexuality and the construction of identities. In many ways, Shepard builds on his first book, *The Invention of Decolonization: the Algerian War and the Remaking of France* (2006), in which he already urged historians to move beyond "methodological nationalism" and to treat France as an imperial nation-state. With empire as the primary unit of historical analysis, colonialism could no longer be reduced to a parenthesis or side project in the construction of the French Republic. Rather, colonialism was integral to the formation of French identity just as it was constitutive of the French state: what happened in Algeria had lasting effects not only on Algeria but also on France. As Shepard

(2006: 9) summarized it, "The history of France in Algeria . . . offers a *mise en abîme* of metropolitan history." While Shepard's first book focused on the effects of decolonization in the immediate aftermath of the war (around the year 1962), this study examines the following two decades, from 1962 to 1979, when Algeria continued to haunt France. Similarly, in relation to the history of sexuality, Shepard is clearly indebted to the work of Foucault, which systematically denaturalized sex by bringing to light the networks of power and knowledge that shaped sexuality as discourse, practice, and identity.

Shepard is, of course, not the first to challenge these "vanilla histories," to use his terms: "Vanilla histories of the West [that] erase the importance of people of color" and "vanilla histories of sex [that] pretend that its multiple valences and diverse forms are best ignored" (16). He is, however, one of the few historians to bring together so successfully these two critiques. Too often, postcolonial history has ignored the crucial ways in which gender and sexuality have served as privileged vectors of power and domination, even after decolonization. And too often, the history of sexuality has considered the colonial organization of gender and sexuality as a mirror or an application of European practices instead of treating it as the very laboratory in which European sexual norms were produced.

Shepard's argument, briefly stated, is that the sexual revolution of the 1960s and 1970s in France was intimately tied to the war in Algeria, to decolonization, and to immigration. As he writes, during this period "invocations of sex, and Arabs" came to "describe people, relationships, and events located within France even as they always also referenced Algeria" (3). "Algerian questions and answers," he writes, "made the sexual revolution French" (1). To support this thesis, Shepard focuses on nine examples of "sex talk," "diverse references to sex, sexual orality, deviance, and normalcy in publications, archived documents, and visual sources" (3). Thus, the Far Right blamed the loss of Algeria on the perceived crisis of French masculinity and depicted Algerian men as sexual criminals responsible for rape, sexual harassment, and homosexual promiscuity. The Far Left also invoked Arab men but to discuss gay liberation, feminist efforts to criminalize rape, and the Third-Worldist revolution. In both cases, the trope of the "Arab man" was prevalent to think through foundational problems of French political, social, and cultural life.

Shepard's framework is not psychoanalytic, yet questions around the unconscious, trauma, and fantasy permeate his book. It is interesting, for instance, to think of this period of "post-decolonization," as Shepard calls it, in terms of trauma and in relation to France's melancholic relationship to Algeria, its inability to let go of the lost object that returns in all these symptoms, in all this acting out.

Similarly, I see this book as a manifesto for the importance of fantasy in political and historical work—fantasy as "social glue," to use Jacqueline Rose's (1996: 3) term. As Shepard shows, Arab men were not actually more involved in prostitution, but it was widely believed that they were, and this fantasy had direct consequences on social policy. Freud referred to fantasies as "protective fictions," and in many ways we can interpret these fantasies around "Arab men" as ways to defer or ignore key political questions that had arisen with decolonization.

Shepard's intervention, however, is not simply historiographical. His book also offers an excellent example of how carefully assembled empirical evidence read with the tools of critical theory can speak to complex philosophical and political questions in different fields, including queer theory. For instance, Shepard's discussion of sodomy as a site of "power, domination, repression, and resistance" (199) will surely be of interest to scholars of queer theory who have thought about the "antisocial thesis." In his 1995 seminal work, *Homos*, for example, Leo Bersani (1995: 127) illustrated his "anticommunal mode of connectedness," his embrace of negativity and the shattering of identity, with an example from André Gide where the main character accesses self-loss and *jouissance* by "fucking an Arab." Similarly, we can read Shepard's book in conversation with recent discussions of homonationalism, in the work of Jasbir Puar or Joseph Massad in the United States or of Houria Bouteldja in France, all of whom have complicated the link between homosexuality and Islam. As Shepard's intersectional approach makes clear, race, class, sexuality, and gender are—and were—constantly entangled with one another. This is a smart and provocative call for a "history of the present" (15) that can help us think through many questions that are still very much relevant for us today.

**Camille Robcis** is associate professor of French and history at Columbia University.

### References

Bersani, Leo. 1995. *Homos*. Cambridge, MA: Harvard University Press.

Foucault, Michel. 1980. *The History of Sexuality*. New York: Vintage Books.

Rose, Jacqueline. 1996. *States of Fantasy*. Oxford: Clarendon Press.

Shepard, Todd. 2006. *The Invention of Decolonization: The Algerian War and the Remaking of France*. Ithaca, NY: Cornell University Press.

Wilder, Gary. 2005. *The French Imperial Nation-State: Negritude and Colonial Humanism between the Two World Wars*. Chicago: University of Chicago Press.

OI 10.1215/10642684-8311983

# WHAT DOES (NOT) APPEAR

**Tamsin Kimoto**

*The Life and Death of Latisha King: A Critical Phenomenology of Transphobia*
Gayle Salamon
New York: New York University Press, 2018. x + 199 pp.

Gayle Salamon's most recent book opens with detailed accounts of events surrounding the final moments of Latisha King's life. King, a Black trans girl, was murdered in February 2008 by a classmate at her school in Oxnard, California. Switching between King's birth and chosen names, between a focus on King and on her murderer, between gender and sexuality and race, Salamon makes clear that this is a case marked by a number of ambiguities and erasures. The question that haunts the introduction and book—"How can one offer a phenomenology of what does not appear?" (22)—is an important one for Salamon to address, given phenomenology's insistence on lived experience and presence; for Salamon, the answer is that phenomenology also demonstrates to us that what appears to us always depends on that which does not, and that this is the productive work of "imagining" (23).

At its best, Salamon's book offers a thoroughgoing, phenomenological account of the "conditions of possibility" for King's murder (10). Each of the four chapters takes a central term in phenomenology and uses it as a lens through which King's actions in life and the circumstances around her death can be analyzed for the transphobic, homophobic, and racist structures undergirding the responses of those around her. For example, chapter 1, "Comportment," analyzes how King's walk and manner of carrying herself were read in the courtroom as a provocation, an "aggressive" act against which her murderer's "defensive" response was potentially justified. In chapter 2, "Movement," Salamon demonstrates how gender and sexual variance appear as disruptive through an analysis of how the sound of King's heels in the hallway produced negative reactions in her teachers and classmates. Taken together, these two chapters give us an account of how the visual and auditory registers of perception come together in the experiences of transphobia, homophobia, or racism to produce subjects who appear as already at odds with the world. This allows us to see how the mere fact of the minoritized subject's existence gets read as an existential threat by subjects aligned with prevailing norms.

This emphasis on the quotidian, even banal aspects of King's life is where Salamon's phenomenological method is at its most powerful. By redirecting the reader's attention from the spectacle of King's death, Salamon demonstrates the ways in which the sedimentation of cultural norms grounded in transphobia, homophobia, and racism made King's death possible. The discussion of anonymity and of King's final day as one in which she was "perfectly anonymous" (130)—dressed in the ways she "ought" to have as a boy and thus unremarkable or even invisible—is one that will undoubtedly resonate for many trans readers of the text. The social demand that we be anonymous and the insufficiency of anonymity to protect us are things with which Black and non-Black transfeminine people of color must be intimately familiar as we navigate the world. Salamon's articulation of this experience makes this double bind starkly apparent.

Whereas classical phenomenology aims primarily to describe the structures of experience as clearly as possible, critical phenomenology turns our attention to the force of oppressive institutions and practices on our lived experiences in order to undermine, transform, or abolish those oppressive forces. In this regard, I have two concerns with Salamon's account. First, what a critical phenomenology of the King case ought to demonstrate is the entanglements of anti-Blackness and transphobia, given her murderer's budding ties to white supremacist movements. While Salamon marks the erasure of race in the court case, "visible even through that absence" (19), beyond a few scattered references to King's Blackness and a lengthier discussion of Rodney King, race is curiously absented from the text. I cannot help but wonder how this phenomenology of transphobia might cover over a phenomenology of transmisogynoir and contribute to the "marginalization of women-of-color feminism" and the possibilities for thinking about Latisha King in conversation with Black feminism (Krell 2017: 236). Second, the *critical* in *critical phenomenology* lacks the power that one might expect, given the harrowing details of King's death in the text. The phenomenological ethos that Salamon offers is ultimately one of self-transformation through the process of "unknowing," the making strange of our everyday experiences in the world through the phenomenologist's careful attention (159). This returns us to phenomenology's greatest vice: the individual, perceiving subject—which Salamon has otherwise tried to avoid. Furthermore, self-reflection is ultimately an insufficient response to the enormity of King's death.

I want to return to the question Salamon gives us in the introduction's reflection on phenomenological method. The answer to how one offers a phenomenology of what does not appear is, it seems, that one does not. Indeed, this limitation to phenomenological method is apparent throughout, as what never seems to fully appear in this book is Latisha King herself. Jean-Paul Sartre (1984: 343–47) describes the experience of being seen by another as something that shifts the universe or decentralizes the solipsistic world of our intentional consciousness by making it apparent that "I am vulnerable . . . in short, that I am seen." In this book, King never gazes back because she never appears as the *subject* of this phenomenological account of her life and death. She only ever appears as object, as something around which various others orient themselves and, as such, is never really seen herself as a perceiving subject in her own right. This tension is apparent from the book's title and subtitle: *The Life and Death of Latisha King* suggests that we might perhaps come to know something substantial of King's life, *her* lifeworld, but *A Critical Phenomenology of Transphobia* assures us that it is only ever *our* lifeworld that will be addressed. The merit of this approach is that Salamon avoids speaking for King. At the same time, it means that King is virtually interchangeable with any other of the many murdered Black trans girls and women.

**Tamsin Kimoto** is a PhD candidate in philosophy at Emory University.

### References

Krell, Elías Consenza. 2017. "Is Transmisogyny Killing Trans Women of Color? Black Trans Feminisms and the Exigencies of White Femininity." *TSQ: Transgender Studies Quarterly* 4, no. 2: 226–42.

Sartre, Jean-Paul. 1984. *Being and Nothingness: A Phenomenological Essay on Ontology*, translated by Hazel E. Barnes. New York: Washington Square Press.

DOI 10.1215/10642684-8311997

# About the Contributors

**Cal (Crystal) Biruk** is associate professor of anthropology at McMaster University. Cal is the author of *Cooking Data: Culture and Politics in an African Research World* (2018). Her research interests are at the intersection of medical anthropology, critical data studies, queer studies, and global health studies. Her current projects—which focus on geographies of aid in Malawi and on theorizing wearables as queer technologies amid the second fitness boom in the United States—take the form of ethnographic treatments of metrics, indicators, and genres of measurement and counting in the era of Big Data and audit culture(s).

**José B. Capino** is associate professor of English at the University of Illinois at Urbana-Champaign. He has recently published *Martial Law Melodrama: Lino Brocka's Cinema Politics*, a book about the political vision of the renowned Filipino director.

**Laura Edmondson** is associate professor of theater at Dartmouth College, where she is also affiliated with the Programs of African and African American Studies and Women's, Gender, and Sexuality Studies. She writes on human rights, transnationality, and state violence in eastern and central African performance. She is the author of *Performance and Politics in Tanzania: The Nation on Stage* (2007) and *Performing Trauma in Central Africa: Shadows of Empire* (2018). Her current project, "Stage Whispers in Central Africa," explores genres of negation—such as absence, silence, and darkness—within performance as a means of articulating buried histories and surreptitious forms of violence.

**Kirk Fiereck** is adjunct assistant professor of anthropology at City University of New York. He works on two long-term ethnographic projects. The first translates three-plus years of fieldwork into a book-length monograph, "Queer Customs: Cultural Authenticity, Sexual Ideology, and HIV Science in South Africa." An open-access account of queer customs, "Queer Customs, Customarily Queer," is available at www.medanthrotheory.org/read/10018/queer-customs-customarily-queer. The second project is a multisited ethnography of biofinance, which examines the rapid, fundamental changes to cultural economies globally that he summarizes as "the derivativization of sociality." *Derivativization* is the transformation of commodity-based, labor-monetized value in industrial capitalisms to derivative-based, information-monetized value in financial capitalisms. His recent coauthored op-ed about biofinance is available at www.forbes.com/sites/alisonbatemanhouse/2018/04/10/why-grindrs-privacy-breach-matters-to-everyone/#1913c6cf67f4.

**R. Galvan** is a Boston-based conceptual artist. They have formal training as a silver-smith and use that sensibility for making artist books, sculptures, drawings, photographs, and performance. Their studio practice is an interdisciplinary engagement with visual research and cultural investigations that focus on the role administrative systems play in the making and understanding of the self. They completed their AB from Brown University and received an MFA from the Rhode Island School of Design. They were the 2018–19 postdoctoral associate at Duke University's Program in Latino/a Studies in the Global South.

**Yessica Garcia Hernandez** is a filmmaker and assistant professor in the Department of Latina/o Studies at San Francisco State University. She has published in the *Journal of Popular Music*, *New American Notes Online*, *Imagining America*, *Journal of Ethnomusicology*, and the *Chicana/Latina Studies Journal*. She is currently working on two book manuscripts: "Intoxicated by Jenni Rivera: The Erotics of Fandom and Sonic Pedagogies of Pirujeria" and "Fat Latina Perversities: Latinx BBW Porn, Dirty Talk, and Gordibuenas."

**Keith M. Harris** is associate professor in the Department of English and Department of Media and Cultural Studies at the University of California, Riverside. His primary research interests are visual culture and gender and race, and ethical constructs of gender and race found in visual cultural production. He has guest edited issues in *Wide Angle* and *Black Camera*. His essays have appeared in *Black Camera*, *Contemporary Black Cinema*, *Wide Angle*, and the collections *The Spike Lee Reader* (2007), *Richard Pryor: The Life and Legacy of a "Crazy" Black Man* (2008), and *War Diaries* (2010). His poetry has appeared in *Callaloo*, *Corpus*, and *Queen: A Journal of Power and Rhetoric* (2000) and in the anthologies *The Road before Us* (1991) and *My Brother's Keeper* (1992).

**Neville Hoad** is associate professor of English and of women's and gender studies at the University of Texas at Austin. He is the author of *African Intimacies: Race, Homosexuality, and Globalization* (2007) and coeditor (with Karen Martin and Graeme Reid) of *Sex and Politics in South Africa: The Equality Clause/Gay and Lesbian Movement/The Antiapartheid Struggle* (2005). He is currently working on a book project about the literary and cultural representations of the HIV/AIDS pandemic in sub-Saharan Africa, in addition to a sequel to *African Intimacies* titled "Erotopolitics: Africa, Sovereignty, Sexuality."

**Keguro Macharia** is from Nairobi, Kenya. He blogs at gukira.wordpress.com.

**Phoebe Kisubi Mbasalaki** is a lecturer in the gender studies program at the African Gender Institute (AGI), University of Cape Town. She is also a postdoctoral research fellow on the GlobalGRACE project housed at the AGI and the Centre for Theatre, Dance, and Performance Studies (CTDPS), University of Cape Town, as well as the NGO SWEAT. She holds a doctorate in gender, media, and culture from Utrecht University in the Netherlands. Phoebe was also a lecturer at Utrecht University, and taught on the Graduate Gender Studies Programme, feminist theory, and feminist research methods. Her research interests are in critical race, gender, class, sexuality, public health, and decolonial thought and praxis. She has also worked in various fields, including those involving gender, HIV, and public health, with agencies such UNDP, UNAIDS, and WHO.

**Mireille Miller-Young** is associate professor of feminist studies at University of California, Santa Barbara and the 2019–20 Advancing Equity through Research Fellow at the Hutchins Center for African and African American Studies at Harvard University. She is the author of *A Taste for Brown Sugar: Black Women in Pornography* (2014) and coeditor of *The Feminist Porn Book: The Politics of Producing Pleasure* (2013) and *Black Sexual Economies: Race and Sex in a Culture of Capital* (2019).

**Danai S. Mupotsa** is senior lecturer in African literature at the University of the Witwatersrand. She specializes in a range of subjects that include gender and sexualities, black intellectual traditions and histories, intimacy and affect, and feminist pedagogies. She has edited special issues, most recently "Visual Interruptions" (*Girlhood Studies*); "Xenophobia and the Techniques of Difference" (*Agenda*); "The Cinematic City: Desire, Form and the African Urban" (*Journal of African Cinemas*, forthcoming); and "Cinematic Imaginaries of the African City" (*Social Dynamics*, forthcoming). She has also published a collection of poetry titled *feeling and ugly* (2018).

**Edgar Fred Nabutanyi** holds a PhD from the Department of English, Stellenbosch University. He is currently a lecturer in the Department of Literature, Makerere University. His research interests converge around issues of public discourses in the public sphere regarding how these channels—fiction and media—are subverted and assimilated by vulnerable and minority subjectivities for self-enunciation. The central thesis of his research is that vulnerable populations like children, women, and ethnic and sexual minorities reconfigure the public sphere with such illocutionary force that they make their issues matter and transform their lives from mere statistical footnotes to critical societal issues.

**Ruth Ramsden-Karelse** is currently completing her DPhil in English at the University of Oxford, where she is Stuart Hall Doctoral Scholar, Merton Prize Scholar, and founder and co-convenor of the Oxford Queer Studies Network.

**Richard T. Rodríguez** is associate professor of media and cultural studies at the University of California, Riverside. The author of *Next of Kin: The Family in Chicano/a Cultural Politics* (2009), which won the 2011 National Association for Chicana and Chicano Studies Book Award, he is completing two book projects: "Undocumented Desires: Fantasies of Latino Male Sexuality" and "Latino/U.K.: Transatlantic Intimacies in Post-Punk Cultures."

DOI 10.1215/10642684-8312013

# Keep up to date on new scholarship

Issue alerts are a great way to stay current on all the cutting-edge scholarship from your favorite Duke University Press journals. This free service delivers tables of contents directly to your inbox, informing you of the latest groundbreaking work as soon as it is published.

To sign up for issue alerts:

1. Visit **dukeu.press/register** and register for an account. You do not need to provide a customer number.

2. After registering, visit **dukeu.press/alerts**.

3. Go to "Latest Issue Alerts" and click on "Add Alerts."

4. Select as many publications as you would like from the pop-up window and click "Add Alerts."

**read.dukeupress.edu/journals**